THE HIDDEN WORLD OF THE LEGAL AID LAWYER

Perspectives on Law and Access to Justice

This series forges a coherent field of access to justice scholarship, drawing connections between research from different disciplines such as civil and criminal law, family law, housing law, immigration law and social welfare law. It facilitates a multifaceted critique of the key issues and incorporates a diverse range of perspectives that will shape the future directions of this emerging field.

Find out more at:

bristoluniversitypress.co.uk/perspectives-on-law-and-access-to-justice

THE HIDDEN WORLD OF THE LEGAL AID LAWYER

Upholding the Heart of Justice

Emma Cooke

BRISTOL
UNIVERSITY
PRESS

First published in Great Britain in 2025 by

Bristol University Press
University of Bristol
1–9 Old Park Hill
Bristol
BS2 8BB
UK
t: +44 (0)117 374 6645
e: bup-info@bristol.ac.uk

Details of international sales and distribution partners are available at bristoluniversitypress.co.uk

British Library Cataloguing in Publication Data
A catalogue record for this book is available from the British Library

ISBN 978-1-5292-3292-9 hardcover
ISBN 978-1-5292-3293-6 ePub
ISBN 978-1-5292-3294-3 ePdf

Cover design: Nicky Borowiec Design
Front cover image: Getty/FotografiaBasica
Bristol University Press uses environmentally responsible print partners.
Printed and bound in Great Britain by CPI Group (UK) Ltd, Croydon, CR0 4YY

FSC
www.fsc.org
MIX
Paper | Supporting responsible forestry
FSC® C013604

Contents

Series Editors' Preface

In recent years, there has been increasing global interest in issues of access to justice and how these issues relate to our increasingly unequal societies. The concept of 'access to justice' – the protection of the law that enables citizens to enforce their rights – is far from new, but has often been approached from a range of different perspectives, methodologies, and disciplines. This series provides a home for socio-legal scholarship that explores issues of access to justice. It will draw important connections between research undertaken across different sub-disciplines, which intrinsically involve issues of access to justice but are not routinely in conversation with one another, such as civil and criminal law, family law, housing law, immigration law, and social welfare law. The series will forge a coherent field of access to justice scholarship; incorporating a diverse range of perspectives to facilitate a multifaceted critique of the key issues, debates and challenges that underpin access to justice, and shape the future directions of this emerging field.

List of Figures and Tables

Figures

Tables

Acknowledgements

This book is based on my doctoral thesis, which was completed at the University of Kent. During this time, I benefited enormously from the support granted to me by supervisors. I would like to thank: Johnny Ilan for encouraging me to pursue this academic pathway and for supporting me since I started out as an undergraduate student; without him, I simply wouldn't be where I am today; Marian Duggan for your constant support and valuable supervision; Kate Bradley for your insightful comments and shared passion for this field; Sarah Vickerstaff for your valuable contributions, particularly within the remit of the study of work. I am also enormously grateful to my PhD examiners, in particular Daniel Newman, who constantly inspires me, motivates me and supports me. This book wouldn't exist if it wasn't for you, so thank you. Jess Mant, thank you for also being there. I can't wait to follow in your footsteps – you are a legal aid legend. To Jo Wilding, I appreciate all your support and guidance with this so much. Lucy Welsh, you are also someone I really look up to in this field, so thank you. Caroline Chatwin, thanks for always guiding me, mentoring me and supporting me throughout my academic career.

This is also my opportunity to express my deepest gratitude to the participants in this research, who gave me access to their precious working world. Without you, this research simply wouldn't have been possible. I owe thanks to every single lawyer who gave me their time, in spite of being constantly pressured and overwhelmed due to the current state of legal aid. I admire you all.

I also couldn't have got to this point without my incredible friends who have travelled alongside me on this journey; you always provide the light at the end of the tunnel that I so truly need. I am so incredibly lucky to have you all.

To Dawn, thanks for getting me through. Thanks for constantly motivating me, listening to me and supporting me. I really appreciate you.

I am eternally grateful to my family for your endless support, encouragement, and love. Thanks for always being by my side no matter what. Mum, Dad and Soph you mean the world.

Arnold, my little buddy, my emotional support and my ultimate sidekick. Thanks for coming into my life at the right time.

The final thought is reserved for Gram, my biggest inspiration, who I miss tremendously. I hope I have made you proud.

Prologue: A Modern-Day 'Legal Aid Lawyers' Story

The aim of this book is to trace the (hidden) world of those at the forefront of legal aid work. What struck me during this research is that it concerns *real* life and *real* people, and the ethnographic methods deployed here seek to encapsulate just that. Of course, this book's consideration of the findings must begin somewhere. What precedes is an over-arching creative chapter in the form of a composite narrative.

There have been an increasing number of scholars who have embraced telling stories through narrative methods (Chamberlayne et al, 2000; Merrill and West, 2009; Miller, 2000; O'Neill, 2020). Bringing together all the collective meanings that lie behind the 30 individual interpretive stories involved in this research, this chapter integrates and restories these into one composite character known as 'Erica', to make sense of their world through the eyes of the lawyers themselves (Crossley, 2000; McCormack, 2004).

'Public Criminology' is concerned with critical analysis that promotes public understanding, and therefore is important not only for the academic good, but also the social and public good alike, and I hope that this book may pave way for such broader understanding (O'Neill et al, 2021: 251–252). Trajectories that emerge through this story-telling chapter span the social, structural, spatial, and cultural/ relational components of legal aid work. Themes emergent from this chapter will fundamentally form the very underpinnings of this book.

Upholding justice

Erica is not one person from the legal aid sample pool in this research. She is part of *every* participant's story. She chose to become a legal aid lawyer when she was in her mid to late 20s, after spending a period working for an overseas charity. She not only identifies as a lawyer but also as a mother, a friend, a social worker, a teacher, and a counsellor. Her experience as a lawyer, however, feeds into and shapes all these identities. Her role as a legal aid lawyer is the identity that takes priority. It is a vocation, a way of living and an all-encompassing career path that always requires Erica's full attention.

Erica cannot go to work at 9 am and leave at 5 pm. Erica is suffering. The clients are suffering. The justice system is failing. But Erica holds on. Erica holds on because so do her colleagues. Erica holds on because she just cannot and will not let go. It is her passion and she *wants* to continue to fight.

Erica: a collective character

Erica studied law at a Russell group UK-based university, which was going to set her up nicely for a solid career ahead. Looking back, she might have expected to be taught all about legal aid during her studies – it was a law degree after all – but it was not quite like that. She was happy enough, though. Erica got by with her criminal law module. Despite it being the only elective on legal aid work, Erica made the most of it. She did not want to follow in the path of the rest of her classmates who were all very much encouraged to go down the commercial route. Erica was committed to her desire to help those in need; to use her legal skillsets in a humanistic manner to make a difference to people's lives. Erica adored helping others. Her mother was the founder of a local legal support trust that provided specialist legal advice for those in need. Erica wanted to follow in her mother's footsteps, and nothing was going to stop her. Her dad, an accountant was not so keen.

In her final year of her law degree, Erica applied for the Legal Practice Course (LPC) to commence her journey to become a solicitor, despite not knowing how she was going to fund it. This was not going to stop her though. She would just take on three or four part-time jobs to try and fund her training. She would go to the library after her shift finished at the pub around 2 am and work until her classes started at 9 am the next morning. Maybe she would finally be able to go back to her own home at 5 pm that next day. She would only be able to pop in briefly though before heading off to tutor Henry down the road for his upcoming GCSE exams. She would drop off the batch of ironing she did for Susan on her way back before heading to the library again. This was Erica's life now. Nothing else mattered but finishing the LPC if she had any chance of pursuing her dream career. Time passed, and Erica was stuck in this continuous loop.

Towards the end of her LPC, Erica had to secure a training contract. Her partner, Isaac would not be happy if she did not have one directly lined up. After all, she had forfeited their time together for her studies. They only saw each other once in a blue moon. She had spent the last quarter of the year living on floor two of the library in the booth in the corner. Her family were also adamant that she would not have a chance of getting a training contract because Laura, her cousin, had already spent five years trying to secure one in the same field of housing law but with no luck. She had opted to become a paralegal with the hope that this would open more doors. But

Erica was not giving up. Even when Erica finally told her parents that she had been offered an interview for a potential training contract in a local high street firm, her dad huffed disapprovingly. He was concerned that there were no prospects to earn a high salary in Erica's chosen career path and that it would not be sustainable if she wanted to have a family. But when Erica was awarded a training contract after a year of searching, she immediately took it. Erica did not care if everyone else around her thought it was a bad idea. This was her passion. Finally, she could apply her professional skills to make a definite difference to someone's life. Erica was willing to put up a very good fight. She knew the impact of the cuts to legal aid would make things harder, but she absolutely loved her role as a trainee housing solicitor, and nothing was going to get in her way.

Legal aid lawyering

Erica had now been working at the firm where she completed her training contract for three years. There had been a lot of changes since she started, particularly surrounding the amount of paperwork she had to fill in daily. She was fed up with spending all her time filling in copious amounts of irrelevant forms. She wanted to be spending that time helping people, but Erica did not have a paralegal anymore – she had been scrapped last year. It was now down to Erica to do everything for her clients, both face-to-face and behind the scenes. This would be ok if she had the right facilities. However, her desk was based in a very stuffy room with three others, and the piles of bundles all over her desk made things extra difficult. She longed for an online case-bundle system where everything could be easily organized and made accessible. Her firm kept promising this, but she was yet to see it in action. Her computer was incredibly slow, and the only working printer was two floors up. Clients were always forgetting the relevant paperwork, so she was constantly chasing. That was ok though, as Jim (one of her clients) had brought her a lovely 'thank you' card and a bar of chocolate last week, despite only having a penny to his name. That really meant a lot to Erica. She had stuck the card up on her desk so that, every time she felt overwhelmed, she could look up and remind herself why she was there. Erica still could not afford to buy herself a new car because hers was broken, but it was the small gestures that kept her going. She was following her dream after all. That was what she kept having to remind herself.

It was the fourth new client meeting of the day. Erica had quickly scoffed down her stale tuna sandwich that she had not managed to eat the day before, in the five-minute break she had before her next meeting. Hopefully, her client would be there on time, as she had another lined up directly after that. Erica was used to waiting around though. Time was not really a priority for many of her clients. Every working day for Erica was disorganized; she had never really been able to follow a linear time structure. After all, her work largely depended on the clients and their problems. If they were late, then Erica had to reshuffle her day around. That was ok though; Erica found that quite exciting. Every working day was different, and the thrill of that excited Erica greatly. If she got everything she wanted done, then the rhythm of her day did not really matter. What really frustrated her about her time, though, was how restricted it was becoming. Her client meetings were being cut short to an increasing extent, as she was becoming more sought after. Erica wanted to be able to see as many clients as she could. A shortage of legal aid providers in the area meant that this was more vital than ever before. But, at the same time, the Legal Aid Agency was making the whole process far more bureaucratized. Erica was now having to climb administrative hurdles that she had never had to climb before. She knew the on-hold music of the Legal Aid Agency telephone helpline from start to finish. She had to listen to it multiple times a week for at least 20–30 minutes per phone call, as every new client meeting required her to ring them up to initiate a case. Every time, she profusely apologized to her client for being put on hold. But she was used to waiting now. This was an inherent part of every single working day.

Erica had now been at the firm for over ten years. Her working life was starting to take shape, and Erica embraced this. An opportunity arose to become a partner of the firm, and Erica applied successfully. She had been waiting for this moment. To be honest, Erica did not think this opportunity would ever arise. She thought that Ned would get it. He started a few years after her, but he was male after all. Erica felt as though she belonged there though. It was her destiny. She enjoyed watching the firm flourish; she enjoyed watching her colleague's flourish. She really enjoyed being in the driving seat. The firm felt like home. Erica knew the firm inside out and relished the unique and quirky features of its working culture.

She enjoyed her chats with Fred, the receptionist at the water fountain every day at around 11 am. She loved her spontaneous, banterous exchanges with Lee, a fellow housing solicitor, as she walked in and out, back and forth to client meetings. She looked forward to seeing Georgi, the cleaner, every evening before leaving the office. She enjoyed hearing about Georgi's daughter, Grace, who had just turned four and was starting primary school the following year. Erica also liked having her own space though. She enjoyed going to the side room in the office if she needed her own headspace. Erica loved having that flexibility in her working space.

After a frenetic week in the office, Erica decided to arrange an office social. It was about time, really. She could not remember the last time she had been out. Erica loved going out with her colleagues, not only because she appreciated them, but it helped her to cope with things. She had had a few difficult cases that week that went beyond her lawyering remit, and she was feeling a bit emotionally unstable. One of her clients had threatened to commit suicide right in front of her, and it had really resonated. She had been having nightmares worrying about it ever since. She could not shift it from her mind. Working in legal aid meant regularly working with emotionally heavy caseloads. The lawyers themselves often had to draw on informal skills they had never had training for, as the emotional side of things was left out of both education and training. More than this, Erica found it difficult to bear witness to her client's pains, which often transcended the legal remit. Dealing with all of this, while also facing low rates of pay, overstretched resources, and unpleasant toxicity from the government and the public alike, lead to a lot of vicarious trauma on Erica's shoulders.

It was ok though; she knew her colleagues would be right by her side. They knew what she was going through more than anyone else. They were living in the same little world and would totally understand. Erica knew that they would not judge her. She knew that they would sit and listen. She knew that they would put her at ease. You see, they were all in this journey together. They shared the same motivations in wanting to fight for social justice, and would continue to do so regardless of the toll it took.

It was a Friday evening. Erica and her colleagues were sat in the local pub, chatting. She had just offloaded her worries and felt so much better. She felt ready for the next working week now. She decided to get in the next round of drinks to thank her team for all their hard work over the past few months. The Legal Aid Agency had continued to batter their firm, yet everyone still clung on. She was not going to lose anyone. She needed her team, and they needed her. As a team they could cope with all the hurdles stemming from the cuts. She could not do that alone. Erica went to the bar and bought a round of gin and tonics. She opted for the finest gin they offered because her colleagues were so worth it. She did not care that she was almost reaching her overdraft. Money did not really matter after all. Her friendships did, especially in this job. She could already imagine how her colleagues would react when she took the drinks over. That made her smile.

On her return, she found herself sitting next to Billy, the new trainee solicitor. Erica felt a very strong connection to Billy. She had been there to guide him through the whole process of becoming a legal aid lawyer, and she felt proud of him. He was so close to becoming qualified, and she could not wait to tell him that she wanted to keep him on because he had been such a committed and hard-working trainee. He was a superstar. She absolutely loved being a role model. She felt that it was her duty to pass down her knowledge to those starting out in the field. This was something Erica strived to do; they were all climbing the same ladder after all. Most people in her firm sought to do the same. This was just the way in which her firm was orientated. It did not stop at just helping the newbies though. Anyone could ask for help, and they would get it, even those who had been there for years and years. Erica encouraged everyone in her department to share knowledge and to lend each other a hand whenever they needed it. She found that this made her firm a much nicer place to work. They identified as a collective, despite the diversity of individuals working for the firm. They were the Silverman and Co housing department, and she was extremely proud of this identity.

The impact of COVID-19

Despite all the challenges Erica and her firm already faced, no one could anticipate what was round the corner – a pandemic that exacerbated literally *everything*. If working in the field was not already challenging enough, add in the detrimental impact of COVID-19 and things became much, much worse. Erica was finally quite content with her position at Silverman and Co, but nothing could quite prepare her and her colleagues for this. It was March 2020, and the world was becoming increasingly impacted by the virus. Erica often did not have time to watch or listen to the news but, given that COVID-19 was so encompassing, she could not really avoid it. Who knew that when she was leaving the office at 7.20 pm on 25 March she would not be returning for *at least* four months.

Accompanying the enforced lockdown was a cluster of problems in the legal aid world. First, working from home had never really been a thing at Silverman and Co. Erica loved going into the office and seeing all her colleagues. They all worked together, as one firm, and that was what kept everyone going. The isolation hit Erica tremendously; who was she going to turn to when things got tough, or when she had to deal with a horrible and hard-hitting case? Sitting at home in the spare bedroom on a makeshift desk – a stolen side table from the lounge – next to pile of stacked washing that had been waiting to be put away for the last three weeks was not the most motivating or appealing work environment. She had tried to shove all the unsightly clutter into a corner that was not visible from her webcam – what would her colleagues and clients think if they saw into her untidy home? She did not have time to clean, she was always working late, but now everyone was going to be able to see into Erica's chaotic, lived reality. Erica did not want everyone to see into her living space, and she did not particularly want to see into her clients' houses either. Personal and professional boundaries were always maintained in the office, but confidentiality became a real problem. Erica now could not predict who was listening in, who else was in the 'room' to ensure the safety of her clients.

Luckily, Erica already had a laptop, but accessing case files and documentation was another matter. Silverman and Co had to quickly sign up to an online case management system to allow remote access. This was completely new to them – the lawyers in the firm had been used to just going up to the shelf full of physical files to locate each bundle. Thrown in at the deep end, Erica had to somehow try and work out how she was going to navigate working from home quite literally overnight. Weekly teams' meetings with her colleagues somewhat helped, but it was not the same. Collegiality was very difficult to maintain on an online platform when colleagues' internet connections kept cutting out, and various kids and animals were repeatedly interrupting the sessions. It was hard for Erica to have, or display, empathy online. Body language and non-verbal cues were so difficult to read through a screen. Erica felt her service became much more impersonal due to increased time restraints, and her lack of ability to support remotely. Erica was used to dealing with clients' problems holistically; she often joked to her friends that she was part-lawyer part-counsellor. This was just part and parcel of being a legal aid lawyer. She could not really do this online; this made Erica worry. Loads of her clients were extremely vulnerable and at risk, and often she was their one and only line of support because all other social support systems had failed them. She was their last lifeline in a lot of cases.

It was extremely difficult for Erica's clients. Huge backlogs started to appear within the courts, and hearings were shifted online. Issues with remote hearings were never ending, as many of her clients tried to appeal them as they viewed them as 'improper' in comparison to in-person hearings. Many of her clients were also simply not computer literate or did not own a suitable device to attend the relevant meetings with Erica. Some had no access to the internet at all. Technology issues and barriers became a problem for Erica, her colleagues, her clients, as well as the wider justice system. Erica was sad as this tended to affect her most vulnerable clients. Access to justice had never been more limited.

As the pandemic went on, Erica got more used to working remotely. Once everyone was allowed back to the office, Silverman and Co maintained a hybrid system of working, which really benefited her and her colleagues. While she could be in the office most of the time to tend to her clients and their needs, she was also able to have a little bit more of a work–life balance and tend to her personal life slightly more on days where she was not either in court or required to be face-to-face with clients. For some clients, this also meant that, if they had suitable access to technology at home, they could save money on transport fares to get to the firm. Erica came to realize that some positives emerged from COVID-19, especially the modernization and flexibility of working practices.

Family life

After a couple of years in her position as a partner of the firm, Erica began to reflect on her life. She had devoted absolutely everything she had to her occupation. At the age of 41, Erica decided that it was about time she focused on herself. Isaac had been nagging her for years about having a family. It was time to take a step back and focus on herself and her family. Erica had always wanted children, too, but her job had restricted her. Luckily, she was in a position where she could now take some time out to have a family – as a partner, she was autonomous. Hayley, her colleague, a very junior solicitor, also wanted to have a family, but, unfortunately for her, she did not have the same safety net as Erica. For those at the bottom levels of high street firms, it was notoriously difficult to take time out to have children and come back. Erica felt so incredibly guilty about this, but could not dwell on it too much. Erica could still work remotely in the first few months of her maternity leave and would return early to work to ensure that she did not take too much time out. She could have her phone on all the time and be logged on to her emails from wherever she was. She still had to be there for her colleagues, and she was willing to sacrifice some of her own needs to make sure her firm did not lose out too much while she was away. While having children was really important to Erica, she did not want this to have any adverse effect on all the hard work she had done up to this point. She would just have to work late into the night once she got home to catch up and keep on top of everything. She was so incredibly lucky to have her mother-in-law down the road if her child was ill or unable to go to nursery, or else she simply would not be able to keep it up. She still had a mountain to climb with regards to the fight for justice. Erica would also miss work while she was away. It had been her life for the past 15 years or so. Erica knew how to be a legal aid lawyer. She was good at fulfilling that role. She could not imagine life without that identity. After all that was who she was – *a legal aid lawyer* – and this was what she wanted to continue to be.

Relevance to this book

Narratives are central to human existence and experiences; actions and emotions connect and integrate (Sandberg, 2015). The potential of ethnographic research (and narratives emergent from that) to reveal silenced experience offers something valuable here. As the poet Adrienne Rich denotes, this involves 'not simply learning the jargon of the elite, fitting unexceptionably into the status quo, but learning that language can be used as a means of changing reality' (Rich, 1980 in Miles, 2005: xii). This combined account of the participants involved in this research cultivates the fragility, variety, and ambiguity of legal aid work on which it is based. Stories from *within* a given field undoubtedly provide us with as much as a direct experience of the ways in which individuals work within it as we can get as outsiders.

'Lives are told in being lived and lived in being told' (Carr-Saunders and Wilson, 1986 [1933]: 61). This chapter has described the nuanced way in which the lawyers experience their world of work based on the empirical evidence gathered. The following discussions will seek to unpick these themes and their relevance to this study. By doing so, they elucidate the findings from the data in more intricate and microdetail. The creative excerpt above evidences the practice of working in the legal aid field, and does so in a way that promotes understanding, knowing, and explaining the lived experience. The following discussions will seek to link this lived experience to broader themes for wider socio-legal analysis, which will feed into the rest of the book. Drawing from lived experience and the 'experiential' can ultimately evoke critical imagination going forward as it illuminates a process of connection to the participants (O'Neill et al, 2021). This can pedagogically facilitate our imaginations as well as our practices as researchers, educators, students, and the public alike in transformative ways, to understand and reveal hidden worlds.

This composite chapter has identified themes that have emerged from the 'data-driven analyses'. The themes speak to all levels of the threefold framework adopted in this research, highlighting the benefit of adopting a 360-degree perspective that combines the overall context, the occupation, and the experience of the individuals on the ground. The themes outlined in Figure 0.1 will be explored in the succeeding empirical chapters in a critical light.

This book marries different themes spanning the macro, meso, and micro levels to encapsulate the world of the legal aid lawyer. Emergent from the narrative laid out above, I argue that existing institutional and professional structural barriers, funding cuts, combined with toxic narratives – most notably lack of understanding of legal aid – have implications on the work, and, resultant from this, I suggest that the moral alignment and collaborative nature of legal aid renews and sustains a sense of purpose in an otherwise alienated field. Considering this, the work can be best understood from the ground level up – the everyday, micro interactions – as opposed to trusting and relying on misconceptions produced by the government, public, and media alike. In sum, the next few empirical chapters draw back the curtains to reveal these inner layers in the depth they deserve.

Figure 0.1: Emergent themes from the narrative chapter

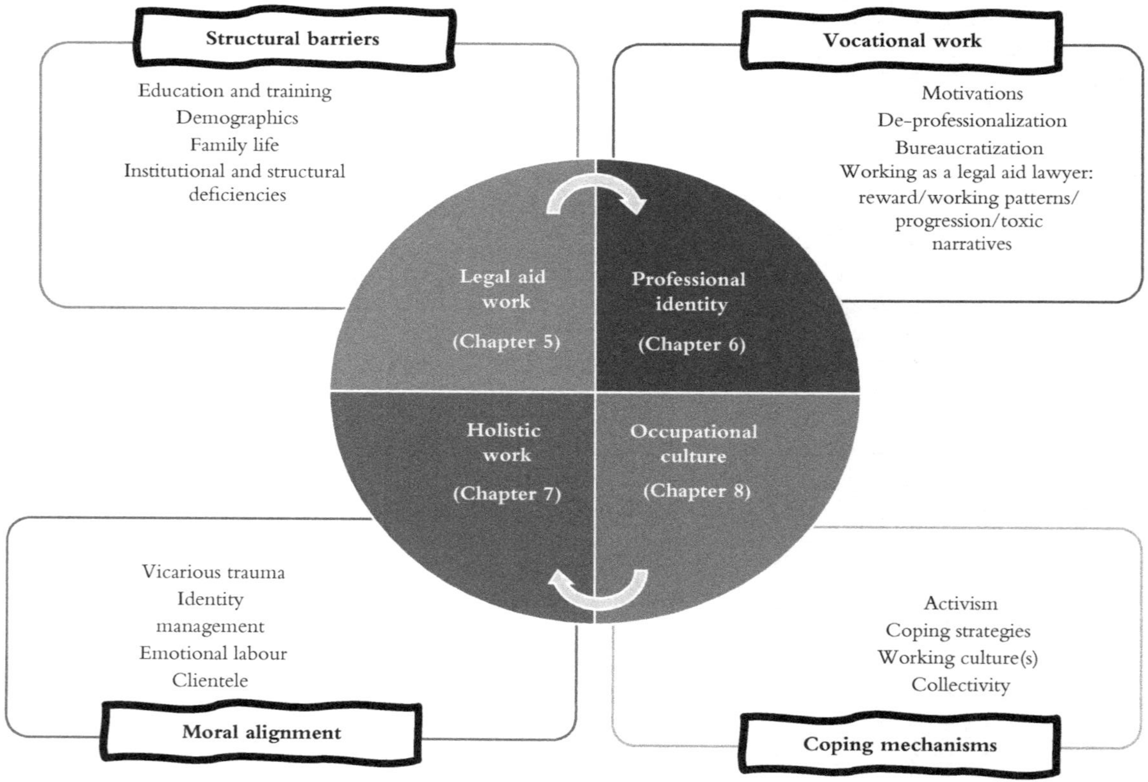

Source: Author's own elaboration.

1

Introduction

'Is there a market for washed-up legal aid lawyers where the light has died behind their eyes, and they're just walking zombies?' (Marcus, a housing solicitor). This may just be the voice of Marcus, one man in a cohort of many, yet, when sharing his insecurity, he speaks for a profession beset by both fragility and precarity. Take this, for example: it is 2023, and criminal barristers across England and Wales working within the legal aid sector were forced to a halt following a dispute with the government concerning legal aid. With incomes falling nearly 30 per cent over the last two decades, criminal barristers working in legal aid now face an average annual income, after expenses, of only £12,200 in their first few years of practice (Criminal Bar Association, 2022). Peter – a criminal barrister – recalls a legal aid case where there was an issue with the charge. The case equated to ten hours of work plus additional hours travelling and waiting in court. He received a total of £126, meaning that he was paid a total of £7.89 per hour, which is £1.61 under the national living wage. Yet, if he had not been there, the defendant would have received a much longer sentence. Becky, based at a firm specializing in civil legal aid was paid £208 for an industrial injury case, even though they carried out £2,800 worth of work. Thirty per cent of the work Becky does is free as it is pro bono. Maria is the only remaining housing legal aid lawyer in Norfolk.

Ten years since the government took an axe to legal aid, justice is increasingly becoming out of reach. Law centres across the country are being closed,[1] and firms have been forced to shut down their legal aid departments. Many people now living in areas where they can no longer access help that they are *entitled* to. The vanishing availability of legal aid across the likes of

[1] Over the 12 months to the end of June 2024, 499 firms have closed (Solicitors Regulation Authority, 2024). Over 100 law firms specializing in criminal work have raised serious concerns about the bidding for new contracts and warn of 'mass rejection' if change does not happen (Justice Gap, 2024).

criminal, family, housing, immigration, welfare, education – the list goes on – is becoming unsustainable for the clients *and the lawyers* alike. This struck me as a researcher, but also as a member of society. We all, in fact, could find ourselves, at some point during our lives, in difficult situations requiring legal representation. Justice should be for all, yet those who qualify for state-funded legal advice are less able to access it, and the public side of the legal profession is becoming less appealing to work within. For many, this may seem particularly absurd. To the public eye the 'lawyering' profession remains elite and well-paid. The branding of legal aid lawyers as 'fat cats' by Tony Blair in 2001 and by Ken Clarke in 2010 has had an effect ever since. Inflammatory headlines such as '500 legal aid barristers earning more than the PM' (Daily Mail, 2011), 'Fat cat lawyers will be banned from mounting last-ditch appeals to stop foreign criminals being booted out' (Hamilton, 2021), and 'Fat cat barristers helping criminals' (Loweth, 2022), painted an unfavourable picture of legal aid work. For most, the thought of a barrister striking may seem unreasonable. Yet people continue to confuse work publicly funded by the state (legal aid) with privately funded work (client funded), and this has led to low levels of public sympathy. Society can justify doctors, nurses, teachers, and train drivers going on strike, but legal aid practice remains hidden, making strike action seem irrational. The work of legal aid lawyers could not be further from the fat-cat stereotype depicted by the broader political and societal sphere. Revealing these inner hidden realities remains vital for scholarly, academic, and public domains given that the sector is at significant risk. While this book focuses on the English and Welsh context, what remains apparent is that, over the last three decades, we have seen drastic cuts to legal aid not only in England and Wales, but also in countries such as the US, Sweden, Iceland, the Nordic countries, as well as the Netherlands (Abel et al, 2022). I am sure that the themes raised here undoubtedly speak to other national/international contexts.

Exploring the legal profession

When considering the above, many questions come to mind. Why should we know more about legal aid? What is the impact on the solicitors and barristers working within the field of the cuts to legal aid funding, and what motivates/allows them to remain working within the field, despite its ongoing precarious state? The motivation to write this book emerged from such questions, as these remain to be answered. To this end, this book seeks to do just that, providing a contemporary insight into the legal aid world, spanning civil–criminal and solicitor–barrister remits alike. In doing so, it critically analyzes, catalogues, and explores the impact of austerity from the perspectives of the workers, and assesses the occupational changes that have occurred in light of the precarious macro backdrop. What is equally important – although too often overlooked or left out from consideration – is to simply capture the hidden world of the legal aid lawyer: to provide the key to open the door to a world that has always been very inward facing, yet so incredibly vital as a pillar of our legal system, and a cog in the very mechanics of justice.

The legal aid occupation holds a substantial amount of appeal for researchers, as a unique and complex working group that sits on the peripheries of the wider lawyering profession, the criminal justice system, the voluntary sector, and the welfare state. Capturing a snapshot of a depleted, and diminishing occupational group also provides a precious resource to aid in understanding and contributing to what it means to be a liberal professional in the 21st century. Funding cuts congruent with demands for efficiency has led to lawyers becoming increasingly alienated (Newman and Welsh, 2019). Increased levels of regulation have disrupted working practices and have interfered with existing work-based identities that, traditionally, were client-focused. Changes to the legal aid regime now encourage the enactment of acquisitive as opposed to altruistic modes of work. Ideal lawyering principles become compromised for practical business concerns, restricting the ability of those carrying out the work to 'do good' or to act under the public service ideal (Sommerlad, 2004). As Thornton (2020: 248) states, this can force lawyers to work in ways 'they find restrictive, distasteful or even ethically uncomfortable', with lawyers themselves reporting a growing sense of crisis.

Studies, have tended to address specific elements of the lawyering role, including: the lawyer–client relationship, legal aid reforms (Hynes and Robins, 2009; Sommerlad, 2004), newly-qualified lawyers (Boon, 2005), entry into the profession (Duff et al, 2000), lawyer mobility (Francis, 2005), lawyer ethics (Boon, 2002; Webb, 2003), or specific fields of law, such as criminal defence (Kemp, 2010; Newman, 2013; Newman and Welsh, 2019; Stephen et al, 2008; Stephen and Tata, 2006; Thornton, 2019; Welsh, 2017; Welsh and Howard, 2019), family law (Mant, 2020; Mant and Wallbank, 2017), and immigration law (Wilding, 2023). Goulandris (2020) explored the Bar profession and its transformation over the last 30 years, identifying key changes to their professionalism and working culture – which will be drawn upon later on. Yet, much of the research on legal aid lawyering can provide only a partial picture of the challenges in the contemporary legal aid sector, as they are either based on the US context, or were published in the pre-2010 era. Literature in this jurisdiction has likewise tended to examine areas of law in isolation, as opposed to assessing vulnerabilities across the wider occupation of legal aid (bar Cooke, 2021; Denvir et al, 2023), leaving something of a methodologically rooted gap that this book addresses.

Abel et al (2020) discuss broader global trends following the acceleration and intensification of global socio-economic developments since the 1980s, challenging the professional form of the legal profession. With the volume spanning legal professions across 46 different countries, this data allows for the engagement of cross-national comparisons. Sommerlad (2004: 15) argues that the 'structure, culture and ethos of the profession' has changed over time as lawyers within it become subject to more surveillance, increased competition, and greater regulation overall. Stephen and Tata (2006) note that, as a result of renumeration changes, those practising in legally aided defence work are spending less face-to-face time with clients, resulting in their work being less effective. This builds on the problems McConville et al (1994) highlighted in their study on organizational practices of criminal defence lawyers in the 1990s, which found that lawyers relied on standardized services provided by lesser-qualified, or non-qualified staff. In an occupation that was already facing significant challenges, the extent to which these problems have been exacerbated further is a significant area of concern, as justice has become temporally situated and limited across the globe (Welsh and Howard, 2019). Socio-legal frameworks have been established as a good starting point for studying lawyers, their practice, as well as how other social factors may shape their experiences (Sommerlad, 2013; Sommerlad and Sanderson, 1998; Webley, 2020). At the epicentre of decades of austerity, it remains essential, however, to unravel how those working within the legal aid field navigate across civil and criminal remits. To this end, practising lawyers are now faced with challenges to both innovate and work more efficiently to maintain their very existence.

A new class of legal professionals?

Reducing public spending comprises one of the latest manifestations of neoliberalism, undermining the professional nature of legal aid work by weakening working values and morals. Yet, the legal aid profession remains a vital pillar of the welfare state. Negotiating the radical impact of cuts to funding, and the associated erosion of legal aid has not only produced structural reform, but rising state intervention has also fundamentally altered the very meaning of legal aid provision. The profession is becoming increasingly detached from its original altruistic remit as it denies the rights of workers within it to serve justice and help people most in need (Newman and Welsh, 2019). Typically, the occupation upholds specific professional values that correlate with the privilege and status of being a legal aid lawyer. A devotion to serving in the public interest and fore-fronting client-centred practice are two key attributes that have typically defined the profession. Under New Public Management (NPM), the emergence of a 'new class of legal professionals who do not have the income, status, prospects or autonomy' has arguably standardized legal product (Sommerlad, 2010: 334).

Lawyers have likewise become increasingly subject to additional administrative duties. Zaloznaya and Nielsen (2011: 10) have coined the term 'task marginality', whereby those in the field now spend more time doing menial tasks than using their advanced professional and legal skills to assist those most in need. Yet, negotiating the professional nature of legal aid work has never been so highly idiosyncratic. Working in the legal aid field has become increasingly onerous for lawyers who now must navigate a difficult allocation system provided by the Legal Aid Agency. The process of acquiring funding has become equally arduous for the lawyer and the client as provisions become more restricted. While lawyers' power is now more constrained as the Legal Aid Agency determines 'what is knowledge', lawyers working within that world are subject to different pressures as they face differing caseloads, funding models, specialisms, and client bases. As the occupation becomes increasingly hollowed out, the 'new' legal aid lawyer faces a more demarcated working environment. Deep engagement with their clients and broader social justice orientations still allows them to 'make do' – in a profession where they are otherwise marginalized professionally in comparison to their private counterparts – despite ever-increasing restrictions (Zaloznaya and Nielsen, 2011: 919). Kinghan (2021: 168) found that lawyers in their study wanted to sustain their identities as progressive lawyers despite these pressures. Evidence shows that a progressive lawyering movement still exists in the UK, which is built around networks of informal interaction, shared beliefs, solidarity as well as collective action, lending itself to the construction of a persistent working culture that will be explored later.

Making sense of legal aid lawyering

As a researcher, I spent a long time thinking about how I could best portray the world of the legal aid lawyer, given its complexities and 'buried' nature. Not only did I want to shed light on the precarious macro backdrop, considering the ongoing cuts to funding, but also on legal aid lawyers as a collective, as well as their individual stories given how diverse the work can be. As such, the conceptual framework adopted in this book is threefold (see Figure 1.1). Influenced by the work of Poelmans et al (2003) and Kwan et al (2016), my own adaptation drawing on macro, meso, and micro variables enables an in-depth investigation into the lived experience of the legal aid lawyer through a data-driven analysis. This framework spans the varying levels of the profession to include: the broader economic context, the occupation, as well as the individuals working within it. This eclectic theoretical approach allows for a more refined and richer understanding of a complex occupation in its entirety.

The macro theories employed here surround themes of precariousness and professionalism. The meso-level variable investigated draws on theories of occupational culture. On the micro level, the examined variables include individual employee experiences, the realities of practice, as well

Figure 1.1: Threefold analysis: macro, meso, and micro

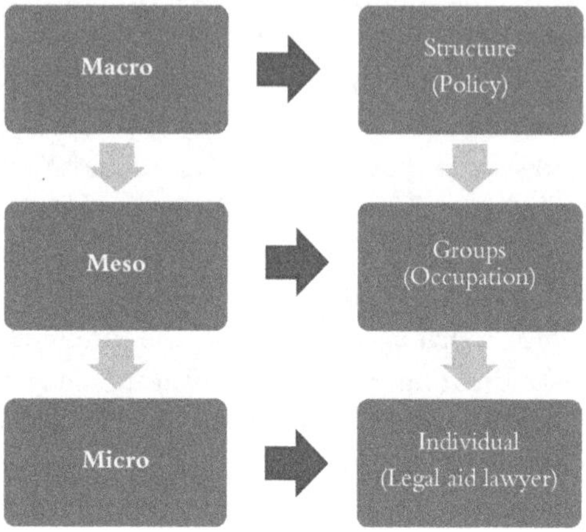

Source: Author's own elaboration.

as day-to-day interactions with different agents. Here, micro interactionist theories (Goffman, 1956) and emotional labour theory (Hochschild, 1979; 1983; Phillips et al, 2020) are utilized. Traditionally, threefold levels of analysis have been used within the remits of human resources, business management, organizational psychology, together with the sociology of work. Through this threefold model, combined with the two sets of gathered empirical data (ethnographic observation and interviews), this book offers a comprehensive insight into part of the legal aid world. A single theoretical standpoint does not encapsulate or understand how broader contextual structures, the profession, as well as the individuals interact in a comprehensive manner. The three levels here complement each other and fill in the gaps that each level in isolation would not identify.

Painting the broader 'macro' picture: a precarious backdrop

On the macro level, the book will explore the impact of precarity. Precarious work or 'precarity' has been a popular focus within the realm of work and labour over the past decade (Hewison in Harper and Lawson, 2003). The origin of the term 'precarity' can be traced back to the 1960s, when Bourdieu initially coined the term 'precarité' to describe the colonial working class, and then later a mode of dominance emerging from 'a neoliberal restructuring of the global economy' (Jorgensen, 2015: 962). The concept of 'precariousness' has also featured in various theories of 'late'/ 'high' modernity (for example, Beck, 1992; Giddens, 1991), and was later used in analyses of poverty (Standing, 2011) and crime (Young, 1999).

The term 'precarious work' is not straightforward to define as measuring the levels of precarity within work is difficult, and temporary work 'does not constitute all the forms of work considered precarious' (Standing, 2011: 434). Sennett (1998) and Beck (2000) have theoretically provided sophisticated analyses of precarious work under contemporary capitalism. These key works view the workplace as enduring 'epochal shifts that have sweeping cultural and personal consequences'. Beck's (2000) work on the 'brave new world of work' likewise draws on issues of precarity in line with issues of job fragmentation and the broader political economy of insecurity. 'The job for life has now disappeared: paid employment is becoming precarious; the foundations of the social welfare state are collapsing normal life-stories are breaking up into fragments' (Beck, 2000: 3). Standing's (2011) work is centred on a new group in the world or, in other terms, a 'class-in-the-making'. In an attempt to revitalize the debate on defining the precariat, Standing (2011: 1) argues that the 'precariat' comprises people without an anchor of stability. It is argued that, since the 1970s, the neoliberal model has called for a return to the market, as market principles come to permeate every aspect of day-to-day life. Of resonance here is the increase in labour market flexibility, which results in the transferal of risks and insecurity to the workers themselves, as well as their families. Likewise, those who have high levels of education may accept a job or occupational role of lower status, or may experience modern labour insecurity, including the lack of long-term contracts or protection of employment.

The precariat is said to experience the four 'As': anger, anomie, anxiety, as well as alienation, and, while the individual may not experience all four at once, individuals can be 'linked to the precariat' through certain features of it (Standing, 2011: 33). Building on this, Standing (2011) denotes that one of the worst outcomes of the commodifying market society is productive 'idleness'. In other words, intensified labour results in passive 'play'. This is the idea that many individuals now find themselves 'spent' because of their employment, and therefore have no motivation or inclination to join in more active leisure activities other than simply watching television. The precariat is now under constant 'time-stress', having to devote all their time to their employment, while not knowing whether this will offer a reliable road to the economic security of a professional career. The workplace is, therefore, becoming or, arguably, has become, an 'unfamiliar zone of insecurity'.

In classical Western sociology, the legal profession played a central role in the construction of modernity, reflecting authority, social solidarity, and moral foundations (Aubert, 1976; Durkheim, 1957; Parsons, 1954; Weber, 1978). Yet, increasingly, those working within the field face the precariousness associated with attempting to cling on to legal aid contracts. It has been argued that, increasingly, liberal workers are being made to manage the risks of their own employment, which leads to 'uncertainty, instability, vulnerability and insecurity' across several different occupations, and which has resulted in the rise of precarious workers (Hewison in Harper and Lawson, 2003: 438; Standing, 2011). As Jorgensen (2015: 961) notes, the precariat is a result of 'decades of neoliberal policy hegemony resulting in flexibilization of the labour markets, insecurity, uncertainty and risks across social strata'. In other words, there has been a shrinking of working rights. As Choonara writes (2011: n.p.): 'All workers can find themselves in a more or less precarious position'. Likewise, while Standing (2011) argues that the development of the precariat is a 'new tendency', 'unemployment, underemployment, insecurity, and precariousness are hardly new conditions for the working class' (Jorgensen, 2015: 963). However, while the precariat is not a new phenomenon, the theory offers a toolbox to understand contemporary work practices and new forms of working identity formations, which this book utilizes. As Abel et al (2020) recognize, the reconfiguration of professional work (to be discussed in more detail below), because of both standardization and specialization, has resulted in increased occupational segregation, and some 'low value work' is outsourced and subcontracted to 'contract' lawyers on zero hours or fixed-term contracts. As their data further indicates, the contemporary legal field has become increasingly splintered, as traditional characteristics of professional autonomy have eroded. The 'profession' remains extremely patterned by social hierarchies, and professional ideals tend to be ever further out of reach for those who continuously struggle to uphold justice.

In turn, the increased precarity of work has also led to a hollowing out of professional ethics and collective norms, leading to what Sennett (1998) has coined the 'corrosion of character'. Sennett examined the impact of New Capitalism to reveal two distinct worlds of work: (1) the vanished world of structured, hierarchical organizations where a sense of personal character mattered; and (2) the brave new world of work based on risk, flexibility, short-term teamwork, and the 'ability to reinvent yourself on a dime' (Sennett, 1998). The latter has led to the erosion of our sense of 'character' and long-term aspects of our emotional experiences (Sennett, 1998: 10). Of relevance, he offers justification for this process in line with the concepts of drift, lack of routine, the restructured and flexible nature of time, the illegible nature of modern forms of labour, the increased pressure to take 'risks' within the context of employment, as well as the changing work ethic in line with how to deal with failure (Sennett, 1998). Sennett (1998) delves further into the meaning of this insecurity felt by many, arguing that, as such, this has not only had a significant effect on individual moral identity, but also on wider collective social relations.

The legal aid lawyer must juggle the spontaneity of their work, combined with the short-termism that permeates their role on a day-to-day basis, because of the clientele they deal with. This book addresses this factor by asking whether this constant control/lack of control dichotomy results in the lack of work-based identity and a broader sense of occupational dismantling, placing them in the position of the precarious worker. Despite this, questions are also asked regarding the extent to which legal aid lawyers have ever had a linear time structure and progression pattern. For instance, lawyers have not necessarily had salaried positions for that long, as legal work has traditionally been paid through billing schemes. Fundamentally, changes to the legal aid regime that encourage the enactment of acquisitive as opposed to altruistic modes of work because of the privatization of public services, as well as the removal of systems of state welfare can, however, also be seen as contributing to the precariousness experienced by both civic-minded lawyers and their clients. This will be situated within the broader remit of the sociology of work and professions.

Katz (1982: 29) states, albeit in the US context, that poverty lawyers have always had a 'limited professional role' as they tend to handle the 'dirty work' as opposed to 'clean law practices' that are the remit of their private counterparts. In the English and Welsh context, legal aid lawyers are likewise marginalized by the wider legal profession, as well as wider society, a theme that is weaved throughout the book. The introduction of the mass legal aid scheme, responsible for the decline in professional status among criminal defence lawyers, has not helped the situation. Cuts to legal aid funding since 2012 have further challenged the legitimacy of lawyering, and concerns surrounding legal aid provision are still yet to be fully resolved. As even more responsibility has been ceded to the government, professional control over legal aid has been further challenged (Sommerlad, 1996). Harnessing access to the law remains precarious, and this has significant effect on the professional identities of those working within the field. As levels of regulation and bureaucratization increase, legal aid lawyers are forced to move further away from the role in which they had been afforded autonomy where the application of rules is reliant on professional judgement' (Welsh, 2017: 559). Increased bureaucratization now results in those practising legal aid spending less time helping people through individualized forms of justice, and more time doing paperwork (Nash, 2018).

An (un)protected profession?

The term 'profession' has been a longstanding focus within the broader field of sociology, and has been explored from Functionalist, Neo-Weberian, Marxist, and Foucauldian perspectives. Defining the term 'professional' has proved to be difficult, with functionalists arguing that professions uphold status in society and, significantly, *protection from the state*, as they were expected to act in the public interest (Parsons, 1939). Carr-Saunders and

Wilson (1986 [1933]) initially classified the five primary professions as: armed services, clergy, medicine, education, and law, all of which produce services as opposed to goods. Professions in this sense were typically altruistic in their nature, and the idea was that these occupational groups would help maintain a collective with a central union of ideals and values. Professions, in other words, had the function of preventing social dysfunction.

There remains a variable relationship between professionalism and modernity and, three decades after Abel and Lewis (1988; 1989) initially offered a contemporary analysis of forms and meanings of the legal profession, the 'profession' has been 'daily assailed by forces associated with globalisation, the centrifugal pulls of the new market economy and the disintegration of cultural or national bonds' (Pue, 1998; 127).

Research following this explored 'idealized professions', which included doctors and lawyers with 'full autonomy, high social status and the power to self-regulate' (Harrington and Seabrooke, 2020; Moreira, 2022). How their services were provided was typically decided by the professionals themselves. The transformation of occupations into professions ultimately means 'an increase of power and societal prestige' (Egetenmeyer et al, 2018). Trail-theoretical approaches later characterized professions. Mieg (2016), for example, suggests that a profession features autonomy, abstractness and flexibility of knowledge base, altruism, and occupational control at the hands of the profession. Egetenmeyer et al (2018) further note that, within societies, professions reach a certain power that governments respect and grant to professions.

Contemporary functionalists, however, soon became very critical of professions because of increasing bureaucracy, managerialism and routinization, as administrative procedure became increasingly embedded in their practice. Weber coined this the 'depersonalisation of work', as those within certain professions began to have less power and autonomy over their working practice (Weber, 1978). Occupations that were traditionally seen as having professional privileges were beginning to be subject to more external pressures and degradation. Hostile spheres created by austerity and neoliberal governance has meant that occupations are now subject to economization, and 'those who have no economic value find themselves disempowered and excluded' (O'Nions, 2020). An increased 'responsibilization' discourse alongside this has pushed self-reliance, and this has affected both the lawyer and the client in the legal aid context (Sommerlad and Sanderson, 2013). Justice has been reframed as a 'privilege' for the worker and the consumer in this context, and the *justice for all* slogan no longer seems fitting.

Not all expert work is now easy to categorize under a traditional professionalization model, and this definition must be loosened to accompany what it means to be a liberal professional in the 21st century (Bellini and Maestripieri, 2018). As Oakley and Vaughan (2019) argue, legal practice is reflective of 'complex relationships of interdependence and interconnectedness'. Different physical working environments, funding model(s), client bases, client relationships, ethical models and distinctive attitudinal components of legal practitioners mean that this opens new challenges to understanding the work (Cooke, 2021). Discussions have, therefore, moved further away from the development of 'professions', to try to understand the development of 'professionalism' instead, as work has been reorganized, restratified, and relocated (Noordegraaf, 2016). The privileges of service and knowledge-based professions have been lost in some ways, due to funding cuts, performance indicators, and the increased measurement and monitoring of activities (Evetts, 2003). The undermining of professional work by managerial and economic principles has meant that traditional characteristics are handed over to the occupation itself, including autonomy, discretion, and self-regulation. Professions are now subject to increased policies, regulations, governance, and educational demands that exceed just the fulfilment of specific attributes or specialized knowledge. As recognized, however, organizations are not static and are responsive to macro and meso-level social change (Bourdieu and Wacquant, 1992).

In the case of legal aid, a natural survival mechanism for firms struggling to stay afloat has been to hire lower-skilled workers. This has meant, for example, that, due to the marketization of justice, skeleton arguments (documents filed with the court and exchanged between the parties in advance of a court hearing) are now being drafted often without the right skills or knowledge. This can often result in lower quality service, as accountability becomes weakened, resulting in more cases being lost. Delays, mistakes, exploitation, and increased levels of self-representation occur as a result. Clients are struggling to locate a legal aid professional in many areas of the country due to legal aid cuts (Wilding, 2019). The consistent downward trend in funding, size, and cost of the legal aid market, with the encouragement of economy and speed over quality of delivery, has damaged, and continues to damage, legal aid work (Smith and Cape, 2017). Current fluctuations have forced those within the field to retreat from zealous advocacy, leaving the role somewhat 'neutered' (Newman, 2016). What was once seen as an idealized profession, the public side of lawyering, is now crumbling and is no longer protected by professional privilege. Treating legal aid work as a 'profession' with its associated privileges feels no longer fitting.

In the national context, Abel et al (2020) note that the increased intensification of work, loss of autonomy, stratification, and commoditization of legal services were recurrent across the data. They further note that the increasing specialization of the field contributes to its ongoing fragmentation, further challenging the field's legitimacy and ethics (Moorhead, 2010).

Sitting at the 'meso' level: occupational culture

The social organization of working relations is an aspect of 'labour constitution', which refers to the historically determined ensemble of rules, institutions, conditions, and social statuses (Coutu, 2020; Dukes and Streeck, 2020). These organizational practices may span departments, occupations, or professions. Social norms and values in the workplace concern how work should be done and how relations and social groups are formed around a common position, such as work and employment (Lipset et al, 1956). Even in fissured workplaces, social and work identities are still built around work relations and shared practices. Social bonds among workers within a given occupation produce and sustain efficacy as they ground normative realities, even more so when working under precarious conditions. As Dukes and Streeck (2020: 636) argue, by focusing exclusively on formal norms such as statutory and contractual occupational rules and neglecting informal social norms in each occupation, a full understanding of the normativity of working life cannot be delivered. 'On the broadest macro level are overt behaviours, written rules, and policy; second, is a sense of what ought to be (values); third those things are taken for granted as "correct" ways of behaving within the organisation' (Deering, 2011: 25).

An 'occupational community' concerns a 'collectivity of workers sharing a common position in work and employment that gives rise to shared social norms and relations of solidarity' (Dukes and Streeck, 2020: 619–620). It concerns work but also social life, and offers a micro perspective in line with the work of Weber (1924 [1894]), which allows for an understanding of collective norms and values, as well as the political capacity to cope with a more fragmented and divergent work structure. Communal social ties, as well as the embeddedness of work life in social life, fosters the emergence of a working culture, as does supportive cooperation among workers in the transmission of skills to new recruits where sufficient education or training may be lacking. An occupational community likewise can act as a 'community of coping' in challenging moments and can further inform 'a curious mixture of consent and resistance to work' (Korczynski, 2003: 59). There remain deficiencies in the literature on occupational cultures, the fixation on limited occupations, the lack of conceptual clarity, and the limited range of studies in the legal setting. Research into how work and culture come to interact within wider legal aid practice is almost non-existent. There has been some research into courtroom working cultures (Carlen, 1976; Welsh and Howard, 2019; Young, 2013). Wider studies have identified a broader 'legal culture' as a form of communicative as opposed to physical culture, unlike other agents working in the justice field, that is police officers and prison workers (Chambliss, 2010; Chan, 2014; Cownie, 2004). Lively (2001) employed an ethnographic approach to explore the 'structurally subordinate positions' of paralegals and their understanding of being referred to as a 'professional' despite the more demeaning aspects of their role. Upholding a sense of collective professionalism was found to increase their 'moral worth'. The paralegals in the study upheld a set of norms independent of their direct occupational positions, which helped them to maintain their sense of professionalism in a role that is often marginalized. Fielding (2011: 97) likewise argues, for example, that over time judges form a culture – which can be referred to as 'judgecraft' – defined as 'an amalgam of working practices' (see also Hunter et al, 2016; Mack and Roach Anleu, 2007). Goulandris (2020) identifies key changes at the Bar, which has altered the working culture of barristers, arguing that a once unified profession has now fragmented: at one end some chambers are operating like businesses, whereas at the other end chambers are struggling to survive day-to-day as they rely so heavily on legal aid funding. Regulatory and procedural reforms are imposing changes and gradually splitting up once-fused professions.

Understandably, not all working environments give rise to an 'occupational community' or working culture due the individualized natures of work, lack of contact among employees, or the separation of workers depending on the design of the physical workplace. Occupational cultures are therefore often elaborate (Christensen and Crank, 2001). As a way of understanding the richness of occupational life, the concept of an occupational culture can help connect the macro and micro in the working context, but they can be difficult to define in a robust manner. Models of 'occupational culture' are expected to both interact and conflict (Johnson et al, 2009), as there are difficulties with objectively measuring culture (Bond, 2004). Allen (2001) argues that employee perceptions always mediate occupational culture; therefore, it is useful to focus on these perceptions as opposed to objective measures to explore its construction.

Nevertheless, the occupational community of the legal aid lawyer has been very much overlooked, despite those within it considering themselves as engaging in the same sort of work, as well as sharing and recognizing job-specific norms and values that extend beyond just work-related matters (Van Maanen and Barley, 1984). LeBaron and Zumeta (2003) argue that 'lawyers' cultural mode of being and behaving is shaped in multiple ways by their training in law, and their associations with other legal professionals. While it has become increasingly difficult to conceive of shared ethical values due to the fragmentation of the profession (Francis, 2005), there remains a collective dimension linking these multiple areas of work spanning specialism, workplace, and legal aid caseload, as will be further outlined. Increasingly precarious conditions within the legal aid world have strengthened solidarity among workers within it, as they become particularly eager to keep the profession alive – conducive to legal aid work becoming more of a progressive 'community of practice' (Dukes and Streeck, 2020: 626). In a job that is typically very client focused, there remains a strong presence of workers within it who are eager to help others even under adverse conditions. In this sense, occupational cultures become catalysts for worker solidarity, cultivating a sense of collectivism in an otherwise fragmented environment. Given the diversity of the occupation – and the wider disruption of the workplace – understanding the way in which work and culture come to interact in the legal aid workplace is certainly not a straightforward matter. Nonetheless, as Dukes and Streeck (2020) argue, more ethnographic research on the 'formation of occupationally and workplace-based communities' among workers is urgently required if we are to understand what is going on 'on the ground' in sustaining work under contemporary conditions. This seems like a particularly fitting time to write this book.

While it may be difficult to speak of a singular, rigid and taken-for-granted culture that applies to all legal aid work, it is likely that different lawyers across both civil and criminal remits, spanning a variety of workplaces, may form 'subcultures', or their work may align in some way or form. This deviation becomes integral to tracing the contours of their working lives. Therefore, rather than trying to shoehorn existing blanket models of occupational culture, this book proposes a new conceptual lens, which seeks to better understand the ways in which the dynamics of culture and work fluidly interact within the context of legal aid work.

Exploring the 'micro' theories: altruism and Goffman

Legal aid lawyers work at the front and centre of the justice system, meaning that they experience significant emotion and therefore must find a way to manage this. Hochschild's (1983) concept of 'emotional labour' is used within this book. Initially applied to the context of the private sector exploring how emotions can be deployed for profit, in more recent years we have seen this term applied as part and parcel of public-sector work (Phillips et al, 2020). As Phillips et al argue, the concept of emotional labour brings forward a focus on public relations with the state, a particularly pertinent link to explore within the context of legal aid. Hochschild provides three criteria that a worker must display: (1) 'face-to-face' or 'voice-to-voice' contact with a member of the public; (2) 'the worker to produce an emotional state in another person'; and (3) to have some level of control over the emotionality of the workers (1983: 147). With a focus on identity, meaning, affect, and subjective understandings of work, this is very relevant here. Hochschild examined how those who are customer-facing in the service sector manage their own emotions in response to the clientele they serve. This stimulated the work of Lamont (2000) and Hodson (2001), who used this as a basis to offer explorations on the complexity of meanings, identities, and values around work. Meaning, identity, and values all feature in the analyses. These all come to inform the working culture of the legal aid lawyer later. Emotional labour likewise 'shifts our gaze away from a top-down understanding of policy' and, in turn, becomes a mechanism to understand a given world, how they seek to achieve certain goals and, more so, how they see their world (Phillips et al, 2020: 11).

As the legal profession has shifted from being almost an entirely private profession in the 19th century to now containing parts that are both public-facing and state-funded, analyses of altruism prove useful here (Andreoni, 1989). Altruism can be seen as a defining value of professionalism, integral to public service in the form of 'the professional ideology of committed service to others' (Mungham and Thomas in Dingwall and Lewis, 1983; see also Friedson, 1973; Erlanger and Klegon, 1976). As will become apparent, altruism or 'do-gooding' plays a significant role in the encouragement of legal aid work. However, as a result of bureaucratic processes and increasing external pressures to legal aid funding, those within the field become increasingly dissatisfied as their ability to practise in a humanistic manner becomes restricted. As Simon (1998: 1) notes: 'no social role encourages such ambitious moral aspirations as the lawyers, and no social role so consistently disappoints the aspirations in encourages'. While Simon was speaking of the US context, this also speaks to the English and Welsh context. As Newman and Welsh (2019) identify, criminal defence lawyers now have to 'churn' out their clients like a production line, and evidence of this can also be seen across other specialisms, as will be explored. There remains an urgent need to 'humanize' the justice system if the 'social good' element of legal aid work is to be saved. To this end, this moral imperative is the very driving force of legal aid work, as will be explored later on.

Being competent in one's work in the altruistic context often requires those within the field to adopt a 'credible front', as identified by Goffman (1967: 75). A credible front 'refers to that element of an individual's ceremonial behaviour typically conveyed through deportment, dress, and bearing, which serves to express to those in his presence that he is a person of certain desirable or undesirable qualities'. Lively (in Harper and Lawson, 2003: 355) notes that paralegals, in line with Goffman's 'credible' front, maintain an ability to separate the 'front' and 'back' regions of social interaction within law firms. Goffman refers to the 'front region' being the performance space visible by all, and the 'back region', a space relative to the performative space, where performers can deal with the hidden components of their lives, which often contradict their actions in the front region (Goffman 1990 [1959]: 23–24). 'Personal fronts', as identified here, may include appearance, manner, and emotion management, all of which feed into the analysis in subsequent chapters. Surface acting often means that the lawyers produce emotional displays that are inconsistent with their inner feelings (Hochschild, 1979; 1983; Westaby et al, 2023). This, in turn, can lead to burnout (Wharton,

1993). In similar vein to Westaby et al's (2023) findings, legal aid lawyers therefore must be 'emotionally nimble' in order to control both their own and others' emotions. Provision of support to maintain wellbeing therefore proves vital, as will be explored later. Interactionist theories here thus prove useful in understanding how legal aid lawyers behave in a 'do-gooding' profession within which emotion plays a very significant role, and further sheds light on the work. The methodological/epistemological value of this research for understanding access to justice, but also for making sense of the future of publicly funded professions, will be elicited throughout this book.

The legal aid world in the limelight

The cuts to legal aid provision since 2012 present a significant threat to traditional legal aid practice in England and Wales. This book examines the changing occupational and professional identity of legal aid lawyers, considering their shrinking industry and significantly diminishing funds. The book offers one of the largest and most novel studies of its kind, capturing the changing occupational terrain spanning civil and criminal, and solicitor–barrister legal aid remits alike. Based on an ethnography, the book captures first-hand the lived experiences of those at the front line of legal aid provision who are seeking desperately to uphold and deliver access to justice. Although the 'profession' has become increasingly precarious, this research demonstrates how lawyers compensate for this by retaining their resilience and demonstrating altruism towards their clients.

This book further offers a nuanced and contemporary insight into the working culture of legal aid lawyers and identifies a 'shared orientation' model as a new conceptual lens with which to refocus the gaze on working life in fissured legal workplaces. The 'shared orientation' vitally acts as a collaborative coping mechanism for those who remain in the field. Through its offerings of a novel and fresh insight into what it means to be a precarious legal professional in the 21st century working for the 'social good', the book seeks to encapsulate both the pitfalls and blessings of those working in the very heart of justice. Chapter 2 offers a detailed insight into the historical development of legal aid provision to provide context, and to set the scene for subsequent chapters. It likewise outlines the different types of professionals who work within the remit of legal aid, as it is a multifaceted occupation – and this remains key to the findings emergent here. As will be made clear, legal aid work has always been subject to cuts to funding, which has had a continuous impact on the provision, access to, and practice of the work. This has been further exacerbated in the post-2012 setting, which will be explored. This chapter therefore lays strong groundwork for succeeding exploration. Combining the historical development of legal aid with changes over time (including the impact of COVID-19) – as well as a detailed outline of different types of legal aid work (role and specialism) – offers clarity for the reader. Different specialisms, as well as different positions and workplaces, will be explored to situate the research. It is vital that the complexities of the profession are noted and mapped out, given the holistic nature of the book and the all-encompassing focus of the research.

Chapter 3 considers the biographies of the participants in this research: their backgrounds, roles, and characteristics. It explores themes such as demographics, work location, and specialisms, as well as providing methodological data surrounding the research locations, as well as the makeup of the legal professionals involved in the research. An overview of the research process is therefore given, to give the reader background insight necessary to allow the subsequent empirical chapters to emerge. A reflective insight on my own research journey and positionality is also provided here. Fuller justification is given to the sampling rationale and focus on both civil and criminal remits. Offering an insight into both civil and criminal remits paves the way for a more detailed examination of the profession overall, and likewise may impact the ways a legal aid lawyer experiences the occupation. Bringing civil and criminal lawyers together in one exploration of working practices is likewise a novel development, which will take forward the study of legal lawyering by allowing commonalities to be drawn across this diverse field, which is a particular strength of this research.

Chapter 4 sheds light on the working culture of the legal aid lawyer, an area that has been previously omitted from the academic gaze. Deficiencies in the literature on occupational culture have been identified: the fixation in the literature on other criminal justice agents, such as police and prison officers; its lack of conceptual clarity and the limited range of studies in the legal setting. This chapter, therefore, contributes to this body of literature through the identification of a working culture of legal aid work, offering a meso-level analysis. This engages well with the books' interest in how culture and work interact in the legal aid context. This chapter critically explores the working culture of legal aid lawyers and develops a novel 'shared orientation' model to better understand contemporary legal aid work and its workers. It examines the emerging relevance and applicability of this new conceptual lens, refocusing the gaze on working life in fissured legal workplaces. This model will anchor the exploration throughout the remainder of the book, acting as a conceptual framework.

A 'shared orientation' model provides a way to better understand the unique and multifaceted workspace of the legal aid lawyer, involving varying caseloads, differing levels of employment and diverse working environments. Driving this conceptual model is (1) the distinctive features of the practice setting, but also (2) the attitudinal component present in the data from the legal aid lawyers themselves. The 'shared orientation' model offers unity as a way of functioning in an otherwise fragmented profession through its preservation of working ideals; it captures the cultural heterogeneity of the work, and acts as an informal coping mechanism. Overall, those practising within legal aid share some similar tendencies across the board, including knowledge-sharing, collaboration, camaraderie, and socialization processes, to name just a few. The wide-ranging sample in this research spanning solicitor–barrister and civil–criminal remits was beneficial to the construction of the shared orientation, as it would have been harder to justify if fragments of the profession were explored in isolation. A shared orientation offers insight into how the wider profession unites beyond individual specialisms, positions, and workplaces. The formation of this conceptual model speaks to the deficiencies in the literature and offers a nuanced insight into this often-hidden occupational world. Findings indicate long-lasting cultural features that originate from the practical craft of legal aid work in resistance to legislative and policy innovation. This study is the first of its kind to provide an exploration of the working culture of legal aid lawyers in the current context. Future empirical work based on the 'shared orientation' model will achieve a deeper understanding of this complex field spanning criminal, family, and social welfare contexts alike.

Chapter 5 lays a conceptual basis to develop and contribute to the macro picture. This chapter is foregrounded with existing secondary literature, data, and statistics, punctuated intermittently with descriptive ethnographic accounts and individuals' experiences as obtained from the interview data. This is done purposely, to provide context for, and to situate, subsequent analysis to tell an over-arching story. This chapter describes the characteristics of the legal aid workforce. To this end, education and training, gender, age, race, and social class all come to construct the rhetoric of the legal aid lawyer. Drawing out patterns and themes can affect how a profession is experienced, which fits well with the intentions of the discipline of the Sociology of Work and Professions.

Chapter 6 determines the particulars amid the journeys of individuals choosing to practice within the remit of legal aid. This proves crucial in respect of recent changes to legal aid work, outlined previously in the earlier chapters. These current fluctuations have forced those within the profession to retreat from zealous advocacy, leaving the resultant role somewhat 'neutered'. Therefore, it is vital for future debates to question why those within the profession nevertheless choose to become, and practise, as legal aid lawyers, by reason of the fundamental role performed by these actors in upholding access to justice. Typically, lawyers working in the field are subject to a 'limited professional role' in the sense that their capabilities, significance, and career development are restricted in comparison to their private counterparts. Consequently, legal aid lawyering requires its own unique analysis acknowledging its position as a vocational pathway.

Chapter 7 argues, that in line with the work of Zaloznaya and Nielsen (2011), the reason why lawyers remain committed to working in an effective and idealized manner, demonstrating altruism, resilience, and determination, is because their deep engagement with their clients and broader social justice orientations allows them to 'make do' in a field whereby they are otherwise marginalized professionally. Focusing on the notion of legal aid lawyering as a 'one-stop shop', the chapter explores the idea that the legal aid lawyers act as a source of multiple services, whereby clients can have their legal (and selected other) needs to be met in just 'one stop', especially in cases situated within the wider theme of access to justice. This analysis aims to understand the consequences that reductions in funding and services will have on the 'lived working experiences' of legal lawyers, and how this influences their ability to continue working holistically (including their views of its effects on their client group, the poor). This chapter likewise outlines how legal aid lawyers are perceived in the wider popular framework. As evidenced here, the legal aid profession faces twofold fragmentation: (1) increased fragmentation and marketization of wider justice services (external), as well as (2) occupational marginalization (internal). The former relates to the impact of the cuts to legal aid funding, and the latter to the marginalized position of the legal aid lawyer compared to their private counterparts, as will be explored. This extent to which this marginalization has been further exacerbated in the context of the post-2012 cuts is examined. This chapter provides discussion in response to the following aim: what consequences have the reductions in funding and services had on the 'lived professional experiences' of legal aid lawyers?

Finally, it is argued here that legal aid lawyering cannot be explained solely through macro theories alone, as this misses out the interactions at the organizational and individual levels. Likewise, without situating the profession in the macro context, an accurate and valid representation of the legal aid world would not be given as the legal aid cuts permeate every layer of the occupation. Social reality in the context of the legal aid lawyer is multifaceted and complex, and therefore such an eclectic approach is needed to give real insight. It is through this threefold model that a richer picture of how precarity and austerity refract down the varying levels of the legal aid occupational terrain emerges. The humanity of lawyers is not something that is regularly spoken about. External characteristics are very one-dimensional, and they ignore the day-to-day working lives. While the individualised legal aid lawyer is presented here as a precarious worker facing marginalization and fragmentation, it is through their 'shared orientation' that they can maintain and attempt to cling on to their ideal occupation to challenge and overcome wider tactics of austerity. Fundamentally, the 'shared orientation' acts as a meso-level catalyst to manage macro-level threats, which in turn affects how legal aid lawyers go about their everyday micro practice.

Encapsulating this occupational world in full was, and continues to be, a hugely daunting task; however, it is a crucial time to obtain a richer understanding of what it means to be a legal aid lawyer in times of precariousness.

2

Research Context: Legal Aid Provision Over Time

This chapter lays the groundwork for succeeding exploration by outlining a contextual basis, exploring what legal aid is, its history, as well as current legal aid developments (see Figure 2.1). This is done to situate the research going forward, but also because many of us – me included prior to carrying out this research – do not truly understand what legal aid actually is or how it works in practice.

What is legal aid?

As recognized in Abel et al's (2020) study on 'lawyers in 21st century societies', legal professions have undergone dramatic changes in recent years, following specifically the impact of globalization, neoliberalism, changes in lawyer demography, legal education, lawyer regulatory bodies, structures of production, as well as access to justice. Increased and unnecessary juridification, resulting in the expansion of regulation, has meant that the numbers of people who feel able to make sense of the world and laws around them is declining. Juridification, in this sense, refers to various aspects of the increase in volume and intensification of legal regulation (Teubner, 1987). Abel (Abel et al, 2022: 624) states that 'all capitalist economies distribute legal services through the market, enabling those who can pay the most to obtain the greatest amount and the best quality (thereby creating the profession's two increasingly unequal hemispheres)' (see also Heinz and Laumann, 1982; Heinz et al, 2005). Most countries established legal aid during the welfare state expansion after the Second World War; however, trends are far from uniform across the globe, and public law provision differs greatly in different contexts (Abel at al, 2022).

Justice is a fundamental principle of any democratic society and, as a society, we expect that our justice system will be both fair and impartial for all involved, despite their means. In order to try and ensure that there is an

Figure 2.1: Legal aid over time

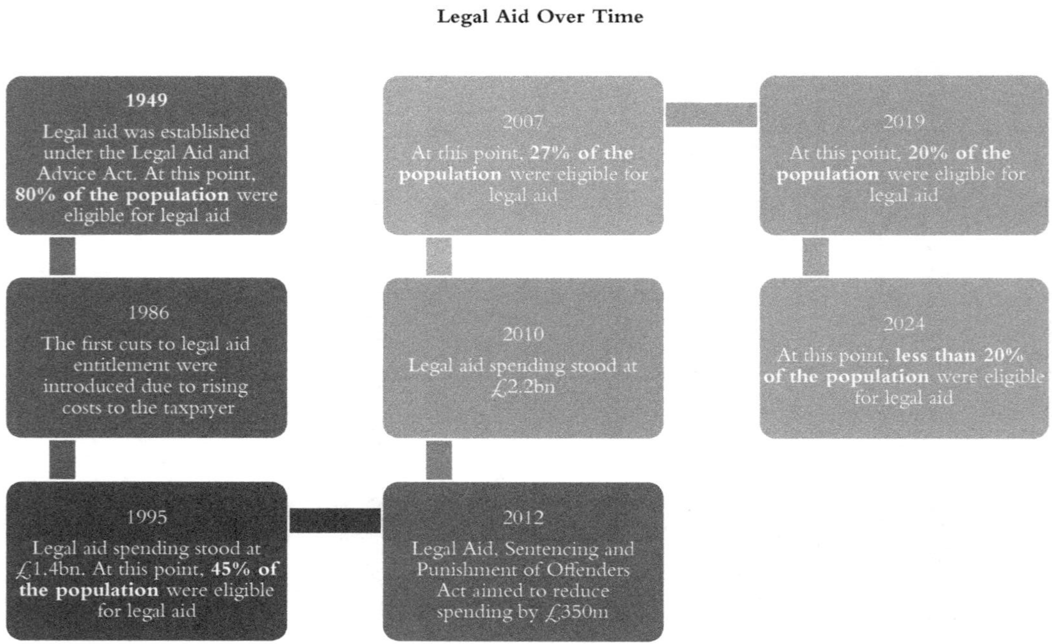

Source: Author's own elaboration.

equality of resources, legal aid was introduced. Legal aid is a publicly funded financial provision administered by the Legal Aid Agency – a Ministry of Justice agency – that provides access to justice in both civil and criminal remits for those unable to afford legal representation. While legal aid was originally available for most areas of law, it is now only available for individuals who meet very specific and certain eligibility criteria, including financial means; it depends also on the merits of the given case, as well as whether the scope relates to an issue that is covered by legal aid provision. It is provided in two ways, via a telephone helpline and via legal aid providers, who then bill the Legal Aid Agency either at an hourly rate or a fixed fee. As outlined in the European Convention on Human Rights: 'In the determination of his civil rights and obligations or of any criminal charge against him, everyone is entitled to a fair and public hearing within a reasonable time by and independent tribunal' (Article 6.1). While this remains slightly murky, as it leaves open to a lot of interpretation, fundamentally legal aid remains a provision that arguably can be regarded as a human right. Legal aid is a right and is required in order to enact the adversarial principles our court system in England and Wales is based upon; yet justice arguably is skewed, as legal representation and resources have never been, and remain, not equally distributed among parties.

The legal aid sector is a unique, diverse, and complex part of the legal profession. This is because the lawyers within it – in a variety of different ways – serve the legal needs of those who are most disadvantaged and marginalized within society. To do so, they rely heavily, if not entirely, on public funding. Consequently, the profession, and the organizations within which they work, have typically felt the impact of longstanding austerity measures and public funding constraints over several decades.

Brief history of legal aid

Central to popular perception, England has had a long tradition of providing access to the legal system for all, with free legal aid constituting a significant social equalizer for those who lack means but are aggrieved (Breger, 1982). However, this has not always been the case. There had been *in forma pauperis* from the 12th century, by which barristers were compelled to act for free; however, criminal legal aid provision was officially first introduced in 1903, with the implementation of the Poor Prisoners Defence Act. This Act empowered courts to grant legal aid to a prisoner with insufficient means 'desirable to the interests of justice' and was an attempt to modernize the system to further avoid any miscarriages of justice (Levenson, 1977: 523). One of the driving forces behind the introduction of civil legal aid provision was the Royal Commission on Divorce (1909–12) (Paterson, 1971; Morgan, 1994; Regan et al, 1999). This drew attention to the demands of the legal profession and likewise questioned its capability of responding to not only divorce matters but also the broader legal needs of the working classes (Bradley, 2019). However, the commission's inability to meet people's legal needs principally around divorce, coincided with the First World War, which reduced the numbers of solicitors. Following on from this, the Lawrence Committee (1919 and 1925) and the Finlay Committee (1926 and 1928) were called in to look at civil provision. While the former report looked at divorce cases more specifically, the latter addressed broader matters of crime and justice. The Finlay Report failed to enthuse lawyers to take on 'poor people's work', and it also did not meet the demands of providing wider access to the law. The Rushcliffe Committee was then formed in 1944 with the remit to improve access to legal advice in England and Wales. It recommended that legal aid should be granted in all criminal cases that met the criteria of being in the 'interest of justice'. In the civil remit, the committee suggested set criteria for eligibility of assistance. This formed the first substantial foundation to legal aid provision.

England and Wales made further attempts to implement legal aid as a public service in 1949 through the partial implementation of the Legal Aid and Advice Act 1949; however, its full implementation was not until 1955. Despite this, it only covered the high courts and not the county courts, which was problematic as this omitted a large bulk of cases (Bradley, 2019). Likewise, while there was no coverage for advice before 1955, Abel- Smith and Stevens (1967) state that provision was already narrowing in the late 1950s despite only just being made available. The Benson Committee (1978) followed, and played a central role in both the provision of legal aid as well as the nature of the profession. The Benson Committee argued that bias-free sources of legal advice were needed and agreed that the Citizens Advice Bureaux, as well as community law centres, would be key providers, working alongside the government to offer more efficient legal advice. The first law centre to open its doors was in North Kensington in 1970. The primary purposes of law centres were to campaign and gain justice for the most impoverished in the community (NKLC, 2019). While they used public funds, they were seen as charities/non-profit firms and could, therefore, be more antipathetic to the state. Alongside securing wider means of justice; law centres were brought about as a response to acknowledged deficiencies in the legal aid scheme that existed at the time, such as the failure to provide funding for those most in need. As opposed to being an impartial legal service, however, the Benson Committee felt that these centres were seen as predominately campaigning organizations for certain sections of the community. The Benson Committee had to wait four years for the (then Conservative) government to respond; however, their suggestions were not implemented in any significant way, and only some of their recommendations, for example the creation of the Legal Aid Board, were taken up (Bradley, 2019).

A consultation paper was published in 1995 and a white paper in 1996, as the Conservative government began to prioritize constraining the legal aid budget within their spending estimates (Brooke, 2016). The Access to Justice Act in 1999 created a new Community Legal Service and Criminal Defence Service, but plans implemented by this Act had failed by 2005 due to cost, which was increasing at an exponential rate. During this time, the crown court absorbed most of the criminal legal aid provision. Between the years 2005 and 2010, the legal aid budget became somewhat stable, but the divide between the needs of the government and the legal profession over legal aid contracts became much wider.

Legal aid spending jumped to £2.2bn in 2010, which was a stark increase from £1.4bn in 1995–96 (Bowcott, 2018). The focus of the Labour Party election manifesto in 2010 was to cut funding, particularly within the criminal remit. The aim was to move away from resorting to lawyers for all justice-related matters and to encourage mediation rather than litigation (Labour Party, 2010). Reducing public spending comprises a manifestation of neoliberalism, undermining the professional nature of legal aid work by weakening working values and morale. The Legal Aid, Sentencing and Punishment of Offenders Act 2012 (LASPO), as well as the Transforming Legal Aid Consultation (2013), continue to significantly limit the scope of civil and criminal legal aid. The Ministry of Justice introduced these reforms to target its limited resources and to reduce the circumstances in which legal aid was payable. They could not continue to pay £2bn for its provision. As a result, many areas of civil legal aid – those related to employment, consumer matters, debt, and clinical negligence – were scrapped entirely. Some funding remained available for eviction, asylum, and special needs provision. Changes in financial eligibility criteria meant that a new upper limit of £37,500 was introduced in the criminal remit (National Audit Office, 2024).

As a result, the process of getting access to legal aid has become far more onerous as new evidence requirements were introduced. LASPO, which came into force on 1 April 2013, has gone beyond its core aims as legally aided assistance is becoming both unsustainable and unattainable for those it seeks to serve. Efficiency has been prioritized over due process, and justice is being denied every day. It has been argued that 'financial status', as opposed to 'legal need', has taken priority, as the latter is no longer seen as a fundable category (Law Society, 2019). Increased efficiency is not only encouraged within the wider criminal justice system, it is also now used as an indicator of success for courts and legal practitioners. In response to cost-shifting, likewise the entitlement and eligibility criteria for legal aid provision has become more stringent, which means that many now do not qualify for help (Law Society, 2019). Issues surrounding both efficiency and accessibility now permeate the system.

As identified by the Ministry of Justice, the main aims of LASPO were to:

1. discourage unnecessary and adversarial litigation at public expense;
2. target legal aid to those who need it most;
3. make significant savings to the cost of the scheme; and
4. deliver better overall value for money for the taxpayer.

The theme of discouraging unnecessary litigation at public expense has always been the central anxiety surrounding legal aid provision, as it formed the justification for earlier committees (Lawrence, 1919, and Finlay, 1926, in UK Parliament, 2025). The government stated at the time of LASPO that the reforms would take three to five years (Law Society, 2017). In the spring of 2013, the legal aid budget was drastically cut by £350 million a year. Before the implementation of LASPO, legal aid was granted in 925,000 cases annually; however, the year after its implementation, this figure dropped significantly to 497,000 cases, equating to an overall decline of 46 per cent. Shortly after this, a further £220 million was due to be cut from the budget, following drastic proposals. Although this figure was contested, overall government spending on legal aid fell by £728 million between 2012/23 and 2022/23 (Law Society, 2024c). Not only has this led to a growing gap between provision and need, but the brunt of this has been placed on the shoulders of the lawyers themselves (Law Society, 2019). The impact of LASPO has undermined access to justice, which in turn has led to wider strains on the justice system (Law Society, 2017). These developments are bringing greater precariousness to both the professionals and the poor who stand to lose vital access to legal dispute resolution and right affirmation mechanisms.

Initially 80 per cent of the general population qualified for funding, but by the early 1990s this dropped to roughly 45 per cent, and it has been suggested that currently as little as 20 per cent of the population are now entitled to legal aid assistance, following the introduction of stringent means testing (Law Society, 2017; Bowcott, 2018). As the fixed allowances for expenditure considered by the means tests have reduced, such changes have also been deemed 'counter-intuitive', as those on state benefits are now considered 'eligible' to pay for their advice and representation (Law Society, 2017: 2). Within the civil remit, the maximum gross income cap for financial eligibility has not considered inflation rates since 2013, which has had an adverse effect. While before LASPO anyone receiving means-tested welfare benefits would automatically qualify financially for legal aid, the new capital means test is now far more stringent than the eligibility for means-tested benefits. The means test has now meant that a large proportion of low-income earners with a minimal amount of capital can no longer receive legal aid support.

Taking all this into account, the legal aid lawyer's role is to mitigate these changes and ensure that those eligible get access to justice via means of legal aid funding. As external pressures increase through restrictions on fees, many are turning away work altogether. The lack of lawyers practising in some areas has resulted in 'advice deserts', meaning that people in certain parts of the UK can no longer find legal experts to consult when in need (Law Society, 2019). Even in areas where access to legal aid is available, some of the initial free legal advice is only available via the 'Government's Mandatory Telephone Gateway' and, evidently, telephone advice provision is not always appropriate as it can be an obstacle for people who may struggle to articulate themselves on the phone, or have the time to stay on hold (Law Society, 2017). Additionally, due to the shrinking nature of the profession because of cuts to legal aid, the quality and quantity of provision has been affected considerably (Law Society, 2019).

This all points to several propositions about the nature of legal aid that will feed into the exploration throughout this book. Legal aid has been through many relentless transformations over the years. The Legal Aid Agency has made the process of obtaining funding far more bureaucratic, which has wider ramifications for the legal professionals working in the field. Provision is restricted, and the quality of the service has been reduced due to pressures placed on the lawyers practising within this field. Not only do the lawyers have to represent vulnerable clients, but they also have to fight for financial support; face bureaucratic hurdles as a result of the Legal Aid Agency, engage in new systems involving telephone gateways and online portals, as well as taking on as many cases as possible due to the shortage of those practising in the field. The occupational terrain of the legal aid lawyer has become far more fragmented during these times. How the profession operates, forms, and upholds its purpose within wider society has altered, calling for an up-to-date exploration, which this book does.

Current legal aid developments

The Ministry of Justice has cut its spending on legal aid by more than a quarter over the past decade, resulting in a fall of 40 per cent in civil legal aid providers, and 22 per cent in criminal legal aid providers (National Audit Office, 2024: 31). The full impact of these cuts is yet to be fully substantiated, but what we do know is that the removal of early advice, as well as the increase in the number of people representing themselves in court, means that many individuals are facing injustices. In their 2019 post-implementation review, the Ministry of Justice noted that reducing the scope of civil legal aid reduces the opportunities to resolve issues early and so problems gradually worsen and become more costly to resolve. Likewise, the increase of 'litigants-in-person' has negatively impacted the court systems, as not only do those representing themselves have a significant lack of legal understanding, but they may require longer, while ever more hearings are being contested (Allamby, 2019). When cases are not rectified as they should be within the legal system, this can have a knock-on effect on other systems, such as healthcare, social services, and local authority provision, as both mental and physical problems arise that require support via other avenues. Other areas of law that were originally pushed out of scope by LASPO have likewise since been reintroduced due to need. These include some areas (but not all) within immigration, housing, private family law, and public family law. As part of their Legal Support Action Plan (2023), the Ministry of Justice have proposed that they would increase income thresholds in civil and criminal areas and will remove the means test for legal representation for children. Additionally, they proposed that the upper disposable income threshold for crown court cases will be removed, arguably proposing that 2.4 million more people will be eligible in civil legal aid, and 3.5 million more in crime (National Audit Office, 2024):

> The Ministry of Justice has set providing swift access to justice as one of its primary objectives. Theoretical eligibility for legal aid is not enough to achieve this objective if there are an insufficient number of providers willing or able to provide it. MoJ must ensure that access to legal aid, a core element of access to justice, is supported by a sustainable and resilient legal aid market, where capacity meets demand. It is concerning that MoJ continues to lack an understanding of whether those eligible for legal aid can access it, particularly given available data, which suggest that access to legal aid may be worsening.

The supply of staff practising within the remit of legal aid is a particular concern, which has long-term implications for the future quality and sustainability of provision. Providers are also increasingly likely to reduce or withdraw entirely from providing services, given its rocky backdrop. With the market becoming increasingly unsustainable, what remains vital is that we understand how the sector is currently functioning, and how best it can (and if it can) stay afloat going forward. Justice is not, and should not be, a choice; it should be a given.

The impact of COVID-19

The legal aid sector in England and Wales has been subject to longstanding austerity measures and funding constraints. A wealth of studies conducted over the past 50 years have shown that this has not only facilitated a fragile working environment but also a growing sense of crisis among legal aid lawyers. The sector was placed under even greater strain by the initial outbreak of the COVID-19 pandemic. On the one hand, lawyers are now supporting a wider range of clients facing increased levels of legal need due to pandemic-induced precarity. On the other hand, these lawyers are also assisting vulnerable clients with amplified legal problems that went unaddressed during the pandemic. The profession is also grappling with the rapid acceleration of digitized legal services and courts that has taken place since the pandemic. Although my fieldwork took place prior to COVID-19, it is important to still consider that the legal aid terrain has been made even rockier as a result.

Mant et al (2023) led the design and implementation of the 'Legal Aid Census', accumulating data from over 1,000 legal aid professionals and organizations. They identified several thematic changes facing lawyers across different areas, including high-pressured work environments, relationships (with clients and colleagues), professional vulnerabilities, as well as barriers to recruitment and retention. In my own paper, I developed an innovative methodological approach for drawing connections across different areas of legal aid work, demonstrating that these lawyers frequently rally against and around similar professional challenges and vulnerabilities, fostering a sense of solidarity despite the differences that segment their work across different areas of law, which will be explored fully in Chapter 4 (see also Cooke, 2021). Mant et al (2023) also explored the role of 'blended' advice (face-to-face combined with virtual) – in conjunction with the Access to Justice Foundation and the Ministry of Justice – from the perspectives of both the providers and the clients; however there remain gaps in research.[1] The Justice Select Committee on COVID-19 (2020) found that the impact on legal professions in England and Wales was quite significant. Trial by jury was paused, fewer civil cases were started and, in spite some urgent cases being heard via video and phone calls, many were put on hold. Not only was this reduction in activity frustrating for the clients, but this also meant that income from legal aid work was lowered, meaning that already strained financial budgets were close to boiling point. Most significantly, some barristers, solicitors, and law centre were unable to stay afloat and collapsed. While some legal aid practitioners adapted very rapidly to the impact of COVID-19 (for example, home working and remote hearings), there remained significant hurdles. Ideally, lawyers would need at least two screens to have relevant documents on one, and the people on the other, Likewise, the HM Courts & Tribunal Service's cloud video platform came with its

1 Cooke, Mant, and Newman are carrying out a BA Leverhulme funding project entitled 'The Profession and the Pandemic: Legal Aid Lawyers in the Era of Austerity and COVID-19'.

own issues. Publicly-funded legal services were already under stress prior to COVID-19; the pandemic has further damaged the terrain.

Having set out a strong contextual basis, in this context of an ever-changing macro backdrop, it becomes vital to identify the role of the legal aid lawyer(s) in withstanding, upholding, and shaping access to justice. Before considering this, I must first outline the way in which this research was conducted: the methods and methodology that underpin the research, and shed light on the participants involved.

3

The Participants: How, Who, and Why?

I could not have written this book if I had not been willing to spend time – a lot of time – with lawyers. From the start, I knew that the only way to truly understand and gain insight into this world was to immerse myself into their working lives: observing behaviours, language, customs, stories, relationships. Immersing myself in their often-hidden world allowed me to uncover at least some of the subtleties and complexities of legal aid work.

This chapter sets out the epistemological and methodological approach of this research. Qualitative research is an inherently unpredictable and complex process of interpretive practices: 'truth emerges and is made visible from engagement with multiple realities in changing contexts' (Denzin and Lincoln, 2011: 42). Within a qualitative interpretivist paradigm, meanings are attributed to experiences. As such, subjectivism is key, and a flexible and open methodology is needed to negotiate the nuances and meanings of a given social world. Considering conceptual, practical, and reflexive matters, this chapter locates the chosen 'liquid' ethnographic methodology and its application to this study, as it is deemed most ontologically and epistemologically appropriate (Ferrell, 2015). All organizations have both 'formal' and 'informal' components, in the sense that legal aid lawyering has formalized tasks and rules to follow, but likewise is subject to interpretation and deviation by the individuals working within those formal boundaries. This particular type of methodology is typically fluid in its nature and can be attuned to broader macro changes. A reflective insight on my own research journey and positionality is also provided here. Fuller justification is given to the sampling rationale and focus on both civil and criminal remits. Offering an insight into both civil and criminal remits paves the way for a more detailed examination of the profession overall, and likewise may impact the ways a legal aid lawyer experiences the occupation. Bringing civil and criminal lawyers together in one exploration of working practices is likewise a novel development, which will take forward the study of legal lawyering by allowing commonalities to be drawn across this diverse field, which is a particular strength of this research.

Despite the possible flaws and limitations of the heterogeneity of such sampling strategy – for example, criminal and civil justice are generally regarded as very different areas of legal practice and, likewise, the solicitor and barrister experiences are generally considered divergent – the choice to span both civil and criminal remits and solicitor and barristers enhanced the overall analysis of the data collected and findings emergent from my research. The aim here is to give a genuinely rich and authentic snapshot of the world of the legal aid lawyer and understand how they go about their day-to-day working lives in the post-cuts context, and this is precisely what this book seeks to do.

Liquid methodology

Interpretivism enables exploration and understanding of a given phenomenon. Mead's (1934) outline of pragmatic inquiry encapsulates this. Importantly, he argues that (1) reality 'is actively created as we act in and toward the world', and (2) we must base our understandings of why people act in a certain way on what the actor actually does. In this sense, interpretivism places emphasis on the importance of understanding. A qualitative methodology is, therefore, more suited from an interpretivist standpoint as it paves the way for the exploration of understanding how people interpret things. This contrasts with a quantitative methodology, which typically focuses on predicted correlations, tests established hypotheses and objective research under the realm of positivism (Guba and Lincoln, 1994). The latter is not appropriate for this field of inquiry; a positivistic paradigm would not encapsulate the complexities, nuances, and meanings of the social dialogues and interactions of the working world of the legal aid lawyer (LeCompte and Schensul, 1999).

Ethnography, which lends itself to an interpretivist paradigm, is an empirical methodology linked to the examination of culture and the wider understanding of the social world. It has undoubtedly enriched sociological and criminological research:

> To tell the story of a life may be one of the cores of culture, those fine webs of meaning that help organise our ways of life. These stories of personal narratives- connect the inner world to the outer world, speak to the subjective and the objective and establish the boundaries of identities. (Plummer in Atkinson et al, 2001: 395)

Ethnography has, therefore, become an extremely popular method within the spheres of crime and deviance, as well as criminal justice. Examples of ethnographies include: Holdaway's (1983) *Inside the British Police Force*, Punch's (1979) *Policing the Inner City*, and Punch's (1985) *Police Corruption*, as well as the work of Reiner (1985; 2000), Loftus (2012), and Newman (2013), to name just a few.

Ethnography is typified by its unstructured means of collecting data; it concerns the prolonged study of groups in natural settings of different cultures and their everyday practices, and therefore it fits the purpose of examining a specific group or community – in this case, legal aid lawyers (Emerson et al, 1995; Brewer, 2000). It ultimately involves entering the field as an outsider and shadowing individuals as they go about their day-to-day business. While it is a methodology and an approach to research, it is also a method and a means of collecting data (Brewer, 2000: 143). As a method and a written product of research, ethnography plays a role in generating knowledge and theory and further allows the research/researched to be placed in a position to assess the application of policy. For the most part, the researcher or ethnographer enters the setting of the study and develops relationships, makes observations, and often participates in the routines and behaviours within that location. As Jupp (1989: 58) notes, 'ethnography adopts progressive focusing via a discovery-based approach', allowing room for the development, refinement, and reformulation of research ideas in accordance with what is found within the fieldwork. The flexibility and 'openness' of this progressive focusing is particularly useful when studying the precarious world of the legal aid lawyer. The occupation is evidently in a state of significant change due to the cuts to legal aid funding. Due to its precarious nature, adapting in line with broader socio-cultural changes to the profession is vital. This flexibility, however, requires a constant interchange between theory and data; however, the fluidity of the observational approach extends to the broader picture of data collection and the research method. Terms such as 'liquid' or 'progressive' ethnography have been used to emphasize the malleable nature of the method, which proved very fitting for this research.

An ethnographic process

The process of initial negotiation into the field of enquiry, as well as 'getting on' within the fieldwork, often evokes feelings of personal inadequacy. Having to overcome uncomfortable situations due to the cultural differences between the researcher and the researched may make this challenging. However, there is also the need to make difficult ethical and emotional choices. The famous Gouldner–Becker debate on the issue of value neutrality within the context of social research provides an insight into values and 'sides' within research. As Gouldner (1968) and Becker (1968) identified, while it is relatively difficult to achieve entirely value-free research, through the lens of a phenomenologist, this vitally makes us more aware of our own morals and assumptions (Ferrell and Hamm, 1998).

For several years, lawyers were largely omitted from the arena of social research. McConville et al's (1994) *Standing Accused* and Travers (1997) *The Reality of Law* both offered ground-breaking ethnographic studies of criminal lawyers. They created a basis for change, as previous studies had primarily focused on courtroom observations (Carlen, 1976; Flood, 1987). McConville et al and Travers maintain their standing as key works within the field. Newman (2013) likewise sought to examine the lawyer–client relationship within the legal aid context ethnographically. This ethnographic study was the largest of its kind in over two decades, and therefore is very influential both methodologically and empirically.

Ethnographic studies outside the legal aid-specific framework also hold significance here. Rogers (2012) employed ethnographic methods to offer an insight into how the Bar presents itself to prospective members. Concentrating specifically on open days for law students run by one of the Inns of Court, an individual set of chambers, as well as other promotional events, Rogers (2012) sought to explore the Bar's professional identity within this context through the ethnographic lens. Goulandris (2020) built on this with her ethnographic study of the increasingly fragmented Bar and its impact on the working culture of barristers. Earlier ethnographic studies in both the UK and US contexts have been undertaken on the interactions and speech of lawyers (Griffiths, 1986), on the courtroom (Atkinson and Drew, 1979), and on the 'poor man's lawyer', as outlined in Chapter 2 (Katz, 1982). However, Flood (2013) sought to offer an in-depth analysis of the world of the corporate lawyer, after a period of prolonged immersion in a corporate law firm. In his work 'What do lawyers do?', which built on his original study in 1987, Flood pays attention to both the interactions between lawyers and clients, as well as the interactions between lawyers and other lawyers. He opts for a data-driven analysis, as opposed to theory-driven analysis, which lent itself to his chosen method of ethnography. Vitally, as these studies have shown, 'ethnographic observation can thus provide us with a yardstick against which to measure the completeness of data gathered in other ways, a model which can serve to let us know what orders of information escape us when we use other methods' (Becker and Geer, 1957: 28).

Straddling two schools of thought

This research differs somewhat from other ethnographic studies within the context of the wider field of justice due to the ever-changing macro backdrop (Holdaway, 1983; Loftus, 2010; Newman 2013). As Newman (2013: 25) argues, previously two contrasting standpoints on the topic of legal aid clientele are taken from firmly held ideological positions, which are separated by their methodological differences. While these studies focused on clients as well as practitioners, their relevance remains influential. McConville et al (1994) utilize a structuralist approach, whereby the reality exists independently from the observer. It therefore looks at the objective broader picture, including structural influences, such as the government, the Legal Aid Agency, as well as inbuilt power relations (Newman, 2013: 27). In contrast, Travers (1997) adopts an interpretivist stance, employing a more subjective comprehension of how the actors themselves conceive a particular situation (Newman, 2013). This study largely employs an interpretivist approach, drawing on structuralist components to provide a well-rounded position on the occupation in question. If either is employed single-handedly, then there is a risk of omitting vital areas of concern from the research in question. Therefore, to consider both the formalities and informalities of the profession, this research follows in the footsteps of Henry (1983: 30), who otherwise labels this approach as 'general pluralism'. This is supported by the process of carrying out the ethnographic observation at more than one location, such as law firms, courtrooms, and law centres, which is essential, as it paves the way for multiple perspectives and insights into the profession in question.

Negotiating the legal aid space(s)

My data collection consisted of a period of a year of intensive ethnographic observation from August 2016 to August 2017, which yielded significant field notes. The research was carried out at several locations in the southeast of England. These included multiple courtrooms, a high street solicitors' firm (Silverman and Co), and a law centre with a range of participants, as will be mapped out below. I entered the field on two to three consecutive days per week consistently throughout the year. The lawyers involved in this research had varying legal aid caseloads as lawyers are not a 'coherent' occupational group. One firm was utilized as the main base, as full access was granted for the entire research period, so I was able to come and go as I pleased. Silverman and Co's funding model is sourced by fixed and conditional fee arrangements, legal aid as well as private funding, so there was a cross-subsidy of legal aid work from other profitable activity. Likewise, the barristers involved in this research were situated in chambers that carried out a mix of privately and publicly funded work. The law centre used within this research carried out work entirely funded by legal aid or pro bono services (without charge). This will allow for the analysis to be contextualized in the subsequent chapters.

I visited Silverman and Co two consistent days every week. This community-based firm was situated in the outskirts of the city in an urban area; however, the majority working there travelled in from the city centre, as well as from other outer and more local districts. The clientele tended to be from the local community because of the positioning of the law firm within the centre of the community. Alongside this, observations were carried out in two magistrates' courts, one county court, and three crown courts in five different locations within the city, as well as in outer towns. While most of my observations were consistently carried out in the firm, I sporadically visited the various courtrooms as and when I was able to. I spent one day a month in the county court with the duty housing solicitor, and a total of 35 days spread across the two magistrates' courts and the crown courts. The county court, one of the crown courts and one of the magistrate's courts were all based on the outskirts of the city. The additional two crown courts, and the magistrates' court were based in other local, smaller towns. While I used the law centre predominately to gain interviewees, I also carried out some additional small observations there. In total, I spent five days observing at the law centre due to access restrictions. The law centre was likewise community-based on the outskirts of the city. This comparative element of carrying out observation in multiple courtrooms, as well as within the solicitors' firm and law centre, helped me to determine the extent to which occupational cultures and patterns are related to organizational structure, physical environments, and working practices. It also provided varying degrees of precariousness to observe, as the various locations have differing levels of legal aid work.

I used my observational periods to gauge further an idea of those who would be useful for my semi-structured interviews. This immersive process allowed me to seek more of an 'insider view', before delving further into my research. Vitally, this first-hand immersion was both timely and multifaceted, as it also enhanced the interview sample, as will be critically explored in the next section. Ninety-five per cent of participants approached during this period agreed to take part in an interview. The small handful who did not nevertheless passed me on to a colleague to assist further with the research process if they physically could not/chose not to be involved themselves. The ethnographic observation was complemented by 30 semi-structured interviews with legal aid lawyers. There was significant overlap with those observed and those interviewed in this research, paving the way for a more in-depth insight overall. This was done purposely in order to cross-check findings and to gain a deeper insight into whether lawyers 'talk the talk' but do not 'walk the walk', a term coined by Newman (2013). While 30 is a modest sample in comparison to quantitative studies, it is not uncommon in qualitative work to have more of a selective sample as it is built upon a different premise. Given that the legal aid world is so overwhelmed and shrinking in size, I also felt incredibly lucky to have the access that I did.

Being in the right place at the right time was key, as often, if a lawyer was on their way down to the meeting rooms and I happened to be in the stairwell, they would then ask if I wanted to join. Employing a liquid methodology in this sense proved to be extremely fitting due to the flexible and adaptable nature of the method. Ultimately, I learned to be very grateful for any opportunity given to me, even if it was the opportunity to attend the tenth new client meeting of the day. After a while, this became quite fatiguing. I soon realized, however, that attending similar meetings repeatedly was particularly valuable for building trust and relationships and increased the validity of my research identity. This was not so valuable with regards to the knowledge-building, however. Fundamentally, to witness first-hand the lengthy process of the lawyers going through the same paperwork hour after hour to meet the requirements of the Legal Aid Agency was eye-opening. Towards the end of the ethnography, I felt like I knew this process inside out. I soon learned that, even if it took multiple, short, and sporadic meetups to get the information I needed, I had to commit myself. I took advantage of coffee breaks, and even just walking to and from different rooms. I used every opportunity I could to elicit information from my participants.

While my focus was on the perspective of lawyers, the study's data was triangulated against relevant documentation. I was granted access to the online case bundle system at Silverman and Co, where I was able to access all client case notes and associated documentation. This access was granted and permitted by the senior partner at the firm. While I did not use the material for direct analysis, this enabled me to see how the firm worked in more intricate detail, and provided context for any meetings that I attended. This saved valuable time on both my part, as well on the part of the lawyers I was observing, as time was not wasted setting the scene before each meeting.

A tricky sample pool

I had set out to research legal aid lawyers practising just within the criminal remit due to my interests, as a criminology lecturer, in criminal justice. However, my sample was gathered by means of opportunity across both the civil and criminal remits. This was for two reasons: cuts to funding have affected both civil and criminal law and, also, due to the shrinking nature of criminal legal aid, it became very difficult to recruit enough participants just within that sphere. I recruited my participants via email, word-of-mouth or Twitter (now X). Recruiting research participants can be very time-consuming, and often emailing people directly can be very imposing. In a similar vein, gaining entry to the legal field for research purposes can also be difficult, and accessing those who work in a secure environment (such as criminal barristers) can be trickier than other research settings. Having 'insider knowledge' of key contacts to identify initial respondents helped immensely. I initially contacted a criminal barrister, who was incredibly helpful, and soon became my 'gatekeeper'. He was the 'key' that I needed to enter the legal aid world.

Working closely with lawyers, however, was very daunting at first, having not practised law personally. Studying 'up' refers to researching those with cultural, economic, and political capital in society (Kivell et al, 2017). Studying up can be a very daunting process, and problems can arise that may not occur when studying 'down'. Studying up seeks to 'create an ethnographic record that takes full account of a wider social circuit' (Nader, 1972 in Souleles, 2018: 51). For example, issues surrounding access, physical barriers, resistance, power imbalances, contested reactions, and uncomfortable encounters had the potential to occur. Moreover, the world of the legal aid lawyer is often one that is both hidden and concealed, which creates the premise for this book. This is for two reasons: on the one hand, there is only a small amount of scholarship surrounding the work of legal aid lawyers. Though there was an increase of scholarship in the late 1980s and early 1990s, only a small amount of research has been done since and, in the intervening period, nearly two decades later, a lot has changed in legal aid and criminal procedure. Secondly, legal aid lawyers are far more 'concealed' than their private counterparts. Those working within the field of public law often get lost in the shadows of those working for large corporations, private clients, or companies. Therefore, due to the restricted nature of the community, I made use of snowball sampling, in line with the work of Newman (2013), to gather further participants. I approached each participant I interviewed for additional participants. I used each respondent as a gateway to the next, as lawyers have a very tight-knit community and uphold some homogenous social traits, which makes the process much more comfortable. This opened many more doors for me. Like many ethnographic studies on exclusive subgroups, my sample was non-random and not necessarily defined by social characteristics. However, demographics such as gender and race feature strongly in both my interviews and will be pivotal to my analysis and findings, as will be discussed later. The interviewees tended to be largely from the outskirts of the city, as well as other local smaller towns in the southeast of England.

- 16 of the 30 participants were female.
- 14 of the 30 participants were male.
- 24 of the 30 participants were solicitors.
- 5 of the 30 participants were barristers.
- 14 of the 30 participants had practised in the pre- and post-2012 cuts context.
- 26 of the 30 participants were white.
- 28 of the 30 participants identified as middle class.
- 4 of the 30 participants practised in a law centre.

As evidenced in Table 3.1, 18 of the 30 participants were practising within the remit of civil law, and 11 of the 30 participants were practising within

Table 3.1: Summary of participants

Name	Age	Gender	Ethnicity	Specialism	Role
Alice	30s	F	White	Welfare	Solicitor (law centre)
Alistair	40s	M	White	Crime	Barrister
Andy	30s	M	White	Crime	Barrister
Anna	30s	F	White	Immigration	Solicitor
Ash	40s	M	Asian	Immigration	Solicitor (law centre)
Becky	20s	F	White	Civil liberties + human rights	Solicitor
Ben	20s	M	White	Housing	Solicitor (law centre)
Eleanor	30s	F	White	Family	Solicitor/partner
Grace	20s	F	White	Crime	Solicitor
Jack	30s	M	White	Housing	Solicitor
James	40s	M	White	Crime	Solicitor (self-employed)
Jane	50s	F	White	Housing	Solicitor
Jay	30s	F	Asian	Housing	Solicitor
John	60s	M	White	Housing	Solicitor
Karen	60s	F	White	Social Welfare	Director[1]
Louisa	30s	F	White	Civil liberties + human rights	Solicitor
Maddie	30s	F	White	Crime	Solicitor
Marcus	30s	M	Asian	Housing	Solicitor
Maria	50s	F	White	Housing	Solicitor
Mary	30s	F	White	Civil liberties + human rights	Solicitor
Nicholas	50s	M	White	Crime	Solicitor (self-employed)
Nina	40s	F	Asian	Housing	Solicitor
Paul	30s	M	White	Crime	Barrister
Peter	30s	M	White	Crime	Barrister
Phil	40s	M	White	Crime	Barrister
Rachel	30s	F	White	Housing	Solicitor/senior partner
Rhiannon	20s	F	White	Welfare	Solicitor (law centre)
Robert	30s	M	White	Crime	Solicitor
Sophie	30s	F	White	Crime	Solicitor
Tom	30s	M	White	Housing	Solicitor

Source: Author's own elaboration.

[1] Director of a membership body that represents legal aid practitioners.

the remit of criminal law. All the participants were given pseudonyms for the purposes of this research, and full ethical clearance was obtained. As Geldart (1995) notes: 'The difference between civil law and criminal law turns on the difference between two different objects which law seeks to pursue – redress or punishment'. While civil law seeks to achieve a remedy, criminal law seeks to punish for an offence. Flagging up the distinction between the two is vital, as this comes to underpin later analyses. Offering an insight into both civil and criminal remits paves the way for a more detailed examination of the profession overall and, likewise, may impact the ways a given lawyer experiences the occupation. Bringing civil and criminal lawyers together in one exploration of working practices is likewise a novel development, which will take forward the study of legal aid lawyering by allowing commonalities to be drawn across this diverse field, which is a strength of this research.

Despite the possible flaws and limitations of the heterogeneity of such sampling strategy – for example, criminal and civil justice are generally regarded as very different areas of legal practice and, also, the solicitor and barrister experiences are generally considered divergent – the choice to span both civil and criminal remits and solicitor and barristers, enhanced the overall findings.

Positioning myself in the legal aid field

I made a conscious decision to stay politically 'neutral' throughout in relation to debates surrounding neoliberalism and the deeper political dynamics at play here. My rationale here was to not skew the data or attempt to match or meet a predetermined outcome that aligns with a particular agenda – in this case a political or moral point of view. Legal aid is inevitably aligned with political agendas from both sides of the fence, as different reactions to the cuts have been put forward. Situating myself in a neutral position, I was able to mitigate any possible personal bias and allow the data to emerge naturally. While this was quite difficult in practice, especially when being faced first-hand with some of the devastating impacts of the cuts on individuals' lives, it was important to maintain a neutral stance, because, as Sommerlad (2001: 336) argues, legal aid lawyers themselves have been described as inherently 'political' because:

> they are distinguishable from their more conventional colleagues in their view of client work as transformative in itself, as well as their basic commitment to using the law in a combative and often innovative way both in order to serve the underprivileged client in the most effective way possible, and also to promote social change.

As such, there remains a link between the role of legal aid in civil and social citizenship and the character and motivation of legal aid lawyers in their practice.

They are often imbued in a public sector ideology. Most lawyers involved within this research had a particular motivation to act as a catalyst for change and reform, seeking to empower their clients. Maintaining moral neutrality on my part therefore remained even more vital in order not to contaminate or taint any perspectives provided by the lawyers involved in this research.

As Newman (2013) states, the more time you spend in the field, the more you are 'accepted' as a researcher, and the more access you are likely to be given. I then began to visit various courtrooms in different locations to shadow both the solicitors and barristers I had met through the legal aid network. I felt reasonably comfortable in my researcher position due to the extremely beneficial experience I had been having at Silverman and Co. It soon became evident that attempting to carry out ethnographic observations within courtrooms required a lot more identity management. I was always mindful of my position as a researcher, as I had to keep continuously reaffirming my presence to make sure I was not lost in the depths of the everyday running of the court. Shuffling from courtroom to courtroom, frantically trying to keep track of the solicitor or barrister I was shadowing, meant that I was continually running into new faces in the field. The court is a very different kind of space compared to the law firm. For example, within the law firm I tended to see the same people repeatedly. However, as the court is part of the state and used sporadically by several different actors, I saw different people every time I went. The continuous process of having to justify my position brought about a severe onset of imposter syndrome. While I had always been aware of my insider/outsider status, as will be further explained below, I soon began to feel much more of an 'outsider' as I did not necessarily 'fit' naturally into the makeup of the court – quite literally. Even down to where I was allowed to sit depended entirely on who was present in that courtroom at that time. While many people 'accepted' somewhat my position as an 'imposter', others made it quite clear that I did not fit in. Managing my relationships with the broader environment soon became vital. At this stage, I was often too busy making sure what I was not outstaying my welcome, as opposed to fully immersing myself into the chosen culture of study. I knew this had to change. Of particular use was my experience of being able to witness the Duty Solicitor Scheme in the county court. I had been invited to shadow Marcus, a housing solicitor I had met via Twitter. Upon arrival, I had to negotiate my way through a very packed waiting room. Locating the solicitor in a tiny meeting room right in the corner of that waiting room, he very quickly explained to me that he only sees/meets these clients as they come into the meeting room on the day. He has no previous information on them, which makes the whole process very difficult. With only five to ten minutes allocated per person, the interactions were a whirlwind of multi-tasking, attempting to build up some level of rapport, while being able to get all the necessary information required to build the legal argument. On one of the days I observed, Marcus saw 15 clients.

What struck me was how the clients often looked at me for advice. While I was able to make those in the field aware of my position as a researcher, quite often, even though the clients would be advised on my position at the beginning of every interaction, I was continuously mistaken for a solicitor. Atkinson and Hammersley (2007) argue that communities tend to assign an identity to researchers and, in my case, because I always wore smart clothing, this confused clients. On the few occasions where the solicitor had to pop out of the meeting room to grab something, I often had to endure legal questions being fired at me. This felt quite intimidating. I found that this often occurred when the client was in a state of desperation and I frequently had to force myself, therefore, to maintain a distance from these clients. Likewise, the broader temporal nature of the whole exchange, however, made it very difficult for the client to have an 'outsider' present, as they must quickly adapt to there being three people in the room as opposed to just the normal one-to-one lawyer–client exchange. On some occasions, particularly within the criminal cases, I could tell that my presence made the client feel quite uncomfortable. In one meeting room in a local criminal court, I was often sat directly next to the client, opposite the solicitor. In the particularly sensitive cases, this often made the environment very uncomfortable as the client would be quite embarrassed to have another person sitting in, listening in to every explicit detail of their case. Clients were always given the option as to whether they wanted me in the room, however, and likewise I was able to leave at any point if things got too tough. Information sheets were always stuck on the wall of the given meeting room prior to the client entering, and the client gave verbal consent to my presence at the beginning of every meeting.

In some cases, it was difficult to tell if a client had just agreed to my presence because they thought it might otherwise harm their chances of representation. In two meetings, I was asked to leave the meeting room as the clients became very distressed and requested me to leave. While this was slightly uncomfortable at first, I was very understanding of this.

One of the regular solicitors I shadowed, James, often joked about my presence once a client had left the room: 'thank God that's over. Bloody hell, you made him a nervous wreck, Emma, although I'm not surprised – he was embarrassed the dirty bastard! … only joking he probably loved it [*continues to laugh*]'. A relationship of mutual respect seemed to grow quite quickly between me and most of the solicitors and barristers I shadowed and interviewed. I was keen to get across that I intended to almost 'live the life of a lawyer'. I wanted to imbue a sense of the effort and sacrifice involved in their chosen line of work. The lawyers, however, often capitalized upon my presence as a researcher. For example, as evidenced in the comment by James earlier, in some cases my presence took the pressure off slightly, as I was almost used as an 'easy distraction' in meetings when things got slightly awkward or difficult. While I would generally try and stay as quiet as possible, some of the solicitors, particularly James, always brought me into the conversation with general chit chat to try and reduce any awkwardness. While this initially made me very nervous as this was somewhat unprofessional considering how clients perceived me, this soon became a familiar practice. I kept my input to a minimum during these exchanges and tried to avoid any awkward chat by quickly changing the subject. Humour proved key in a lot of situations, as will be explored later.

Despite not being a lawyer or having any form of legal qualifications myself, the ethnographic process meant that I got a glimpse into their working world. This privileged viewpoint definitely would otherwise not be achieved if other research methods were deployed. Understanding the reality of the profession within the context of the lawyers' social space, however, undoubtedly involved a process of identity management. I had to be aware of my positionality constantly. It was very hard not to build friendly relationships with the lawyers I was interacting with on a regular weekly basis. I had to be careful not to mix the professional with the personal. I was always wary of my position as a 'researcher'. Identity management is still an issue for the ethnographer (Atkinson and Hammersley, 2007: 83), and I did not want to overstep my involvement with the lawyers. I was often invited out for lunch with these individuals, or to social events. After a while, however, I began to attend more social events as my confidence built up, and I regularly joined a couple of the lawyers at a local pub. After a few drinks, these participants began to tell more intricate and emotionally driven stories that permeated their lives as legal aid lawyers. The closeness achieved during these moments was often not replicated in the cold light of day, and so this proved to be very valuable. These 'friendships' resulted in very fruitful interviews at a later date, as the participants felt very comfortable talking to me.

I had a good relationship with the majority of solicitors, particularly the 'gatekeepers'. Beyond this, however, not everyone accepted me within the courtroom setting. Self-monitoring ultimately became a continuous process. Other barristers would often shout at me across the courtroom while waiting for the next case: 'Who are you then?', 'What are you doing here?' or 'Why are you still here?' While this was very uncomfortable at first, I soon learned how to manage these situations. Having a gatekeeper was fundamental for reasons beyond just getting access. Once in the field, I encountered problems from people who did not trust my presence as a researcher. 'Researching up' into a professional setting can be a very daunting experience. I encountered resistance from some lawyers who argued that my research was 'a waste of their time' while others completely refused to engage with me as they could not see themselves as subjects of research. The process felt very uncomfortable at times, as many of those I encountered in the field were extremely guarded and unapproachable. I overcame this by speaking to my gatekeeper, who advised me about whom to contact/avoid. This advice proved invaluable to my research process.

Quite often, depending on which solicitor or barrister I was with, any awkwardness often turned into a light-hearted 'banterous' exchange:

Opposing solicitor:	So do ya wanna be a criminal solicitor then, love?
James (criminal solicitor):	No, she is not like us thickos, she is a PhD, she's going to be a doctor you know. Leave her alone.
Opposing solicitor:	Ah, check you out, what you doing here then with us weirdos? Haven't you got anything better to do?

This made the ethnographic process a whole lot easier. It was weird to comprehend this 'inversion' of power in a sense. While I was there looking up at professionals and valuing all those individuals within it, bizarrely my status as a 'PhD researcher' was often deemed to be above that of the lawyer, as regularly highlighted by the lawyers themselves. I attributed this to the rarity of having someone researching their community or the fact that very few practising lawyers hold a PhD themselves. As Ben (housing solicitor) stated, to some extent I was highly respected, as those within the field were excited to have someone shedding light on what they do every day. While this gave me a confidence boost, it was somewhat intimidating, as ultimately my cultural lexicon and social habitus are somewhat different from that of a legal professional. Likewise, I wondered whether my age or gender influenced their reaction to my presence, given how I was 'passing' in the field. Being a young female in the context of the solicitors' firm did not have much of an impact, as many of the solicitors and paralegals I was interacting with were female. In the context of the courtroom, however, I often found myself among predominantly male barristers, which in some cases had a positive effect and in others a negative effect. Gender bias in this sense could be either explicit or subtle. In some cases, I found this uncomfortable and could not participate in the 'banter' between the male barristers. Being referred to as 'love' or 'darling' became rather wearing, and I did not appreciate the condescending tone of some of the barristers I engaged with.

Early one morning in the field, it dawned on me that I was on the 'other side', as a researcher looking in toward the field, observing and not participating. I caught myself thinking that, as academics, we sometimes feel like we do not 'fit in' – feeling vulnerable researching a field that we may have no prior experience within, having anxiety about being in the wrong place, or interfering as an 'alien' in the participants' everyday environment. Although these feelings all exist in a transitory way I can handle, this is research and, however much I feel I can give the field justice, I cannot do so without drawing on insider narratives to contribute and enrich socio-legal knowledge.

Due to the sheer nature of the task of documenting the world of the legal aid lawyer in a threefold manner, I was likewise aware of the fact that I had taken on a lot considering the multifaceted nature of the work. Divisions across specialisms, workplaces, and position all add further dimensions to the task. While this research has offered a surface-level insight, to adequately accommodate the breadth and depth of their world undoubtedly requires further research. However, the aim was to give a genuinely rich and authentic snapshot of the world of the legal aid lawyer and understand how they go about their day-to-day working lives in the post-cuts' context. And that is precisely what this inquiry has done.

Different types of legal aid lawyer

This section seeks to outline and thereby clarify the variations within the profession. It likewise offers insight into the multifaceted nature of the occupation, outlining the different types of lawyers and the distinctions in their specialisms, positions, and workplaces to ease understanding. Solicitors are qualified legal professionals who perform most of their work in a firm and/or office environment. Their clients include individuals, businesses, charities, and public sector organizations. Solicitors are primarily litigators; however, some can 'advocate', that is represent clients in court. Their day-to-day roles tend to include conversing with clients, taking clients' instructions and advising them on the specific area of law about which they are seeking advice. They also gather evidence in preparation for court cases, negotiate with both clients and opposition parties, supervise agreements, as well as coordinate the work of all parties in each case. They typically prepare a case and then pass it on to a barrister or specialist who will advocate for the client in court. A barrister, therefore, advocates both on behalf of the solicitor, as well as the client. Over 80 per cent of barristers in England and Wales are self-employed and typically work in chambers, despite all being independent of each other. Solicitors, on the other hand, tend to be employed by one firm and therefore work together as one entity. Solicitors can also be self-employed if they choose to be. A private lawyer is paid and retained by the client, whereas a legal aid lawyer is appointed on behalf of the client via a firm, law centre, or the Legal Aid Agency, and is government funded.

Legal aid funding follows the division in law of types of case, typically falling into two categories, civil and criminal. Civil includes: family (public

+ private); immigration; housing; mental health; other non-family matters. Eighty per cent of housing matters are legally aided, which explains the significant weighting of housing lawyers in this research (Ministry of Justice, 2018: 10). Criminal is split into 'crime lower' and 'crime higher'. The former covers: police station advice, magistrates' court and prison law, and constitutes the majority of cases. The latter includes all work in crown and higher courts.

There are variations in the amount of legal aid work each workplace offers and, therefore, different varieties of professionals practising within the field exist. These include private practitioners who accept legal aid work as a side-line, lawyers who do legal aid work predominantly and accept pro bono work (free legal advice), as well as those who work at neighbourhood law centres or firms whose existence largely depends upon legal aid funding. Law centres have existed since the beginning of the 1970s and are community focused. They exist to defend the rights of local people who cannot afford a lawyer themselves. They all act entirely on a not-for-profit basis; however, they can use legal aid schemes. Likewise, legal aid is provided through private law firms, and the government pays for this. This can also be known as a form of legal aid called 'Judicare' in which private lawyers are paid to handle cases from eligible clients. Legal aid caseloads in this context can vary. While some may take on a lot of legally aided work (90–100 per cent of their workload), others may only take on a minimal amount (10–20 per cent of their workload). Pro bono (unpaid) work may also be offered alongside this.

Having set out the contextual basis, it is now time to delve into the nitty gritty of the research and to truly open up the door to the hidden world of the legal aid lawyer.

4

Moving Beyond 'Occupational Culture': Introducing the Concept of the 'Shared Orientation' Model

Robert's indication of a collaborative working model shows that he considers a form of working culture exists, a stance held by most respondents in this research:

> There's definitely an ethos of people helping each other out in this field; there's a real thing of … if you're in a position to help someone sort of further down the ladder from you, who may be trying to get established themselves, then you'll naturally just help them … and I always just say, 'don't thank me, just do the same to someone else when you're in that position' and that's just how this occupation works. (Robert, criminal barrister)

Lebaron and Zumeta (2003: 468) argue that: 'Lawyers culture mode of being and behaving is shaped in multiple ways by their training in law and their association with other legal professionals'. However, it has become 'increasingly difficult to conceive of shared ethical values (however illusory) or impose a uniform detailed code of professional conduct' due to the fragmentation of the legal profession in England and Wales (Francis, 2005:189). The viability of having a set of uniform 'core values' that unite the field is improbable, but there remains 'a collective dimension' linking these multiple areas of work. The austerity, toxic narratives, and the moral imperative to be revealed in subsequent chapters, ultimately fabricate the glue that holds this collective together. This chapter, therefore, sheds light on the working culture of the legal aid lawyer, an area that has been previously omitted from the academic gaze. This will act as a conceptual framing device for the rest of the book, allowing themes to be unravelled.

Deficiencies in the literature on occupational culture have been identified: the fixation in the literature on other criminal justice agents, such as police and prison officers; its lack of conceptual clarity; and the limited range of studies in the legal setting. This chapter, therefore, contributes to this body of literature through the identification of a working culture of legal aid work, offering a meso-level analysis.[1] This engages well with the books' interest in how culture and work interact in this context. To this end, all occupations develop some kind of lasting culture. The small amount of research concerned with documenting legal culture serves as an essential reminder of the ongoing significance of 'culture' as an enduring theme. Elements of traditional occupational culture models apply to the legal aid world, such as the idea that an occupation upholds written rules, values, and accepted behaviours. The notion that a form of working culture is transmitted to new members is also pertinent. Previous work suggests a drop in 'morale, recruitment and retention' within the sector, so this collective imperative becomes even more important. The nature of legal aid work, however, means that a working model that cuts across different occupational groupings, crosses boundaries of barristers, solicitors, paralegals, and wider members of the justice field, is needed.

This chapter critically explores the working culture of legal aid lawyers and develops a novel 'shared orientation' model to better understand contemporary legal aid work and its workers. This chapter focuses on the development of a new conceptual framework, a model that better serves an occupation that has altered from its original remit. It examines the emerging relevance and applicability of this new conceptual lens, refocusing the gaze on working life in fissured legal workplaces. It is argued that the 'shared orientation' model upholds multiple functions. Firstly, it captures the cultural heterogeneity of legal aid work, across civil–criminal and solicitor–barrister remits alike. Secondly, the model functions as a form of cohesive coping mechanism in response to both the changing professional identity of lawyers, as well as the existence of vicarious trauma and occupational burnout. Moreover, the 'shared orientation' offers unity as a way of functioning in an otherwise fragmented occupation through its preservation of working culture ideals. The chapter concludes that recent changes to the terrain have challenged the professional and working identities of legally aided work, in so far as existing scholarship is no longer entirely fit for purpose. I suggest that we need to refocus the gaze away from traditionally rooted and rigid notions of working cultures – which no longer accommodate fragmented, diversified, and precarious working conditions – while allowing

[1] An article on this chapter was published earlier – see Cooke (2021: 704–724).

for shared normative beliefs, values, and processes that are integral to the occupation emerge.

Overall, those practising within legal aid share some similar tendencies across the board, including knowledge-sharing, collaboration, camaraderie, and socialization processes, to name just a few. The wide-ranging sample in this research, spanning solicitor–barrister and civil–criminal remits, was beneficial to the construction of the shared orientation, as it would have been harder to justify if fragments of the field were explored in isolation. A shared orientation offers insight into how the wider profession unites beyond individual specialisms, positions, and workplaces. The formation of this conceptual model speaks to the deficiencies in the literature, and offers a nuanced insight into this often-hidden occupational world. Findings indicate enduring cultural features that originate from the practical craft of legal aid work in resistance to legislative and policy innovation. This study is the first of its kind to provide an exploration of the working culture of specifically legal aid lawyers in the current context. Future empirical work based on the shared orientation model will achieve a deeper understanding of this complex field spanning criminal, family, and social welfare contexts alike. Its value, however, lies not only in the field of law but in its applicability to wider geographic, economic, and demographic domains. As the macro context becomes precarious to an increasing extent, for example considering COVID-19, the ability of a shared orientation to withstand external pressures, respond to marginality, and provide a coping mechanism merits further exploration.

Negotiating the professional nature of the work has never been so highly idiosyncratic. Legal aid has become increasingly onerous for the lawyers who now must navigate a difficult allocation system provided by the Legal Aid Agency. The process of acquiring funding has become equally arduous for the lawyer and the client as provisions become more restricted. While lawyers' power is now more constrained as the Legal Aid Agency determines 'what is knowledge', lawyers working within that world are subject to different pressures as they face differing caseloads, funding models, specialisms, and client bases, as will be explored. As the occupation becomes increasingly hollowed out, the 'new' legal aid lawyer faces a more demarcated working environment. Deep engagement with their clients and broader social justice orientations *still* allows them to 'make do' – in a profession where they are otherwise marginalized professionally in comparison to their private counterparts – despite ever-increasing restrictions (Zaloznaya and Nielsen, 2011: 919). Kinghan (2021:168) found that lawyers in their study wanted to sustain their identities as progressive lawyers despite these pressures, as will be further indicated later on in the book. Evidence shows that a progressive lawyering movement still exists in the UK, which is built around 'networks of informal interaction', 'shared beliefs and solidarity', as well as 'collective action', lending itself to the construction of a persistent working culture.

How do work and culture come to interact?

The social organization of working relations falls under the term 'labour constitution', which refers to the historically determined ensemble of rules, institutions, conditions, and social statuses (Coutu, 2020; Dukes and Streeck, 2020). These organizational practices may span departments, occupations, or professions. Social norms and values in the workplace concern how work should be done and how relations and social groups are formed around a common position, such as work and employment (Lipset et al, 1956). Even in fissured workplaces, social and work identities are still built around work relations and shared practices. Social bonds among workers within a given occupation produce and sustain efficacy as they ground normative realities, even more so when working under precarious conditions. As Dukes and Streeck (2020: 636) argue, by focusing exclusively on formal norms such as statutory and contractual occupational rules and neglecting informal social norms in each occupation, a full understanding of the normativity of working life cannot be delivered.

An 'occupational community' concerns a 'collectivity of workers sharing a common position in work and employment that gives rise to shared social norms and relations of solidarity' (Dukes and Streeck, 2020: 619–620). It concerns work but also social life and offers a micro perspective, in line with the work of Weber (1924 [1894]), which allows for understanding of collective norms and values, as well as political capacity to cope with a more fragmented and divergent work structure. Communal social ties, as well as embeddedness of work life in social life, fosters the emergence of a working culture, as does supportive cooperation among workers in the transmission of skills to new recruits where sufficient education or training may be lacking. An occupational community likewise can act as a 'community of coping' in challenging moments, and can further inform 'a curious mixture of consent and resistance to work' (Korczynski, 2003: 59). There remain deficiencies in the literature on occupational cultures, the fixation on occupations, the lack of conceptual clarity and the limited range of studies in the legal setting. Research into how work and culture come to interact within wider legal aid practice is almost non-existent. There has been some research into courtroom working cultures, for example (Carlen, 1976; Young, 2013; Welsh and Howard, 2019). Wider studies have identified a broader 'legal culture' as a form of communicative as opposed to physical culture, unlike other agents working in the justice field, that is police officers and prison workers (Cownie, 2004; Chambliss, 2010; Chan, 2014). Lively (2001) employed an ethnographic approach to explore the 'structurally subordinate positions' of paralegals and their understanding of being referred to as a 'professional' in spite of the more demeaning aspects of their role. Upholding a sense of collective professionalism was found to increase their 'moral worth'. The paralegals in the study upheld a set of norms independent of their direct occupational positions, which aided them to maintain their sense of professionalism in a role that is often marginalized. Fielding (2011: 97) likewise argues, for example, that over time judges form a culture – which can be referred to as 'judgecraft'- defined as 'an amalgam of working practices' (see also Mack and Roach Anleu, 2007; Hunter et al, 2016).

Understandably, not all working environments give rise to an 'occupational community' or working culture due the individualised natures of work, lack of contact among employees, or separation of workers depending on the design of the physical workplace. Occupational cultures are, therefore, often elaborate (Christensen and Crank, 2001). As a way of understanding the richness of occupational life, the concept of an occupational culture can help connect the macro and micro in the working context, but they can be difficult to define in a robust manner.[2] Models of 'occupational culture' are expected to both interact and conflict (Johnson et al, 2009), as there are difficulties with objectively measuring culture (Bond, 2004). Allen (2001) argues that employee perceptions always mediate occupational culture; therefore, it is useful to focus on these perceptions as opposed to objective measures to explore its construction. Nevertheless, the occupational community of the legal aid lawyer has been very much overlooked, in spite of those within it considering themselves as engaging in the same sort of work, as well as sharing and recognizing job specific norms and values that extend beyond just work-related matters (Van Maanen and Barley, 1984). LeBaron and Zumeta (2003) argue that lawyers' cultural mode of being and behaving is shaped in multiple ways by their training in law, and their associations with other legal professionals. While it has become increasingly difficult to conceive of shared ethical values due to the fragmentation of the profession (Francis, 2005), there remains a collective dimension linking these multiple areas of work spanning specialism, workplace, and legal aid caseload.

Increasingly precarious conditions within the legal aid world have strengthened the solidarity among workers within it, as they become

[2] Referring to 'macro' here as structural influences such as formal working practices, regulations from the Legal Aid Agency, economic provisions, governmental control. 'Micro' here refers to working practice on the ground level, including informal working practices, working and social relations, norms and values, as well as interactions and behaviours.

particularly eager to keep the profession alive – conducive to legal aid work becoming more of a progressive 'community of practice' (Dukes and Streeck, 2020: 626). This is an interesting finding compared with the presumed competition between different law firms, which is particularly evident in private practice. Yet in the context of legal aid, in a job that is typically very client-focused, there remains a strong presence of workers within it who are eager to help others even under adverse conditions. In this sense, occupational cultures become catalysts for worker solidarity, cultivating a sense of collectivism in an otherwise fragmented environment. Given the diversity of the occupation – and the wider disruption of the workplace – understanding the way in which work and culture come to interact in the workplace is certainly not a straightforward matter. As Dukes and Streeck (2020) argue, more ethnographic research on the 'formation of occupationally and workplace-based communities' among workers is urgently required if we are to understand what is going on 'on the ground' in sustaining work under contemporary conditions.

While it may be difficult to speak of a singular, rigid and taken-for-granted culture that applies to all legal aid work, it is likely that different lawyers across both civil and criminal remits, spanning a variety of workplaces, may form 'subcultures', or their work may align in some way or form. This deviation becomes integral to tracing the contours of their working lives. Therefore, rather than trying to shoehorn existing blanket models of occupational culture, this research proposes a new conceptual lens through which to better study and understand the ways in which the dynamics of culture and work fluidly interact within the field.

Transcending traditional occupational boundaries

Occupational culture tends to signify singular occupational groupings, job titles, static occupational boundaries, standardized working spaces, and has been criticized for its lack of theoretical development (Chan, 1996: 41). Heidensohn (1992) states that: 'all occupations develop some kind of lasting culture'. The small amount of research concerned with documenting legal culture serves as an essential reminder of the ongoing significance of 'culture' as an enduring theme. In line with the work of Schein (2010) and Deering (2011), elements of occupational culture apply to the legal aid world, such as the idea that an occupation upholds written rules, values, and accepted behaviours. The notion that a form of working culture is transmitted to new members is also pertinent (Van Maanen and Barley, 1984). Previous work suggests a drop in 'morale, recruitment and retention' within the sector, so this collective imperative becomes even more important (Kemp; 2010; Newman, 2016; Thornton, 2020). The nature of the work, however, means that a working model that cuts across different occupational groupings,

Figure 4.1: Interactive bodies constituting the legal aid world

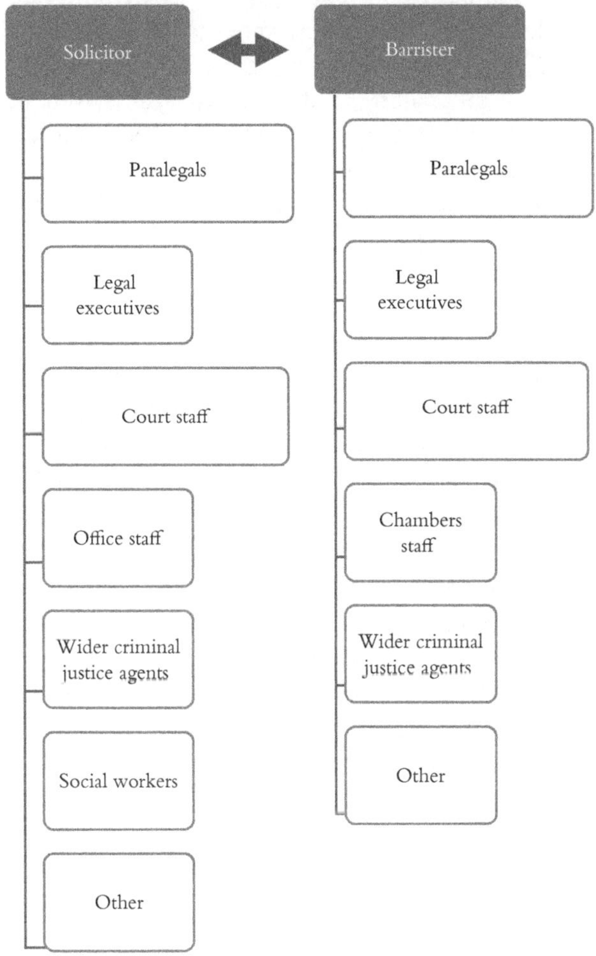

Source: Author's own elaboration.

crosses boundaries of barristers, solicitors, paralegals, and wider members of the justice field, is needed. For example, collaboration between a barrister and a paralegal crosses different occupational boundaries than collaboration between a solicitor and a paralegal, as each role has its own identity and its own way of operating. Exchanges within the legal aid world can, therefore, occur on multiple levels. These can be in the form of solicitor–solicitor, barrister–barrister, solicitor–barrister, para-legal–solicitor–barrister exchanges, or likewise interaction with other salient members in the field (as evidenced in Figure 4.1).

When an individual becomes a lawyer, they have to be prepared to carve out their own approach rather than seeking a template way of operating, due to the individualized nature of the work, as well the deficient levels of education and training.[3] Boon (2005: 254) notes that 'the "liberal" focus of law degrees leads to limited opportunities to educate for the realities of professional life'. Legal aid work is not given much attention within the remits of education or training, and therefore legal lawyers have to 'find their feet' themselves very early on as will be explored in more depth in the subsequent chapter.

Different legal specialisms also mean different working environments. Heterogeneous working spaces also impact how the work is experienced. For example, a housing solicitor who works in a high street firm and a housing solicitor who works for a law centre will experience vastly different working practices. They may think and interact in a completely different manner. A solicitor's firm often consists of a range of other legal specialisms, whereas a law centre operates in a different, more charitable sphere, seeking to address broader socio-structural issues.

Solicitors tend to be employed by a firm or organization; barristers tend to be self-employed and affiliated with a set of chambers, which can, likewise, uphold varying cultural attributes. Peter and Alistair, both barristers specialising in criminal law, refer to the role as 'individualized' because of their self-employed basis. Consistent with this, both respondents expressed the prospect of being able to 'do whatever they like', 'whenever they like', as they were not necessarily tied to a traditional employment relationship, unlike some of the solicitor respondents within this sample. As Peter suggests: 'just because we're self-employed, it doesn't mean that we don't share concerns and practices. It is even more vital that we do so in *our* positions'. Those self-employed still face the same challenges because of their wider marginalization, and equally require support from their peers. James (criminal solicitor) places emphasis on the need for both individualism and collectivity in their work: 'Lawyering is both an *individual*, as well as a *group commitment* … It's the only way you can pull through and succeed at the same time'. What becomes apparent is that, while legally-aided work is a unique practice, there remains a collective element to it. Grace (criminal solicitor) highlights the impossibility of categorizing those practising together because 'each person deals with their cases individually'. Jane (housing solicitor) stresses that, 'where historically, lawyers have all been shoved together under one branding, important variations within the profession have been ignored'. Several lawyers in the sample highlighted the ignorance of attempting to

[3] Highlighting issues of (in)adequate training and preparation for working with clients demonstrated that the participants were alert to potential failings beyond their control early on in their careers. This inadequacy further indicates how their personal investment may not be matched by professional or institutional provision, a gap that continues to widen.

'homogenize' their work. Respondents likewise told a consistent story, of the desire to be 'recognized' in a way that truly encapsulates the profession. In the words of Nicholas (criminal solicitor), 'we are not like any other occupation really'. Maddie (criminal solicitor) stated that 'being all in it together' makes it easier to get by in the job:

> There's definitely an ethos of people helping each other out in this field; there's a real thing of … if you're in a position to help someone sort of further down the ladder from you, who may be trying to get established themselves, then you'll naturally just help them … and I always just say, 'don't thank me, just do the same to someone else when you're in that position' and that's just how this occupation works.

Robert's indication of a collaborative working model in the excerpt above shows that they consider a form of working culture exists, a stance held by most respondents in this research. The need for an accurate representation of legal aid working culture is twofold: (1) to address the gap in scholarship, and (2) for the benefit of the practitioners in the field, as it was in their interest to identify a suitable form of working culture. Two-thirds of the practitioners in this research sample identified a form of working culture, which the vast majority suggested is fluid, adaptable, and unique in its nature. They found it difficult to define specifically. Ash, an immigration solicitor, reflects on this: 'Yes, I would identify a working culture, but I wouldn't say it's a *standard* working culture like you would get in say a police station. I can't necessarily describe it in clear terms, but it's definitely there, and it's definitely unique'. Given the confirmation that some form of 'occupational community' exists by the participants in this research, what follows is a novel exploration of their working culture that considers the dual fragmentation of the occupation. Internal fragmentation encapsulates the varying specialisms, varying caseloads, different job titles and different workspaces. External fragmentation refers to the increased fragmentation and marketization of wider justice services, as well as occupational marginalization.[4] An attack on the legitimacy of legal aid lawyering makes the lawyers undoubtedly more entrenched in their professional ideology (Sommerlad, 1996), and what this research shows is a distinctive attitudinal component present in the data that helps generate this model of working culture.[5] Emergent from the data is

[4] Occupational marginalization refers to the subordinate positioning of the profession. The profession tends to sit on the peripheries of the wider legal profession as a result of the way in which it is perceived by wider society, as well as the rest of the legal profession.

[5] This refers to the perception present in the data that legal aid lawyers are a profession separate to their private counterparts, with their marginality, their holistic orientation, and their subscription to an alternative ethical paradigm.

a working culture that I propose is best thought of as a 'shared orientation' as will be fully explored in the next section. This is a vital framing device, which conceptually grounds the themes discussed throughout the remainder of this book.

The emergence of the shared orientation model

Maddie (criminal solicitor) emphasized the term 'orientation' as something shared among the different bodies practising within the remit of legal aid. Described as the 'lay of the legal aid land', an 'orientation' can be described as an informal mechanism that both affects and explains how the occupation functions beyond the walls of formalities, that is procedures, rules, and regulations, as well as education and training. Maddie further states that such 'orientation' is learnt on the job, as those in the field transmit and/or pass it down to newcomers. As observed, some lawyers may cling on to this imperative tightly, whereas others may dip in and out depending on their job title, funding model, client base, working environment, as well as stress levels. In this vein, an 'orientation' is a shared working model that emphasizes diversity rather than conformity, shifting away from more blanket conceptualizations of occupational cultures as outlined earlier.

This fluidity is important as Nina (housing solicitor) states: 'I might do my job one way, but the person sitting right next to me in the office might do it differently, and that's absolutely fine. Different cases undertaken vary in terms of legal requirements, and all of our clients bring different needs to the table'. John (housing solicitor) reflected on the role of a working culture: 'multiple cultures may exist within the workplace, depending on firm, organization, law centre, courtrooms, or even whether you are based in an urban or rural area', echoing the work of Schein (2010). Marcus (housing solicitor) spoke about the unusual position of legal aid lawyers: 'it's like being alone in a crowd, you know, we all have similar tendencies and do share morals and values surrounding justice and the desire to want to help those in need, but we are all on our own paths really'. The complex array of organizational and performance spaces generates a large amount of cultural heterogeneity. As a conceptual model, the shared orientation model identified in this research accommodates these fluid occupational boundaries. It is sustained by both teamwork and individualism. For some, working alongside others can be tense and unnecessary, and for others it can be productive and necessary. Occupational boundaries can be defined as, 'the process of setting and negotiating boundaries which differentiate between fields of knowledge and expertise' (Kuna and Nadiv, 2018: 849). Lawyers face a multifaceted working environment in the sense that they sit on the peripheries of the legal profession yet uphold a dual responsibility to act on behalf of both their clients as well as the state, which means they

Figure 4.2: Differing features of the shared orientation to occupational culture

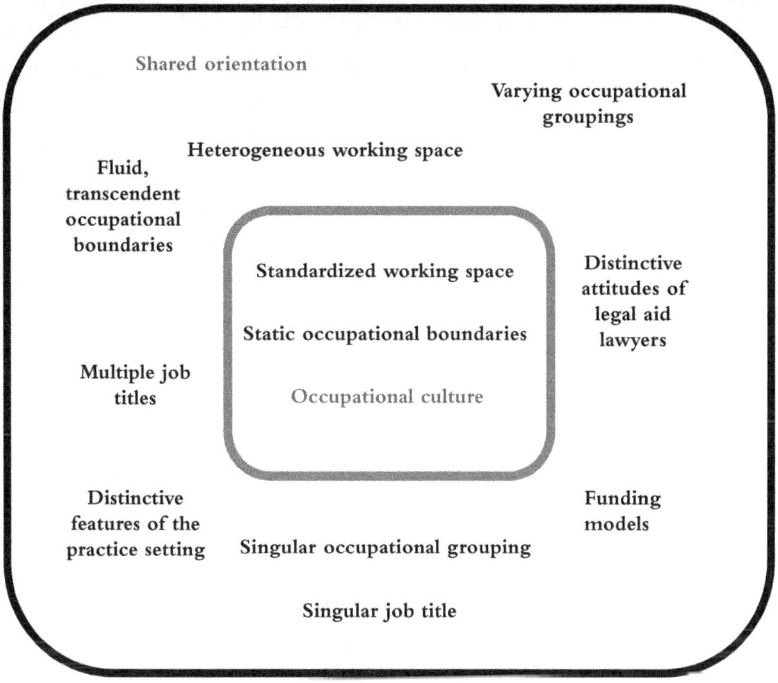

Source: Author's own elaboration.

have to negotiate both boundaries. Additionally, they face an increasingly complex web of controlling bodies, including the Ministry of Justice,the Legal Aid Agency, as well as the Law Society, and regulations that influence their everyday practice. The 'modern' lawyer who thrives (or survives) in this field, is one who still engages in some form of collective in spite of these negotiations. A 'shared orientation' upholds four broader functions, which include its ability to: (1) offer unity as a way of functioning in a multifaceted and fragmented occupation; (2) fortify support systems and collegial relationships in the face of diversity; (3) transcend personal and professional occupational boundaries; and (4) offer a way of 'finding your feet' beyond the remit of formal education and training. The fluidity and varying levels of engagement with the shared orientation are influenced by macro barriers, including management practices and increased pluralization of the workforce. Tom (housing solicitor) encapsulates this fluidity in a positive light:

> While my working culture is extremely important to my firm and me, it might not be important to the firm down the road. Likewise, their working culture might be very different to ours, and *I like that.*

> We *enjoy* that sense of being different to each other. It makes things more exciting.

Figure 4.3 explores the differences and similarities between 'occupational culture' and 'shared orientation' models for purposes of clarification, building on the scholarship outlined previously. Both can be defined as shared internalized dispositions, in the sense that they occur once the individual is within a given field and not during the formal stages of education and training. Both models have core characteristics that become timeless qualities as they are handed down through generations, from the more experienced professionals to the less experienced. Both are durable against macro changes to the field and allow stronger identities to be formed in the face of diversity.

Figure 4.3: Similarities and differences between occupational culture (OC) and shared orientation (SO)

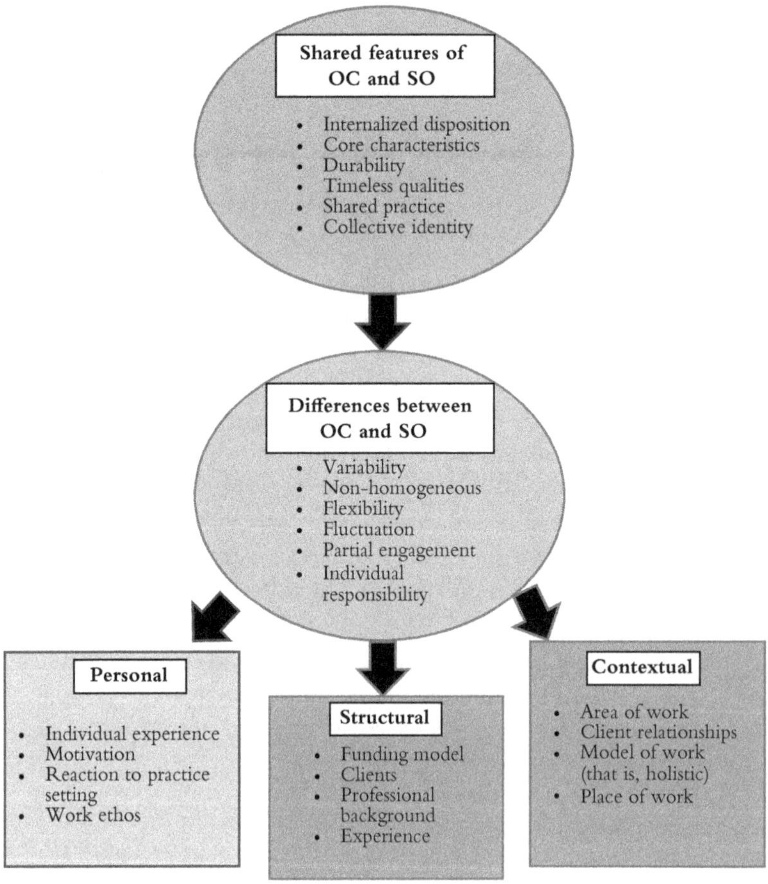

Source: Author's own elaboration.

However, shared orientation, as a concept, is far more variable and non-homogeneous to accommodate distinctive features of the practice setting. The following are distinctive of the shared orientation model: the physical working environment, funding model(s), client base, client relationships, holistic approaches, as well as ethical models. There is also the attitudinal component present in the data, the distinctive attitudes of legal aid lawyers.

Core characteristics of the shared orientation model

Collaboration featured as a core characteristic of this model. Andy (criminal barrister) referred to the orientation as 'the glue that holds the occupation together'. Participants regularly cited that 'knowledge sharing' among peers was significant to the success of their everyday practice. This can be contrasted with private lawyers, where competition for promotion, status, and clients impede people from sharing knowledge. In line with the words of Nina (housing solicitor), the legal aid industry is particularly 'knowledge heavy' due to the holistic nature of the work, which calls for elements of both legal and socio-capital knowledge. The learning process undoubtedly continues as a tenancy, or a training contract, is secured because of this knowledge-reliance. Tom (solicitor) compared this to driving: 'while you are safe enough to get on by yourself, thanks to a basic grounding, you are not perfectly able to drive'. The encouragement of knowledge sharing was observed within both the firm and the law centre. Respondents were particularly keen to make their colleagues feel comfortable in a reciprocal, as opposed to obligatory, manner. In a 'knowledge-driven' profession, this was even more important; Jane (housing solicitor) summarizes that those practising in legal aid often get 'thrown in the deep end': 'when you qualify, no one really shows you how things are done … You only get one advocacy assessment on your LPC,[6] one interviewing assessment and the next thing you know you're on your feet representing people. We literally get thrown in the deep end'. It is the absence of obligation here that makes the consensus work. A level of connectivity was likewise observed among the barristers in the sample: 'for me, it's all about coming together and sharing our knowledge. I've never been a solicitor, but if I can help then of course I will' (Peter, criminal barrister). This internalized disposition featured broadly across the wider sample, and was therefore not specific to solely barristers, solicitors, civil or criminal circles. Knowledge demands have been exacerbated by ever-changing protocols and legalities, as well as the increasing levels of paperwork and administration. James, a criminal solicitor, emphasizes the ability to help each other out when you get stuck, stating that he 'doesn't

[6] 'Legal Practice Course.

know what he'd do without his colleagues'. He further stressed the importance of having events like breakfast meetings to help keep each other up to date, and to allow colleagues to 'vent' if needed. The shared orientation model, in this sense, provides hope that people do not 'throw in the towel' when faced with difficulties. Thornton (2020: 250) reasons that 'the tension between what one values and *wants* to do versus how one actually *has* to do' can lead to 'frustration and low morale'. Newman (2013) reported a culture-shift away from client-centered values. Evidently, there remain several indirect factors that have affected the way the job must be done. Marcus (solicitor in housing) noted: 'I can't explain how important it is to stay close to your team members. Treat them like family, together we are stronger. I for one, couldn't survive in this profession any more alone'. The appreciation of each other's working practice keeps them going. 'Being 'liked' by our own colleagues and being part of a 'collective' makes us feel wanted, makes us feel like we belong to something and that our work is actually being appreciated' (Jay, housing solicitor). This coincided with the thoughts of Phil (criminal barrister) and Nina (housing solicitor) who spoke about the need to be 'resilient' on the inside 'to stick together in the face of adversity'. The shared orientation model in this sense offers a 'central core' to an otherwise 'hollowed out' profession, as emphasized further by Rhiannon (welfare solicitor). More so, it also acts as a form of coping mechanism in an occupation where very little in the way of formal support systems exist: 'Police officers who deal with indecent images or rape or something along those lines, I think they do get sort of a degree of counselling or assistance. Defence lawyers just a case of, well, living it, go and deal with it'. Participants stressed the issue of having to take on their client's traumas, and the effect this had on them. As Jane (housing solicitor) further stated, in many cases education and training does not teach you how to deal with the ongoing traumas and harms that their clients face. Due to the holistic nature of many of the cases within the legal aid remit, legal problems are not the only problems the clients often face; significant vulnerabilities can exist within the broader personal and social realms. As evidenced in Erica's story earlier, facing issues such as suicides, illness (both physical and mental), and significant traumas leading up to the legal issue can take a serious toll. Scott and Freckelton (2024) state that workplaces should be obligated to inform their employees about these risks, but also to develop and create policies and procedures to respond and mitigate pathologies that may arise as a result in the form of vicarious trauma. Additionally, as Alistair (criminal barrister) notes, often in the cases of criminal law, themes such as sexual violence, child abuse, and death regularly occur on a day-to-day basis, and thus exposure to such trauma can have a cumulative effect on both the lawyer's professional and personal life. Therefore, as further stressed by Scott and Frekelton (2024), as well as Fleck and Francis (2023), the need for a supportive culture that encourages someone to reach out remains crucial. Yet, while many individuals cited and/or displayed camaraderie in practices for reasons including socialization, moral support, motivation, or morale raising, in practice this was not always upheld by all lawyers in the sample. A couple of participants presented a glowing, idealized picture, yet my observations sometimes contradicted this. For example, an interaction observed following a difficult client meeting between a lawyer and a paralegal ended up turning into a bit of a disagreement as it was compounded by stressors. The client had offloaded significant amounts of their trauma onto both employees, and the impact of this had led to the client making unreasonable demands. While the paralegal argued that they would attempt to meet these demands, the lawyer had reached boiling point due to the imposition of time pressures and showed outward signs of being distressed to the point they had to remove themselves from the office environment. This highlights that, in some cases, camaraderie can be presented as a performance front. Goffman's (1959) dramaturgical perspective emphasizes the importance of settling on the appearance and manner of one's behaviour. 'Front stage' behaviour reflects internalized norms and expectations, whereas 'backstage' behaviour is often uninhibited or free of expectation. Evidence of this was also observed in the firm, as colleagues diverged between more public and private conversations. Maddie (criminal solicitor) likewise spoke of a sense of predestined fatalism that almost goes hand in hand with representing the 'underdog'. But the key argument to emerge here was that most of the lawyers tended to support each other when other people might not, potentially making them more susceptible to external pressures. Sophie (criminal solicitor) stressed the importance of motivating one another and keeping one another afloat, against those who 'damn the profession every single day', reminiscent of the narratives of fragmentation that will be fully unpicked later on. Financial restrictions placed on the occupation acted as a significant motivator on the existence of the shared orientation. Online and social networks have been fortified in response to fiscal cuts. The importance of these networks was confirmed by Peter (barrister), who spoke about the pressures of trying to keep abreast of any legal aid developments: 'it's me and my colleagues that keep cobbling it all back together'. Andy (barrister) reasons further: 'historically, lawyers have always upheld some sense of cohesion. In the face of adversity, legal professionals have always rallied together to avoid stagnation'. As noted, occupational cultures have previously been used in a progressive manner against an external threat from the 'outside'. This resonates with Bennett's work in the legal context:

> The legal profession sometimes behaves as if it is waiting for a knight in shining armour to rescue it from the forces of the marketplace .... But the practice of law is not a fairy-tale, and there is no knight in

> shining armour coming to the rescue. There is only we, its members. If the legal profession is going to save itself, we are the people who must do it. We are the wounded king, and our profession is the wounded kingdom. (2001: 12)

Despite the pressures or the perception of a stacked deck, there remain some positive values. Three-quarters of the sample stated that a form of collaboration was encouraged by senior staff across the board of firms, law centres, as well as chambers, to uphold their united concern for justice despite external challenges. Ben (housing solicitor) summarized this: 'definitely politics comes in, like everyone feels very much the same way, that society is unjust and that we want to make some form of positive contribution to that. Kinda charitable right?' This charitable sense was shared by 29 out of the 30 participants. External pressures can push for standardization of working practice (Rutherford, 1993; Tata, 2019). Newman's (2013) likening of criminal defence work to a 'sausage factory' and uniformed production line highlights the impact stringent regulations are having on the profession. The shared orientation model aligns to the commitment to justice, as it allows and enables the formation of networks to encourage continued campaigning, the promotion of interests for new entrants, and the ability to publish joint briefings, reports and responses to wider legal changes, allowing them to still generate impact despite increased standardization. Yet, some participants, for example, continued to adopt more of an 'informal' approach to their practice in terms of mannerisms and language employed, relying on humour and light-hearted exchanges, whereas others would practice in a more formal remit. Socialization processes likewise featured as a core characteristic. Picturing the world of the legal aid lawyer in the form of a loose cultural web can further bring to light the 'core set of assumptions, understandings and implicit rules that govern day-to-day behaviour in the workplace' (Deal and Kennedy, 2000: 501). This was true for Alistair (barrister), who affirms the existence of 'unwritten' rules:

> These rules aren't going to be found anywhere on paper, but you can get an awful lot just by watching; you've just got to open your eyes to it. There are different rules for different firms and chambers, so they can only be learnt once you immerse yourself within that specific working environment.

Several participants referred to these 'unwritten rules'. The UK does not have a written constitution, therefore much of our law – that is common law – is 'common sense' rather than codified. So it stands to reason that the wider legal aid arena follows suit. 'Unspoken strategies are essential if you want to progress. It is not about sticking to the book, necessarily; it is about picking up on the nuances that are going to allow you further inside the walls of the profession' (Robert, criminal barrister). Being part of the 'pack' was important: 'if you are a newbie, you need to pick these rules up quickly, don't hang about. Look at those who have been in the profession a long time and learn from them' (James, criminal solicitor). The sense of passing down shared characteristics was pivotal to the maintenance of the shared orientation. An example of an unwritten rule in the solicitors' firm was that 'if you've got work to do, then you just stay late and finish it as cases can't wait', and 'if you know, you *know*'. Robert (criminal solicitor) labelled this as a form of 'insider culture', maintaining that 'image is important, to our clients especially. What goes on "inside", compared to the public image we portray is very different'. Chambliss's (2010) concept of the insider–outsider legal culture is relevant here. On the outside, while the wider firm practises to meet the needs of the public's imperative, such as joining in the wider fight for justice, within each specialism or department they may also uphold separate smaller internal orientations. The partner of the firm noted that she encourages her team to work holistically in the housing department, whereas in the crime department they are told to take a narrower view on cases. This dual dimension is not only crucial to the functioning of the firm, but also to the firm's image, which is observable to the community exercising transparency. This could be attributed to the intention or desired outcome to warrant higher levels of trust from the clients. This desired 'image' differed for each workplace. As Ash (immigration solicitor) highlighted: 'that's why we can't all ascribe to a *singular* working culture, because we might all be striving for a different image. We have different specialisms, and different internal goals within our firms; therefore this needs to be taken into consideration, and far too often it's not'. While the existence of working cultures in their various forms existed, these were 'not forced' by any means. One of the partners in the firm, for example, observed that she did not *have* to spend 30 per cent of her day aiding her colleagues; she opened her arms because she chose to do so to increase her job satisfaction. This sense of 'always having an open door' was more outwardly evident among the female solicitor pool. Heidensohn (1992) argues that gender is pivotal to the formation of a working culture. The number of women working in the legal aid sector in England and Wales continues to show an upward trend. Seventeen out of the 30 participants in this research sample were female. Rosener has argued that women are more likely to utilize their socialization experiences as women in the form of a 'transformational' leadership style to reach the 'top'. This involves transforming self-interest into a vested interest in the group goals. Females also tend to focus on skills such as charisma, contact-building, or interpersonal skills, evidenced when observing two of the female partners at the firm (Rosener, 1990). An essential function of a working culture is its ability to transcend work and social boundaries. Three-quarters of the participants in this sample stressed the importance of socializing with others practising within the remit of legal aid. Maria (housing solicitor) enjoyed the fact that she had a social lounge and bar built within the basement of their firm. Participants also highlighted social events such as five-a-side football leagues against other firms and summer parties as part of wider legal aid networks. Two of the barristers in the sample, however, stressed that they would not tend to interact with those outside their own chambers. Davey et al (2001) found that alcohol consumption plays a key part in high-pressured jobs, sometimes in a negative manner. Ash (immigration solicitor) stated that he felt like he 'didn't fit in' because he did not drink, but he typically went along to social events anyway because he felt they were integral to strengthening relationships with his colleagues at the law centre. Sophie, a criminal solicitor, stated that the ability of a culture to strengthen collegial relationships can also assist with external relationships within the wider justice system. Eleanor, a partner of a firm specializing in family law, spoke of a system she set up at her own firm that involves a local trainee police officer coming into her firm to show them what it is like 'on the other side' of cases, to facilitate more positive relationships in their community. For others, relationships were slightly more difficult to build both internally and externally. Humour was typically used to alleviate problematic relationships. James (criminal solicitor) echoes this: 'I feel so much more at home when I recognize the others in court, a bit of banter helps so much'. Humour has likewise traditionally been used in police and prison officer working cultures as a form of communicative performance (Holdaway, 1983). Humour was more likely to be employed by those practising within the criminal remit. This could be attributed to the more extreme nature of their cases and the stricter rules of the courtroom, acting as a form of release. Different legal aid lawyers engage and interact socially at varying levels. Humour was particularly evident among the barristers in this research, as evidenced in the two examples below:

[*Context: banter with court clerk. Barrister (B1) walks in*]
B1: Damn it am I in the right court?
Clerk: This is court 4. Come on, mate, I thought you had a degree? Do you need some help with your reading?
B1: Yep, wrong court, I'm just learning to read you see.
B2: Ha-ha loser, see ya! [*said in a sarcastic tone*]
B1: Yeah, bye for now, nice to see ya. Hope your case goes well.
[*Excerpt from ethnography*]

[*Back in court*]
B1: Can anyone smell coffee? [*laughs*]
B2: [*Holding a plastic cup of coffee*] It's just water! [*winks at B1, knowing he's not allowed hot drinks in the court room*]

B2: So how long do you think your speech will be?
B1: 43 minutes.
B2: You don't earn your money by doing a long speech you know! [*laughs*]
B2 [*Continues*] You practise your speech in the mirror don't you! I don't know how you always get it at 30 mins. You look in the mirror, get your timer on and practice, you saddo.
B1: Yep, well of course … what else would I be doing at weekends …
B2: [*Laughs*] Come on mate you need to get out more, you geek.
B1: Enough of this … I was actually in the middle of a very important interview you know [*as he turns round and winks at me – referring to our conversation*].

The use of humour was often visible within interactions between various members of staff, such as court clerks, barristers, and social workers – something that I was not expecting due to the strict nature of the courtroom. Humour, however, allowed a better rapport to be built among the various professionals, which in turn improved the overall mood, resulting in increased efficiency. James (criminal solicitor) echoes this:

> If I am having an alright time in the court and I get on with the others, then I'm more likely to come out the other side with a successful result you know … that's just how things go …. if people are on your side, and they like you then it definitely helps with things in the court context. It's still a lot about who you know and who you get on with.

Humour has likewise traditionally been used in police and prison officer working cultures as a form of communicative performance (Holdaway, 1983). James (criminal solicitor) notes that the informal side to the work makes the work more enjoyable overall:

> I think it's quite a nice way of earning a living really. You go to court, you have a bit of banter with the other lawyers that are there, and the court staff that are there so it is quite social in that respect, you see loads of different people, but you also see loads of the same people day in day out. You know, and you have a bit of banter with the prosecutors as well because obviously you're up against them quite a bit.

James makes use of humour daily, both with other staff as well as clients in one-to-one meetings. Fundamentally, it is his way of building relationships and, as observed, it seemed to have a very positive effect on all sides. For example, from entering the court to leaving at the end of the day, it was noticeable that James had very good rapport with all parties present in the courtroom, which ultimately made his job a lot easier. Not all respondents had good relationships with the court staff, however. As Robert (criminal barrister) states: 'Some of my colleagues are so rude to the court staff, and I just cannot fathom that.' Likewise, Grace (criminal solicitor) reasons: 'but not all legal aid lawyers are friendly. Some of them hate it if they hear laughter in the courtroom. You have to be very careful'. Those practising in the remit of crime in this research more commonly employed humour. This could be attributed to the more extreme nature of their cases, as well as the stricter rules of the courtroom.

How does shared orientation manifest within the physical working environment of the legal aid lawyer?

The final section of this chapter will seek to address how the physical working environment can both facilitate and hinder how shared orientation is experienced and/or maintained within the legal aid world. In this sense, it will address the notion of why the element of group work – the shared orientation – functions as it does. This section draws more specifically on the physical space at Silverman and Co – the main firm used within this research – to illustrate this.

Attention must be given to the office environments of the solicitors' firm used within this research, Silverman and Co (see Figure 4.4). In this firm, the 'operational core' of the practice was designed to be conducive to specific

Figure 4.4: Layout of office at Silverman and Co

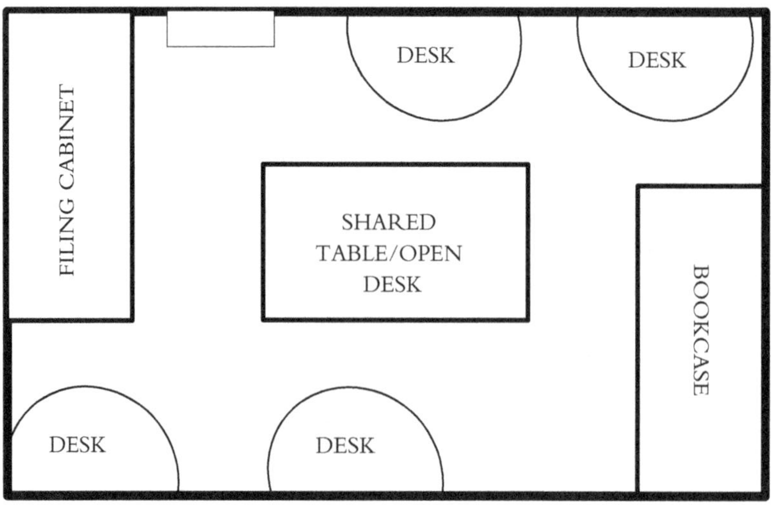

Source: Author's own elaboration.

types of cultural practice, such as knowledge sharing and collaboration. For example, all the desks were situated in a large open space, situated around the edge of the room and, in the centre, was an open table and chairs, which colleagues regularly used to have open discussions and to go through cases/ documents with each other in a very open manner. An enormous shelf with case bundles and relevant books likewise was accessible to all. There were no noise restrictions, and the radio was often kept on during the day to keep up morale. Colleagues were able to chat freely whenever they wanted to, and this assisted with knowledge sharing and collaboration. Emphasis was therefore placed on transparency, openness, and communication within this physical office environment. Alongside this, outside this working space there were multiple water dispensers in the hallways where colleagues often gathered to chat and refresh. Likewise, there was a small kitchen featuring sofas and free communal tea and coffee facilities for all, which were regularly used throughout the day. A plethora of research places emphasis on office environments, most significant to this research the work of O'Hara and Ribstein (2009). The office environment can have a significant effect on office culture. While the office described above was open-plan, exercising transparency, as well as team-based and communicative tendencies, other offices (such as the law centre) were more enclosed, with separate offices accommodating a maximum of three people per office space. In response to being asked whether the layout of her office in the law centre was practical, Rhiannon (welfare solicitor) responded:

> It is not always ideal because it's quite cramped, and lawyers always have a lot of files … but its good at the same time because it means that if I want to bounce an idea off someone I can just look up from my computer and get it answered right away.

Unpicking this further, Rhiannon stressed the ability to be able to knowledge share due to the close proximity of her colleagues. She went on to state that she preferred having a shared office because it enabled more collaboration to occur at once as more individuals could join in the conversations when there was more room. Likewise, being able to bounce off ideas while sitting at her computer ultimately facilitated quicker exchanges of knowledge sharing. Traditionally, however, as Marcus (housing solicitor) recognizes, lawyers tend to get assigned a client, and these clients are met in individual office spaces. However, with the onset of 'team-based structures', particularly within solicitors' firms, the physical designs often intentionally move away from this tradition. Now the client often progresses through the firm, seeing multiple individuals in one visit, from receptionists to paralegals, to legal secretaries, to various lawyers, depending somewhat on who is on duty. Therefore, in many respects, the office environment reflects this nature of progression to aid both the client and the more fluid nature of the work. In this sense, this type of environment fits the type of lawyering explored in this book.

That is not to say that all firms are like this. It is important to remember that the shared orientation model exists in deviated forms according to the specific environment it is being applied to. The barristers within this research highlighted that, because most of them are self-employed, often the chambers are empty, as people mostly tend to work from home when they are not appearing in court. Peter (criminal barrister) says that 'one advantage of going into chambers is that there are other people there, so socially it's good; and more importantly, with regards the work, if there's people there who do a similar type of work to you, then you can bounce ideas'. He further stated that he only really went into the chambers when he was preparing work, and that is when he got the most benefit out of knowledge sharing. However, he went on to stress:

> Some barristers go in more than others though; but a lot of people do tend to work from home, and I'm one of those people. If I wanted to speak to someone about a case, I'm more likely to just pick up the phone or send an email around. I mean, if you are in, you could put out a question to the robing room, and people will always help if they can. It's very collegiate. There's still a strong culture of people helping each other out, and you repay the favours done to you, not to the person who helped you, but to someone else down the line. Being in the robing room, that really helps as you get people with all different levels of experience.

As stressed by Peter, he is still able to collaborate when working from home via email. Some firms likewise now have instant messenger services, as evidenced by Tom (housing solicitor), which makes communication a lot easier as it is far more informal. He further states, however, that it is most beneficial to be present as you can physically share knowledge and ask questions in the robing room. Traditionally, robing rooms have been designed for barristers to change into their robes, discuss cases, and hide from troublesome clients. Yet, the Bar Standards Board has been known to suspend individuals for misbehaviour – including a Mr Khan (an experienced barrister) for seven months for 'gossiping' in the robing room (Legal Futures, 2018). Gossiping about fellow colleagues can make the robing room much less desirable, also further discouraging a collective working culture. In addition to this, typically robing rooms have always been very gendered. In 2017, the all-male robing room was opened up to female barristers in Southwark Crown Court following a judicial intervention, which has aimed to open up pre-case discussions to all (Connelly, 2017). However, if it took a judicial intervention to open this space for women, this highlights the persistent patriarchal nature of the barrister profession (see Chapter 5). Offices being empty is not just a feature of barristers' chambers, however. James (criminal solicitor) echoes a similar notion:

> Where I am now, because of the way it's laid out, it's all different rooms. You can discuss cases and you do discuss cases but because everyone's … everyone's always out all the time … you're not in the office very often because you're always out. Literally I'm out every day and in the evenings, I catch up with my work. where I'm working at the moment, so you don't tend to see anybody. I might only get in the office one day a month … It's great! [*laughs*] … the problem with crime is *if you're in the office you're not earning money so …* . [his emphasis]

Identifiably, it is very much dependent on the type of law that you are specializing in as to how conducive the office or working environment might be. For example, as James stated, if you are practising as a criminal solicitor or barrister, then if you are not in court, ultimately you are not earning money. So offices may not be particularly useful for those practising in the criminal remit. However, as stressed in previous sections, James identified the importance of having good working relationships with other members in the court. The ability of a shared orientation to suit heterogeneous working environments proves vital here as it can accommodate varying physical structures. Having a suitable working environment to facilitate a healthy working culture is necessary. For solicitors, this comes more in the form of an open-plan office, while for barristers it seems that the courtroom has more influence on the collaborative elements of their everyday interactions. Different individuals, however, have varying opinions about the types of environments that work correctly for their firm; this is very important because it further encapsulates the individualized nature of the work (Beck, 2000). Ash (immigration solicitor) prefers to work in a less open-plan environment, as his type of work in immigration often entails a lot of private one-to-one engagements behind closed doors, whereas Becky (civil liberties/human rights) stresses the need for having an open-plan space to maintain a 'strong working environment' because it encourages group work and knowledge sharing. Variations in office layouts were highlighted among participants responses, with 75 per cent of respondents stating that open-plan offices created a healthier working environment overall. This contrasts with popular perception, given that often open-plan offices tend to be the least popular in other professions. Likewise, the open-plan working environment speaks to the 'sausage-factory' model identified by Newman (2013), which reinforces the idea that legal aid lawyering can be likened to a form of production line.

This chapter will now conclude, summarizing what contribution it has made to this book, and vitally acknowledging that the working culture of the legal lawyer is best understood in the form of a 'shared orientation'. While it is argued that collaboration, shared values, active socialization processes, and working relations (to name just a few attributes) are not entirely exclusive to legal aid lawyers or likewise exhaustive in their list, these features remain core to *their* working culture.

Kinghan (2021: 168) found that lawyers in their study wanted to sustain their identities as progressive lawyers despite these pressures. Evidence shows that a progressive lawyering movement still exists in the UK, which is built around networks of informal interaction, shared beliefs, solidarity, as well as collective action, lending itself to the construction of a persistent working culture, and this study has helped confirm just that. As Marcus (solicitor) summed up: 'We are our own kinda tribe, and I really like that'.

Summary: A useful conceptual framework?

There is no doubt that legal aid lawyers are facing a more demarcated, fragmented, and difficult occupational terrain due to sustained under-cutting, toxic narratives, and misconceptions of their work. This research has presented a new model to better understand the working culture of these lawyers that considers the macro backdrop. This will be used as an anchor for the remaining chapters to develop; a useful conceptual framework to ground this research.

A 'shared orientation' model provides a way to better understand the unique and multifaceted workspace of the legal aid lawyer, involving varying caseloads, differing levels of employment, and diverse working environments. Driving this conceptual model is (1) the distinctive features of the practice setting, but also (2) the attitudinal component present in the data from the lawyers themselves. The shared orientation model offers unity as a way of functioning in an otherwise fragmented profession. Through its preservation of working ideals, it captures the cultural heterogeneity of the work, and acts as an informal coping mechanism for the likes of emotionally driven labour and vicarious trauma. Overall, it remains clear that those practising within the field share some similar tendencies across the board, including knowledge-sharing, collaboration, camaraderie, and socialization processes, to name just a few. The wide-ranging sample in this research, spanning solicitor–barrister and civil–criminal remits, was beneficial to the construction of the shared orientation, as it would have been harder to justify if fragments of the profession were explored in isolation. A 'shared orientation' offers insight into how the wider profession unites beyond individual specialisms, positions, and workplaces. The formation of this conceptual model speaks to the deficiencies in the literature and offers a nuanced insight into this often-hidden occupational world. This study is the first of its kind to provide an exploration of the working culture of legal aid lawyers in the current context. Future empirical work based on the shared orientation model will achieve a deeper understanding of this complex field spanning criminal, family, and social welfare contexts alike. The value of the 'shared orientation' model, however, lies not only in the field of law but in its applicability to wider geographic, economic, and demographic domains. As the macro context becomes increasingly precarious (considering, for example, COVID-19), the ability of shared orientation to withstand external pressures, respond to marginality, and provide a coping mechanism merits further exploration. Also, the impact of remote working practice, and the extent to which it impacts worker relations, will prove interesting here. The 'shared orientation' model will also prove valuable in the study of other complex occupations that have multiple categorizations (medicine, social work, or education, to name just a few), where a blanket model of occupational culture may not suit.

5

Navigating Entry to, and Barriers Within, the Legal Profession: Exploring Institutional and Structural Deficiencies Within the Legal Aid Field

The process of becoming a legal aid lawyer is often difficult for several reasons. This chapter is foregrounded with existing secondary literature, data, and statistics, punctuated intermittently with descriptive ethnographic accounts and individuals' experiences as obtained from the ethnographic data. This is done purposely, to provide context for, and to situate, subsequent analysis, to tell an over-arching (macro) story. This chapter describes the characteristics of the legal aid workforce. To this end, (ever-changing) education and training, routes into the profession, as well as lawyer demographics all come to construct the rhetoric of the legal aid lawyer. Drawing out patterns and themes can affect how the field is experienced, and further highlights that existing structural institutional and professional deficiencies still exist. This exploration also speaks directly to the 'shared orientation' model explored in the previous chapter.

Demographics

> I think race, gender and class are the three factors which, you know, play a big role in determining whether you can become a barrister, and very importantly whether you can *continue* as a barrister. (Alistair, criminal barrister)

Insight into how the legal aid profession is shaped and constructed can be gleaned from addressing factors such as gender, social class, and race. The pool of research participants used within this research is skewed towards white

(26/30) and middle-class (28/30) participants; however there was almost an equal split of females and males (16–15). All female participants involved in this research were practising as solicitors, whereas the male participants in the sample pool were a combination of barristers and solicitors. While I admit that the sample here is quite limited in its size, and is by no means generalizable, considerations of this sample will still be interweaved within the discussion below as I still feel it has significance here.

Gender

Noteworthy demographic changes have occurred within the wider lawyering profession, with the significant growth of the numbers of women within legal practice. In the US, women were barred from the field right up until the mid-20th century (Sanchagrin, 2014: 2). In the UK, the Sex Disqualification (Removal) Act 1919 allowed women to enter the legal profession for the first time (Gosling, 2017). Ivy Williams became the first female called to the Bar on 10 May 1922, followed shortly by Helena Normanton, the first practising female barrister. In the same year, Carrie Morrison was the first solicitor in England and Wales to be admitted. The lawyering profession, in general, has always been known for its incredibly stringent recruitment practices and lack of demographic diversity, despite the onset of late modernity bringing about a broader consciousness over equality (Kadushin, 1962; Loftus, 2010).

For most of its history, the legal world has been very much a male-dominated space. This is now in some sense seen to be 'atypical', particularly in respect to solicitors practising within the legal aid remit, as evidenced within the sample in this research. Within this context, there has been a significant influx in the number of females within the solicitor pool at the entry level. Women now make up 62 per cent of the solicitor pool (Solicitors Regulation Authority, 2024). For example, 12 out of 15 female solicitors in this research hold 'entry-level jobs', meaning that only threee of the female participants in this research hold senior positions, such as firm partners or deputy heads of departments. This is likewise in congruence with their experience/length of service. Differences become more apparent when we look at seniority in firms, as women tend to be less represented at senior levels. However, the proportion of women at partner level is 37 per cent, which is up from 32 per cent in 2015 (Solicitors Regulation Authority, 2024).

Yet, women still face some barriers with regards to progression and reaching those higher positions: 'I think it would be extremely difficult for one of the girls to become a partner … positions of power here tend to be dominated by males, unfortunately … I suppose it's a bit of a boy's club attitude' (Maddie, criminal solicitor). All the barristers that responded to the call for participants were male. This finding can also be attributed to the fact the Bar remains male dominated in practice but not in training. In their recent *Diversity at the Bar* (2024 :12) report, the Bar Standards Board found that there were 52.6 per cent females at the pupillage stage, but only 19.9 per cent had been given the title of 'Kings Counsel', compared to 77.9 per cent men.

To this end, there are far more applicants for tenancy in chambers[1] than there are places, and those who do not practise as a barrister tend to venture out to other work whether that be as a solicitor or within other business fields. On average, the number of females practising as a barrister is less than the number of males, with a total of 10,520 men and 7,186 women across all levels recorded (Bar Standards Board, 2024: 13). Several reasons have been attributed by the Bar Standards Board. They found that the general culture of chambers is not conducive to having children. Around 80 per cent of barristers operating out of chambers are self-employed, which can also be difficult for family life. All five of the barristers interviewed in this research were self-employed and based in well-established Inns of Court, which fits with the findings. The Bar Standards Board also highlighted the issue of power within the occupation, as the gap between policy and practice remained quite vast, particularly concerning maternity rights. For example, it was cited that women felt intimidated about evoking maternity rights due to stringent policies and chamber practices, which have typically been very androcentric in their nature. A significant issue, identified by Alistair (criminal barrister), was the inability or unwillingness of the Bar to take action to improve such issues:

> I realised early on that there is a narrative that the Inns of Court puts forward and the Bar Council and other providers put forward about encouraging people from diverse backgrounds to access the Bar, but you realise it's just actually a load of rubbish. They're not actually doing anything. There was a group of women a few years ago who tried to get one of the Inns to rent at a lower rate or give them some space. I don't know if you know how the Inns of Court operate, but basically, they own all the property. The women asked the Inns to give them some space so they could set up a nursery and, you know, what you have to do is make a basic report from the Bar Council about diversity to see that there is discrimination against women, because even women who manage to get pupillage and get taken on, then inevitably statistically at some point will have children, and then they lose out. And one way to address this is childcare. I thought it was a really positive thing getting the Inns of Court involved with allocating space for a nursery, but they said no, and now the women went ahead but built it outside the Inns

[1] Chambers refers to the rooms or workspaces used by barristers.

> of Court with a private provider. I thought it was so disappointing because that's where they can make a difference. Having a nursery in the Inns would make things so much easier. It would be right on the doorstep and would just give more flexibility around our working hours. It's not the fluffy talks they give, but it's those kinds of real-life practical things that can really make a difference. They could have really shown their desire to change things there.

As Alistair notes, there remain significant developments to be made within the chambers to ensure those who have families can manage childcare arrangements. Even when presented with the opportunity to make a change, the Inns of Court, in this case, did not take this on board. Attrition rates for women continue to be much higher than their male counterparts due to institutional failures to accommodate family commitments and caring roles. It remains a very traditional world in many senses; the male lawyers indicated that they were not expected to engage with family or ask for paternity leave, as confirmed by Alistair, Robert, and Phil (criminal barristers). As noted by the Solicitors Regulation Authority (2024), women are also more likely to specialize in areas other than criminal and corporate work, such as litigation, family, property, and private client work, due to the increased stability and more flexible working environments.

However, family law – for both solicitors and barristers alike – has been particularly affected by cuts to funding, which has led to much more instability within the workplace. Working in a high street firm likewise comes with its challenges as there tends to be a much smaller workforce, who become very reliant on each other. As Eleanor (family solicitor and partner) outlines:

> I think that working at a high street firm on the ground level makes it notoriously difficult to be a woman and take time out to have children, and then come back at the level you left it because there's just no one there to pick up the work whilst you're gone. I think LASPO has had a massive effect; I mean, because I'm a partner here I am quite lucky in so far as I'm fairly autonomous … but for females in junior positions, it has had a profound effect. They have no control over anything. It's really hard to go part-time, let alone to take maternity leave.

Women are also less likely to practise criminal law because it is so uncompromising and impossible to balance with other responsibilities. As Phil (criminal barrister) notes:

> Crime is the most brutal for families, hence why it is a majority-male profession. The macho sitting hours, and the phallocentric

> fundamentals that underpin it undoubtedly have a very significant impact. I wish I could say it's changed over time but, unfortunately, the Bar is very much set in its historic ways. The courtroom itself still has issues surrounding over-dominant male power.

As noted by Phil, due to the 'macho sitting hours' within the Bar, it makes it difficult to balance childcare and practice. For example, the unpredictability of court sitting hours can be seen as a significant disincentive; sometimes barristers must be in court until 8 or 9 pm in the evening. Barristers are required to work very long and unsociable hours, which does not lend itself to flexible working practices to fit around family life for both women and men alike. Phil confirmed that often he finds himself working 12–14-hour days, which means he works well into the late evening. Likewise, he further stressed that his working hours were not flexible due to needing to be in court at all hours. Often, when a trial is on, it has to be five days a week, and this will very often be away from home. This is a crime-specific problem as trials go on much longer than court hearings in other areas of law.

Differences existed between criminal solicitors and barristers, as confirmed by the female criminal solicitor respondents. In one criminal defence firm associated with one of the participants, over half of the solicitors were female. One of the managing partners there was also female. The flexibility of time is more conducive to the solicitor remit; the proportion of women in law firms has risen from 48 per cent in 2015 to 53 per cent in 2023 (Solicitors Regulation Authority, 2024). As further outlined by Mary (civil liberties and human rights solicitor):

> My workplace is more accessible to women, particularly women who have childcare responsibilities, because they're more flexible about your working hours. There's far less emphasis on presenteeism, you know this idea that someone needs to be at their desk between 8 and 6 all day every day. This doesn't really exist in my place of work, so it's excellent for women who have children.

Anna (immigration solicitor) likewise spoke about the gendered features of her working environment and the more 'female-friendly' features of her workplace:

> I think there's less focus perhaps on targets and competitiveness in this sector and place of work, and I think targets and competitiveness and the sort of one-up-man-ship, I think those are very masculine characteristics traditionally; however, there are definitely women in the legal profession who definitely exhibit, you know, that tendency

> to get one up on her colleagues. Legal aid I think is probably broadly speaking a bit more female-friendly, whereas private practice is much more masculine as there is a lot of emphasis on being there all the time and it's all about competitiveness.

Anna's account resonated with other areas of legal aid work. When speaking about the divide between legally aided work and privately funded work, she expressed that funding played a significant role in the nature and competitiveness of the work. In some places, legal aid work is funded through grants as opposed to being based on business being passed down, which takes away the pressure of having to compete with colleagues. This contrasts with the extensive competition that exists within areas of private practice, in particular commercial law. Likewise, the immigration lawyers involved in this research also had a stream of commissioned work from charities and social services, which made it a lot easier as the competitiveness of trying to secure business was lowered. These external forms of funding pave the way for more flexible working practices overall and, as such, can be more conducive to family life.

There remain significant differences in the feminization of the solicitor and barrister professions. For example, in the latter more elements of patriarchy persist in practice. While this research only offers a snapshot of the legal aid profession, this section has highlighted gender differences supported by secondary data, which will be fed into the analysis later. Alongside the adverse effects of the cuts to funding, the field still faces broader challenges surrounding gender equality, particularly within the remit of practising as a barrister.

Ethnicity

> They tend to use people like me as a poster charm. I'm not English you see; my family came here as refugees … and I really don't like to be used like that. (Alistair, criminal barrister)

Following on from our discussions on gender, diversity continues to be a significant challenge facing the legal industry, and always has been. The data taken from the Bar Standards Board (2024: 15) shows that most individuals practising at the Bar (77.2 per cent) are white. While we have seen an increase in diversity within solicitors' firms, there is still significant work to be done. Even up to 1995, solicitors from a minority background only accounted for 2 per cent of the profession. The Solicitors Regulation Authority highlighted that the number of black, Asian, and minority ethnic (BME) lawyers in firms went from 14 per cent in 2015 to 19 per cent in 2023, recognizing some widening in diversity (Solicitors Regulation

Authority, 2024). As evidenced in these figures, BME practitioner numbers are steady. Four out of the 30 participants in this research identified as being from BME backgrounds: 'yes, they are hiring ever more people like me, but there remains to be a lot of work to be done with regards to widening the diversity in relation to those from BME backgrounds' (Marcus, housing solicitor). Evidently, as stressed further by Marcus, having more representation in the field, as well as potentially challenging issues in recruitment and education, may encourage more inclusivity. Helping to provide opportunities for minority groups will also be beneficial to clients, as in a lot of cases they will want to see the same representation in the legal teams that choose to support them (Solicitors Regulation Authority, 2024).

Age

With an increasingly ageing profession, in some areas of England and Wales criminal duty solicitors are now pretty much non-existent. Duty solicitors exist to ensure that suspects' legal rights are observed; they are there to assist those who do not have access to a solicitor. Duty solicitors come in two forms: police station duty solicitors and court duty solicitors. Their role is to provide services to clients free of charge. This scheme allows someone who has already been charged with an offence to consult and be represented by a solicitor for their first appearance only. As a result, it is difficult to know how many clients a duty solicitor will get on any given day. For example, while Marcus typically had seven to eight clients in his working day, some days he would have none and others he would have nearer 15. The uncertainty of the role makes it extremely difficult for lawyers to plan out their days, and likewise means that their time is never really under control. Also, in most cases, they may not have met the offender prior to attending court; but they are still a key bulwark between the client and the justice system. Their role remains vital as they ensure the protection of rights and a fair trial. Yet, as noted by the Law Society (2024a): (1) 4 per cent of duty solicitors are under 35 years old; (2) there are now no criminal law solicitors under 35 in Cornwall, Lincolnshire, Wiltshire, or Worcestershire; and (3) only one exists in Norfolk, Shropshire, and Warwickshire. Their data further shows that in many places (Bristol, Lincolnshire, Cornwall, and Devon, for example) 60 per cent of duty solicitors are over 50. As Nicholas (criminal solicitor) notes:

> This is just a result of the lack of increases in fees, drastic cuts to legal aid, and people being pushed to the edge. It is now so so *so* hard to have a viable career as a criminal duty solicitor. If we're not careful, there's going to be no one left practising in this field.

Over half the respondents in this sample raised concerns over the lack of duty solicitors available due to ageing demographics, lack of pay, increased workloads, as well as damaged reputations. As external pressures build, many are turning away legal aid work altogether, and the lack of lawyers practising in some areas has resulted in 'advice deserts', meaning that over 15 million people in the UK are living in areas where there is little or no local representation. However, three-quarters of the respondents in this research are under 40. Of the 11 participants practising in the criminal field in this sample pool, four of these are aged 40 and above, which fits in with the trends outlined above.

Social class

> I think class is one thing that permeates everything at the Bar. Even chambers that have 95 per cent white male tenants will have 5 per cent that are not. But when you look closely at the CVs, you see that one thing that unites 100 per cent of the tenants is social class. (Alistair, criminal barrister)

Historically, the legal profession has tended to be dominated by those from the middle and upper classes. Bar training costs on average £15–£19,000, so that accounts for some of its prohibitive nature. There has been very little development in terms of widening the diversity of social class, because of high course fees, low entry salaries, and the cost of accessing the Bar in the first place. Alistair further notes:

> Amongst people who tend to practice at the English Bar, yeah, there is a lot less diversity, a lot more male-heavy, a lot more white, and a lot more private school … actually diversity at the Bar is terrible. It's just awful. Ninety per cent of (higher court) judges are male, privately educated Oxbridge. I mean that's just *insane*. [his emphasis]

Phil and Andy (both criminal barristers) agreed with this sentiment. In contrast, however, Peter (also a criminal barrister) noted:

> Class doesn't really play any kind of role in my set of chambers. In terms of the profession, what I understand is that it would be very difficult to sort of get a job by the old boys' network now. But now you are up against a pool of very talented applicants, and I am not sure how much it's going to help you what your social class is. But I would count it a lot less … if you were applying for a top commercial set, then maybe it's not inconceivable to be considered as more important, but I still think it's inevitably much less important than it used to be. If anything,

> it might count against you if you were posh, and you applied to a set of chambers if it was legal aid work.

Peter's response, however, was seen as atypical in comparison to the responses from the other participants in this sample. There is a divide in opinion about the role that social class plays between those who practise as a solicitor and those who practise as a barrister. Marcus (housing solicitor) recognizes that barriers remain within the solicitor profession:

> You kind of must be from a wealthy background. It was tough before with student loans, it's tougher now with £9,000 a year, the training costs, and the competitiveness for training contracts, and plus even getting a training contract nowadays is such a tough thing to do. You either must be supported by someone wealthy, as they have even removed the minimum salaries as well for trainees, or you have to be extremely lucky and find someone who is going to sponsor you well enough so you can actually survive.

Karen (director), as well as Rachel (housing solicitor and partner), maintain that class issues remain, particularly due to the sheer cost of education. One of the key challenges that undoubtedly remains in the legal sector is the financial pressures of accessing education, as further explored in the next section. However, in contrast, others, such as James (criminal solicitor), noted a different story:

> I mean it's traditionally such an elitist profession and like I still don't quite believe that I've got a training contract. But I'm not part of the elite; I am so far from it. I went to a normal state school, I had poor attendance at school, and there were times in my life where I've been, you know, street homeless.

I recognized and appreciated James's openness and honesty in describing his background, which, crucially, deviates from and challenges the dominant narrative in his eyes. This insight has demonstrated that the lawyering profession may somewhat be moving away from being such an 'elitist' profession. However, there remain differing opinions on the role that social class plays with regards to both entering and practising in legal aid, both as solicitors and barristers. While some of the sample recognize significant discrepancies in inequalities, others attribute the difficulty of getting access to the profession to having the right skills to do so: 'ultimately if I'm not good enough, and if I just don't have the right skillset, then I wouldn't be let in to be a barrister. That's what it all comes down to really' (James, criminal solicitor). Fundamentally, 28 of 30 participants within this research identified as being middle class. Social class, without a doubt, plays a significant role in terms of being able to afford access to legal education and training, as lawyers acquire ever more debt during their training as fees increase.

Education and training

This section highlights the various educational and training routes into the profession and the features that come to underpin it, given that, for many, this still seems to be barrier. It is worthwhile to look at entry into the occupation as, traditionally, significant inequalities have existed within the legal profession. Likewise, changes to legal education and training have altered the field, therefore paying attention to legal graduate recruitment is also key for the future of legal aid work.

Among my participants, out of the 30 respondents involved in the interviewing process, ten had attended a private or fee-paying school. Three out of the four barristers involved in this research were among the ten who were privately schooled. While this is not surprising, recognizing that 20 of the participants did not have this start is of great interest here, considering the historical tradition that law has traditionally been dominated by the privileged. Katz (1982), in the US context, distinguishes between 'poverty lawyers', who tend to attend local state law schools, vs 'commercial lawyers', who attend more prestigious schools. There remains a gap in the research on the correlation between private schooling and legal aid lawyering more specifically.

In some ways, the Bar is still somewhat dominated by the privately educated, especially at Kings Counsel level, which can pose some accessibility issues. The Bar Standards Board (2024: 25) reported that 27.9 per cent have been privately educated, as opposed to 23.6 per cent being state schooled. The Solicitors Regulation Authority gathered data on the diversity of law firms in 2023. Their survey includes information from 203,000 people working in 9,276 law firms in England and Wales (Solicitors Regulation Authority, 2024). It was noted in the results from this survey that 21 per cent of the lawyers in their sample pool attended fee-paying schools, in comparison with 7.5 per cent in the general population, highlighting a significant gap between lawyers and the general population. Fifty-seven per cent of lawyers were found to have come from a professional socio-economic background.[2] It was also found that nearly three-quarters of solicitors in firms practising within the criminal and

[2] Professional socio-economic background, referring to modern and traditional professional occupations and senior, middle, or junior managers or administrators (Solicitors Regulation Authority, 2024).

litigation fields were state-educated, in comparison with corporate law, where only half of the solicitors in the pool were from state schools. It was also found that 22 per cent of lawyers in firms that mainly do criminal work were from a lower socio-economic background, compared to only 11 per cent in corporate fields.

Regardless of whether the candidate has been privately schooled, for any solicitor looking to practise both within and outside the remit of legal aid, locating a training contract post-education can be difficult, as confirmed by Rachel (housing solicitor and partner), Grace (criminal solicitor), as well as Ben (housing solicitor). Maria (also a housing solicitor) further summarizes this:

> I mean it was so *so* hard to get a training contract;[3] there's so much competition regardless of what school you went to and, with being slightly older as well, it just makes it harder. So I just ended up getting a training contract with a local firm who happened to be legally aided, so that's how I ended up here. [her emphasis]

Likewise, for a prospective barrister, attaining a pupillage[4] can be an extremely competitive process, as outlined by Alistair (criminal barrister):

> Sometimes you hear this kind of 'false sense' of security, whereby during your education, you get told that you are good enough to go ahead and train as a barrister, and you get accepted onto the BPTC.[5] But once you leave the safe walls of education, you realize you aren't even really experienced enough to be a paralegal, let alone a barrister. The pupillage chase is not fun, and it's not easy. It can be a very gruelling process, and it is not for the faint-hearted.

Not only that but, often, individuals spend significant amounts of money getting a legal education to then face the prospect of a low salaried job. Marcus (housing solicitor) put this into perspective:

> Why put money into helping students train, when there's either nowhere for them potentially to go, and there's only a minimal amount of training contracts to go around, which isn't enough to sustain the providers. Or alternatively, putting money into something which you are never going to earn enough to get back.

---

3 A training contract is a compulsory period of practical training in a law firm for a solicitor.

4 Pupillage: final, vocational stage for those who are becoming barristers.

5 BPTC: Bar Professional Training Course: for those who want to qualify as a barrister.

Identifying that debt, combined with low salaries, is often a barrier to the profession as a result of high tuition fees throughout the education and training journey of a legal practitioner, regardless of specialism, is significant. Consistently, individuals get paid meagre salaries once they secure a training contract. In 2018, for example, over 53 per cent of solicitor respondents from Young Legal Aid Lawyers stated that they were earning less than £25,000 five years PQE (post qualified). Both the Solicitors Regulation Authority's[6] decision to scrap the mandatory minimum salary for trainees in the sector, as well as the cuts to legal aid funding, has meant financial difficulties are rife. Nicholas (criminal solicitor) confirmed this; he stated that he was on £25,000 and he was in his mid-60s, having been in the profession for over 40 years. He had previously worked for a firm that had then shut down; as result he had become self-employed and had since been struggling with the low salary. He indicated that he had lost his family, car, and house, and that the financial and psychological impact of this had made him suffer tremendously. He suggested that if he had gone down the route of becoming a barrister, which he had the option to do, he would not have been placed in his current position, as self-employed solicitors are more likely to face financial insecurity. James (criminal solicitor) expresses a similar notion in his response: 'I think we are better qualified than barristers because we do two years of training, rather than one … but they are paid so much more'.

Recent changes to legal education have meant that candidates starting a law degree from 2022 onwards have to follow a different route to become a solicitor. Law degrees will no longer be labelled as 'qualifying degrees'; rather, to qualify, students will need to complete a degree, followed by the completion of the 'Solicitors Qualifying Exam' (SQE), plus two years' qualifying work experience. Arguably, the primary benefit of having the new SQE route is that all candidates will be assessed equally by sitting the same exam; this not only ensures consistency but will also encourage people from outside the legal sector to enter the field, potentially assisting with the diversity issues outlined previously. The SQE route is designed to remove the formal/conventional training contract route, which has been infamously difficult to secure, to allow more flexibility, with lower tuition costs and a shorter qualifying period. As a result, hopefully we will see a larger uptake of new solicitors over the coming years. For aspiring barristers, they will still need to complete a degree, followed by the Bar training course, as well as work-based training, otherwise known as a pupillage.

Despite there being differences between solicitors and barristers concerning pay, it was commonly noted that legal education, particularly

6 The Solicitors Regulation Authority regulates solicitors and law firms in England and Wales, setting qualification standards, as well as training and other requirements.

at degree level, was often lacking modules that focus on legal aid, as confirmed by Peter and Andy (both criminal barristers). Over half of my interview participants cited that there was an absence of any focus on legal aid in legal education more generally: 'Legal aid work is not really highlighted in education and training. Legal education is very much set in its traditional ways … I only really knew what I was doing because of my work experience' (Marcus, housing solicitor). 'Legal Aid seemed to be looked down upon in the LPC, even the elective on housing law was cancelled, so the only option to even study legal aid was within the criminal module which is very restrictive' (Jack, housing solicitor). Jane (housing solicitor) also stated that her legal training was somewhat outdated, which highlights how advantageous the new SQE route for prospective solicitors will be:

> The LPC is so 'old fashioned'. Two-thirds of the course were taken up by stuff I had absolutely no interest in whatsoever. I know it is meant to be a general course, but they should make it equal and open to all prospective lawyers, regardless of if you want to practise as a legal aid lawyer or a commercial lawyer. Then the training contract you are really thrown into the deep end.

These training inadequacies play a significant role in the extent to which those in the field feel equipped to carry out day-to-day tasks. Several other research participants further stated that legal aid work was not encouraged within their education; instead, commercial work was always at the forefront of the agenda. Rachel (housing solicitor and partner) referred to this: 'During my law degree, I was always constantly encouraged to go into the commercial/ private sector. There didn't seem to be any other interesting ways of "doing law"'. Robert (criminal solicitor) stated that his training contract equipped him well, as it was very much 'hands-on' straight away. Tom (housing solicitor) said that the training contract was very much dependent on the firm, and therefore everyone would have different experiences. Differences between commercial firms and legally aided firms or law centres also affect how a training contract is experienced. Lack of resources, alongside the ever-shrinking nature of funding, can make the experience quite diverse:

> Some solicitors at the same level … their experience is so much better because they trained elsewhere … *but* the nature of the work is so diverse so there are always things that are going to come up that you've never covered before. Add in wider changes in legal aid as well; it's just impossible to keep up sometimes. (Tom, housing solicitor; his emphasis)

As Tom outlines, education and training are, however, only part of the learning curve. The shift from being newly qualified to become a more experienced legal aid lawyer requires further development once actually in the role: 'It [the training contract] is like a driving test – it gives you a basic grounding, but it's not like you are perfectly able to drive … it's just you're in a position where you're safe enough to get in by yourself'. As outlined further, 'every day is different and therefore you never stop learning', as lawyers are consistently faced with new challenges due to the sheer diversity of cases and clients.

The training for legal aid lawyers was often described as inadequate by participants, with most of the learning done 'on the job'. As Marcus (housing solicitor) notes: 'There is a considerable gap between studying and practising law. Legal Education needs to catch up and adapt to what's happening around us now. We are all diverse, the work is diverse, and our motivations are diverse. Change needs to happen in education'. Highlighting issues of (in)adequate training and preparation for working with clients demonstrated that the participants were alert to potential failings beyond their control early on in their careers. This inadequacy further indicates how their personal investment may not be matched by professional or institutional provision, a gap that continues to widen. 'The "liberal" focus of law degrees leads to limited opportunities to educate for the realities of professional life' (Boon, 2005: 254). The professional socialization here creates somewhat unrealistic expectations and, as Sherr and Webb (1989) note, those entering the legal field need to be educated to understand its true operation better, as expectations can have significant impact on how the occupation is experienced (in Boon, 2005). The distance between education and training and the realities of practising law, however, is not limited to the legal aid remit, but exists across the wider realm of the legal profession. It can be argued that, while education and training is not always 'comprehensive', potentially a form of working culture has the potential to fill in the gaps that legal aid education and training otherwise do not fill, through the encouragement of knowledge sharing and informal learning and socialization practices.

This section has mapped out the characteristics of the legal aid workforce. As has become clear, demographic barriers remain to some extent within the legal field. Legal aid lawyers face marginalization within their education and training. Highlighting issues of (in)adequate training and preparation for working with clients has demonstrated that participants were alert to potential failings beyond their control early on in their careers. This indicates how legal aid lawyers' personal investment may not be matched by professional or institutional provision. Understanding how this deficiency is addressed feeds into the broader examination here in this book. However, the new SQE route for solicitors sheds a potentially positive light on the field.

The extent to which the reductions in funding and services has further exacerbated these existing inequalities and further places these lawyers in an even more precarious position feeds into the subsequent analyses. As will become apparent, legal aid lawyers have always faced, and will continue to face, barriers to their work. Yet the question remains why those working within the field remain doing so given such a rocky backdrop.

6

The 'Precarious' Legal Aid Lawyer: Consequences that Reductions in Funding and Services Have Had on the Legal Aid Lawyer's Lived Experience

Not only do representational and educational challenges exist within the field, as identified in Chapter 5, but legal aid lawyers are also subject to a 'limited professional role' in the sense that their perceived capabilities, significance, and career development are restricted in comparison to their private counterparts. Legal aid practitioners also continuously come under disparaging attention from society, the media, and the broader profession alike, further condemning them and restricting their work. This chapter argues that legal aid work needs to be understood and portrayed in its own right to negate its misconstrued reputation, as opposed to being categorized under the broader heading of 'lawyering', as this fails to differentiate the nature and the challenges of the work.

This chapter, therefore, looks at the consequences of reductions in funding and services on the legal aid lawyer's lived experience, in addition to exploring the relationship between their precarity and professional identity. This sits well with the aim of the *Perspectives on Law and Access to Justice* series in highlighting and documenting the changing role of lawyers in the contemporary climate.

Lawyering is very dynamic, in the sense that professionals across the various specialisms, including crime, family and civil matters, uphold varying levels of legal caseloads, and work in a variety of different workplaces, from solicitors' offices to courtrooms, to housing centres and charity organizations. Diversity in the legal industry has evolved over the last decade. Francis (2005: 175) argues that 'the increasing variety of workplace arenas within which discreet ethical choices confront lawyers means that fragmentation within the legal profession is exacerbated'. In this sense, while professional control may still be exercised centrally through the Legal Aid Agency, this occurs on a contingent and individualized basis, fluctuating between the varying workplace arenas. While in the past we have had more regimented control, through the likes of the Law Society, as Francis (2004: 322) notes, they no longer serve as the 'fulcrum of the professions collective advancement'. In this sense, negotiating the professional nature of legal aid work remains highly individualized and idiosyncratic as it spans different job titles, working environments and specialisms. This workplace diversity drives the profession as it allows for different funding models, attitudinal components, and stronger support systems to be maintained across the board in both public and private spheres.

Yet while, more than four decades ago, Samuel (1983) called for a clear distinction to be made between public and private legal work as this offers a valuable distinction to understand how lawyers work in different fields, this is still often omitted from both academic and public remits. As the field becomes increasingly hollowed out, the 'new' legal aid lawyer currently faces a more demarcated, restricted, and difficult working environment. The affects that reductions in funding and services have on the 'lived professional experiences' result in workers being placed in a position of the precariat, or precarious worker. Legal aid lawyers now face work overshadowed by restricted time, practice, and monetary reward, which is very different from their private counterparts. This has significant ramifications on the micro day-to-day practice of the legal aid lawyer, as will be explored. Emergent here is the need to look at legal aid work as more of a 'vocational pathway' than a traditional 'profession'. This also speaks well to, and justifies the need for, the 'shared orientation' model presented earlier in this book.

The popular image of the legal aid lawyer: fat cat vs church mice

Popular images of the lawyer often capture the barrister/solicitor distinction of private work. On the one hand, images of barristers, and the broader judiciary within the English criminal justice system, often depict middle and upper class, white males in wigs and robes in courtrooms, with posh accents, engaging in conversations from perplexing textbooks on their desks (Friedman, 1989; Post, 1987). On the other hand, images of solicitors characterize individuals in smart suits, carrying briefcases, and working in large and elaborate offices within the city. Examples of this can be seen in TV shows such as *Suits*, *Law and Order*, *LA Law*, *The Practice*, *Boyd QC*, *Trust and Boston Legal* (Robson, 2017). Television lawyers have nearly always been criminal law practitioners, with very few practising in civil areas. As Miller (1994) recognized, this cultural production is very much 'the composite of the "ideas, attitudes, values, and opinions" about law held by people in society', and therefore often the public tend to categorize lawyers into one of these popular adversarial frameworks (Friedman, 1989). Often, contemplations on the public image of law end at adversarialism. From the perspective of the media, courtrooms are far more interesting than office spaces. For example, most people would know what an office looks like, but not many would have necessarily experienced a courtroom, which gives it an air of mystique (Robson, 2017). Sophie, a criminal solicitor, considered this a 'misconception' in the perception of what it means to be a legal aid lawyer to the general public, noting how many clients think that *all lawyers* do the same work, day in day out, despite their position as either a 'public' or 'private' legal practitioner, or as a solicitor or a barrister. What remains clear is that the perception versus the reality of the legal aid world is vastly different.

Another problem here is that, typically, lawyers are often portrayed as 'money-grabbing' or 'fat cats', as briefly touched upon earlier. Headlines in tabloid newspapers, such as the *Daily Mail*, regularly wield such terms: 'Legal aid pay-outs to fat cat lawyers will be slashed by a third, says Justice Secretary' (Daily Mail, 2013) or '£500,000 lawyer tops legal aid fat cat league' (Daily Mail, 2007). Louisa (civil liberties and human rights solicitor), spoke about the media headlines:

> The worst stereotype from the media is that we are all just 'lawyers' and that lawyers are after money. So it does not matter if you are a legal aid lawyer or not; if we're all just lawyers, then we're immediately seen to be paid a lot of money, and that's a perception that's very difficult to challenge unfortunately.

Apparent here is that there seems to be a general lack of understanding from the public about how money flows through the legal system. The problem we can see more broadly is that the lawyering profession has always been seen as unabridged; the public tend to place *all* lawyers – whether that be solicitors or barristers, publicly or privately funded – under one heading. This naturally encourages assumed extensive wealth, professional privilege, and well-regarded status. Differences in service between legal aid and private work are vast. While this is dependent on the private firm, concerns nevertheless arise around some charging for work and doing it badly and, in other cases, the fact that the lack of legal aid funding pushes clients to the lower quality private firms that are cheaper, meaning they are not subject to the checks inherent in legal aid work. But, ultimately, in the private sector you tend to have more time to prepare, read, and advise on cases; the physical working environments differ greatly in both size and quality; reward exists in the form of either financial gain (private) or social gain (legal aid); and the clients could not be more polarized. The 'fat-cat' lawyer narrative has been used by the government to devalue the work of legal aid lawyers as part of a wider (neoliberal) programme of dismantling public services. In the new legal landscape, the sphere sees access to justice reframed as a privilege and is one of the many public services that has been subjected to competing public interests and cuts (O'Nions, 2020). Both the lawyers ('fat cats') and the clients in this context therefore face simultaneous toxic constructions (Newman 2013; Welsh, 2017). A central aim of my research was to understand the extent to which the lawyers are aware of the way they are sometimes stereotyped as 'fat cats',[1] in spite of the precarious terrain outlined. A key finding was the confirmation and awareness of stereotyping among the participants. Participants demonstrated that they felt doubly discriminated against as they were simultaneously struggling in a financially austere work environment, as well as experiencing a lack of understanding or empathy from both public and professional perspectives. In general, they felt that the proliferation of this stereotype had contributed to an erosion of legal aid services and, ultimately, a diminishing of justice to many members of society. Lawyers also do not always get good press because of the social role that they perform (Boon, 2015). Traditionally, the wider lawyering profession has been viewed as having high social standing; however, this has not been the case for the legal aid lawyer. The combined outcome of cuts to funding, low salaries, and increased amount of administrative work is worsening their social standing even more. It has likewise been noted that individuals should work to resolve their own legal problems, as opposed to resorting to litigation that creates 'significant cost to the taxpayer'. This toxic narrative which encourages 'responsibilization', is the driving force of austerity, as it suggests that those who cannot be in control of their own failings should be deprived from full participation in civil society (O'Nions, 2020). James (criminal solicitor) offered further reflection on this, stating that, on the one hand, the general public judge as undeserving lawyers who specifically help 'criminals', but also stressed the lack of respect from lawyers in the commercial sector who view their public counterparts as 'second-tier lawyers' as a result of working with the 'undeserving' in society. As noted by Dehaghani and Newman (2021: 41), legally aided criminal defence lawyers' clients make up 'an underclass distinct from the good, law-abiding citizens of the general population' who are often viewed as a burden on the state. A further example of this was outlined by Anna (immigration solicitor): 'for many, having a legal aid lawyer assumes guilt'. Working with the 'undeserving' also brings light to unwanted attention and an increased level of stigmatization. As James (criminal solicitor) further states: 'You've got to love the clients

[1] See also Cooke (2024).

… because nobody else does. People always just make comments like "why are you doing all that work for poor people when they don't even contribute to society?"'. The theme of discouraging unnecessary litigation at public expense has always been the central anxiety surrounding legal aid provision and its implementation, and has been a key target under the grip of austerity. The impact on this neglected sector of lawyers has been phenomenal; access to justice leans significantly on legal aid practitioners themselves and, therefore, the rule of law would and could not be upheld without them as key drivers of justice (Bar Council, 2023).

The legal aid client

Despite this book's focus on the legal aid lawyer, their working credos cannot be adequately understood in isolation from those at the receiving end of their services. To this end, the legal aid client is often vastly different to the private client, as the solicitor can afford to spend much more quality time with the client when they are paid privately:

> I enjoy meeting the clients that I have because I learn so much from them, I feel very privileged to represent them, and they always challenge me. I just enjoy being able to help them and, you know, to gain courage in themselves and to give them a voice. That's my main objective, to help people who haven't had the same benefits that I've had in terms of education and training to give them the opportunity to put forward their case when they might not be able to do it themselves. Private clients can just pay for their services, but those who require legal aid are often so incredibly troubled and desperate. They couldn't be more different. (Louisa, civil liberties and human rights solicitor)

Jane (housing solicitor) therefore stressed the importance of client-centred practice; placing the client and their needs at the forefront is 'both rewarding and challenging', and 'it creates a closer community between not only us and the clients, but also with colleagues as we seek to address an array of wider social issues'. It brings together those in the field, resonating with a form of working culture. Jane further emphasized that she 'feels privileged to represent the most vulnerable clients'. In the context of the lawyer–client relationship, Jane is the powerful partaker. In this sense, feeling privileged to represent her clients makes Jane feel important and worthwhile. Social justice prevails over monetary return, as evidenced in Jane's response. This links to the very reason individuals are drawn to the occupation in the first place. James (criminal solicitor) states that, within the context of legal aid, 'individualized, and dignified justice' is more important given the more precarious state of the clients:

FIELD NOTE

James's story

The client (Fred) walks into the meeting room looking extremely distressed, behaving very erratically. He has been charged for being caught in possession of class A drugs. As James (solicitor) asks him to sit down, he asks Fred where he has been and why he is subsequently late for court. Concerned Fred wasn't going to turn up at all, James began questioning him further on his whereabouts and current home address. It was at that moment that James realized Fred did not have a permanent home address. His heroin addiction had become out of hand, he had just lost his mother due to long-term illness, and Fred was going from shop doorway to doorway, trying to seek shelter and survive the night. James's next client was waiting outside, but that didn't deter James from continuing to help, advise, and comfort Fred. James spent an hour with Fred that day when he should have only seen him for five minutes. It was at this p.oint that James prioritized the client's need over caseloads.

A few years later, James is walking down the high street, and he bumps into Fred. Fred has just been released from prison and is starting work at his father's auto mechanic business. Fred runs up to James and hugs him, says 'thank you so much, you changed my life' and walks on to go about his day-to-day activities.

James prioritized the individual client over caseloads, despite having a long list of clients waiting to see him that day. This would not be possible in a commercial profit-orientated law firm. The outcome of this was extremely positive for his client. Yet, this can also come with risk; as Nicholas (criminal solicitor) states, 'often we are overvalued by our clients'. Most lawyers in this study shared the view that their clients relied far too heavily on the lawyers for all kinds of problems. Over-reliance can cause difficulties in keeping the relationship professional: 'it can sometimes be difficult to manage the client relationship because sometimes they get a bit too needy because you can be their only hope' (Rhiannon, welfare solicitor). Maintaining an outwardly professional front, despite emotional pressures, proves to be even more vital in these situations. Often lawyers are not equipped to deal with the complex needs of clients, and the ability to empathize with clients becomes lost as increased efficiency overrides the ideal lawyer–client relationship (Dehaghani and Newman, 2021). Rhiannon (welfare solicitor) also highlighted the need for the lawyers to be aware of their own safety: 'you have to be really good at managing your clients because sometimes they're vulnerable, and sometimes you get quite aggressive clients'. It is often forgotten that lawyers are usually left in a room with just themselves and the client, and this can have significant implications. Rachel (housing solicitor and partner) explains:

> It's very different from dealing with … business clients. You don't have to go to a meeting with business clients and … be worried that you're going to have to press the emergency help button at some point … . I've never had to use it, but ultimately in our building there are emergency buttons in each interview room. I mean, there have been situations where I have felt extremely uncomfortable, but that's one of the skills you need to have – to be able to know and detect when things are going to escalate and being able to remove yourself from the situation before it goes too far.

Being able to pre-empt behaviours mirrors the work of Brotheridge and Grandey (2002), who argue that the 'regulation of feelings' is implicit in being in an emotionally charged role. Legal aid lawyers fundamentally face significantly different hurdles and challenges when dealing with their clients, in comparison with their private counterparts. 'Lawyers must often be more than lawyers' (Natt Gantt, 2004: 365). In this sense, they can often face issues that push the boundaries of being 'legal' as defined by traditional standards. However, 'it is these relationships that primarily inform lawyers' use of discretion' (Oakley and Vaughan, 2019: 111). This is even more apt when the client is vulnerable and holds an inability to resolve their issues themselves because of illiteracies. The reliance on the client for information is even more important when the legal aid lawyer and the client have no previous history. Client illiteracies can likewise further exacerbate client crises: 'It's sad because a lot of the clients that come to me can barely write their own name, let alone attempt to solve their own crises. Half the reason some of these clients come to us is because they are unable to resolve other problems on their own' (Maddie, criminal solicitor). Legally aided clients face unique vulnerabilities. As Maddie further alludes, legal aid clients are often demonized. She further explains that the more funding is being withdrawn, the more it turns into a narrative that people using legal aid are 'antisocial' or a 'burden' on society, as opposed to them being deeply troubled because of wider structural failings in society. Maddie said that, even from her own family, she often hears discourse such as 'eww, why are you working with them?' when her clients are mentioned. There are two sides to the coin when considering how legal aid is viewed. On the one hand, it is sometimes seen as being a way of helping these vulnerable people to get back into society; but on the other, there is often a concern that those being assisted via legally aided means should not be accepted back into society, as evidenced by Rachel (housing solicitor and partner). As Boon (2015: 3) maintains: 'Professions perform a vital role in society. They are often inducted into a moral system that seems to stand at odds with standards of everyday life'. Ensuring that these individuals, therefore, make the right decisions on 'problems with a moral dimension' requires specific practical measures to be taken, which are undoubtedly informed by ethics (Boon, 2015: 3). Lawyers uphold one of the most controversial moral systems in the sense that it requires them to 'defend murderers, abusers, and terrorists with the same vigour as they would defend an innocent child in their social role' (Boon, 2015: 4). To this end, legal aid lawyers uphold a unique and special relationship with their clients in the sense that they are almost expected to dedicate and devote themselves to the client despite how morally undeserving they happen to be (Green, 2016). An essential aspect of this is professional detachment; lawyers are prohibited from judging their clients and are instead required to serve them as part of their professional responsibilities. A vital role of a profession is to make decisions that may go against what others think is right (Boon, 2015). Yakren (2008) argues, therefore, that: 'Prevailing norms of legal practice teach lawyers to detach their independent moral judgements from their professional performance – to advocate zealously for their clients while remaining morally unaccountable agents of those clients' causes'. Maintaining independent moral judgements can lead to both personal and professional dissatisfaction for lawyers, particularly the former as they are forced to submerge their personal feelings on a day-to-day basis, linking here to the concept of emotional labour. 'No social role encourages such ambitious moral aspirations as the lawyers, and no social role so consistently disappoints the aspirations it encourages' (Simon, 1998).

Assessing the correct level of client support that is required is sometimes tricky. Lawyers practising within the legal aid remit must curb their ideological commitments to 'professionally' manage their client–lawyer relationships (Katz, 1982). This management of relationships is now more critical than ever before. – not only due to time constraints and the need for efficiency due to increased bureaucracy because of LASPO and subsequent cuts, but also for the sake of their own needs. To this end, the 'new' legal aid lawyer is very much in a vulnerable position, as not only has the relationship between the lawyer and client been tarnished, but so also has the relationship between the lawyer and the state. The legal aid lawyers' ability to 'do-good' is becoming increasingly limited, which, as you will see in Chapter 7, is rather problematic in practice.

The 'neutered' lawyering role

Dealing with clients can not only be difficult, but professional regulators also have a significant impact on the everyday practice of a legal aid lawyer. As Karen (director) states: 'You now have to literally tick every box, cross every 'T' and dot every 'I' and that's just no fun'. Not only are legal aid practitioners facing judgement battles as outlined above; Andy (criminal barrister) notes that, because of managerialism implemented by the Legal

Aid Agency and other regulatory boards, their professional status has also been weakened by the stringent nature of the work continuously confining legal practice. The lawyer's power is further constrained as the Legal Aid Agency now determines what is knowledge and, therefore, their working practices are both dictated and constrained by strict processes. For example, Jane (housing solicitor), spoke of how she now feels she is just 'churning out' cases as quickly as possible, without fully utilizing the extent of her skillset:

> The pressure on us being efficient and keeping up with the rules and regulations has become so overpowering that I often wonder why I am still sat here. I came to the job to use my skills, I suppose to give something back, in a kind of philanthropic way, but now it seems I am just feeding into a bureaucratic cycle which gives me no time to individually and compassionately deal with those who need it, the most vulnerable people in society.

In further conversation with Jane, she stated: 'I always say, it's like you have two opponents on every case, the *actual opponent,* and then you have the Legal Aid Agency who are trying to *squeeze* all the funding out … and it's got so much worse since I've been doing it … much *much* worse!' (emphasis hers). Likewise, as Nicholas (criminal solicitor) notes: 'I now have to tell all my clients that it is no longer the other side that is your biggest opponent, but it is the Legal Aid Agency'. He further added:

> The CCMS[2] just causes problems after problems, from system failures, such as not being able to log on, to the building up of backlogs of cases as a result, and therefore leaving people in extremely dangerous situations … the CCMS can only deal with one amendment at a time which means that anything urgent becomes extremely difficult.

As Karen – director of a membership body representing legal aid practitioners – recognizes:

> Even once you have submitted your claim to the Legal Aid Agency, they are now turning down cases for the silliest of reasons, looking for any grounds to deny funding such as going through piles and piles of extremely outdated bank statements, and asking for numerous follow-up statements, before assessing whether or not the client's income is

[2] The Client and Cost Management System (CCMS) is an online system for civil and family legal aid providers covering the entire process from submitting legal aid applications to paying bills. In 2016, the use of CCMS became mandatory.

> above the threshold for legal aid eligibility, even though they quite evidently don't come anywhere near to the line.

John (housing solicitor) elaborates: 'It's a rigid system with no way it can be sorted out … bureaucracy, lack of access to courts, urgency, no capacity to make local links – for instance, you can't just ring up now, it is all online. The whole process should be written bottom-up, not top-down'. This has meant that a lot of the day-to-day work of a legal aid lawyer is subject to huge delays as a result and, consequently, 'even if there is a legal argument to make, it becomes all about the funding and the means at the end of the day' (Rachel, housing solicitor and partner). Legally aided work has become unnecessarily onerous on the lawyers who now must navigate a difficult system alongside unhelpful clients produced within a precarious environment. As Rachel further notes, the process of acquiring funding is equally as arduous for the solicitor as the client. This is evident in the extract outlined below, taken from my field notes during a new client meeting at Silverman and Co, with Rachel and Tony (a paralegal), spending most of the meeting attempting to get through to the job centre, as per the legal aid application:

	[Based in a small meeting room situated near the reception desk]
Rachel (R):	Okay, so Tony is going to just ask you a few questions but, just so you know in advance, this could take a while. [Client nods in agreement, and looks particularly anxious, staring down into his lap]
Tony (T):	Okay … so, I am going to ask a few intrusive questions as part of the legal aid application, you can choose not to answer but this may hinder your overall application. [T proceeds to ask questions regarding the client's ethnicity, background, financial situation, and domestic situation for about ten minutes]
T:	Okay … so, I am going to need to see evidence. I need the letter of notice of the house in question from the housing association, all of your bank statements dating at least ten years back, as well as your documents on income support and benefits. [Client scrambles through a pile of papers on his lap. He keeps dropping pages as he is frantically trying to get all his evidence together]
R:	[In a reassuring manner] Take your time, [client's name], it's okay. [The room is silent for at least five minutes while the client continues to sort out his papers]

T: Right, while you are doing that, let's call the job centre now together to find out what type of allowance you are receiving, and whether or not you are still in receipt of income support … let me just get their phone number.
[T gets through to an automated system on the phone which takes a while to connect. It then plays music for over 15 minutes while waiting to connect to someone at the job centre]

T: [*Looks and smiles at the client*] I promise we will get there eventually! [*They both laugh*]
[*T continues to fill in the legal help forms while they wait for someone to pick up the phone. He begins to go through the details of the case*]

T: Okay, so can you go through exactly what has happened …
[*The client speaks about his legal issue in great depth, including his own personal issues, which have aggravated the situation. He suffers from chronic depression and lost his father the previous year, with whom he lived in the house in question. He has nowhere else to go if he loses his house and therefore will be homeless*]

T: This seems to be taking ages, you might have to pop back another day.
[*Client states that they really struggled to get here today and not sure they can physically come back due to significant anxiety and lack of money for travel. The client states that they normally don't leave the house for months on end*]

T: Sorry it's just the systems are so difficult these days, you might have to I'm afraid, we might not have a choice.
[*The client holds his head in his hands and looks incredibly distressed, meanwhile Tony remains on the phone waiting for someone to answer. He has been on hold for nearly 30 minutes now*]

For both lawyer and client, the emotional impact of dealing with and undergoing the lengthy process of obtaining funding is often even more overwhelming than the requirement for intrusive questioning. As Rachel emphasized: 'It's turned into such a horrible situation, whereby you often must tell clients that there is literally nothing else you can do within the realms of the law if funding isn't granted, even though they might be on the edge of disaster'. Marcus (housing solicitor) recognizes that funding cuts are the biggest problem, because it means that 'either the client must go out and look for, you know, free advice to help them or do it themselves, or legal aid lawyers have more pressure trying to do it themselves pro bono [for free] in order to defend the possession proceedings if legal aid isn't granted'.

Often the process can be just as demoralizing for the solicitor, subject to increasing administrative duties, filling in and submitting forms, and doing their best to procure funding. Louisa (civil liberties and human rights) encompasses this within her response:

> The biggest negative is working with the Legal Aid Agency because we spend so much of our time trying to get funding, or justifying why we need to have funding, or arguing at the end of a case why we should be paid. You know, I'm sure you're familiar with this but … a lot of the work that we do … we … especially where I work now, we try and … basically, we just work as much as the client *needs* it and so that means that a lot of our cases go over the fixed fee level.

Therefore, the Legal Aid Agency puts undue pressure on the lawyer, and this has worsened in the post-2012 cuts context. Conversations in corridors or during lunch and courtroom breaks often revolved around the fiscal cuts from the Legal Aid Agency and their impact. In an exchange between Rachel (housing solicitor and partner) and Nina (also housing) at their office, Rachel said that she is fed up with hearing about the cuts. Nina replied, 'So am I, I know we have to watch our backs, but it's depressing hearing it day in day out'. Every day I was present in the office, the cuts were mentioned. Likewise, conversations around possible access to legal aid arose on a regular basis:

	[*Sat in the office*]
Tom (T):	Some clients ask, 'how do I make myself eligible for legal aid?' and we just must laugh it off because, in reality, it's not even a ridiculous thing to ask! [*Tom and Rachel laugh*]
Rachel (R):	Yeah, it's just ridiculous … I mean, I try and see if people are eligible before they physically come into the office, but some just have too many sources of information. The threshold is just so low, so many things are out of scope because of LASPO or people now 'earn too much', which often seems ridiculous.
	[*Tom pulls out a case bundle to show me*]
T:	Okay, so, so far we've signed a form for advice and the initial consultation, but if we want to actually put a case forward, we need to apply for a public funding certificate … and, for that, we need to show that there is more than a 45 per cent chance of it being successful … and, at the moment, we don't have a very high chance as they've already had two eviction orders. It's quite hard to put all the pieces of the puzzle other …

R: Yes, you need to constantly act on your feet within client meetings as they sometimes don't have the same level of autonomy/comprehension as others may have, so it can be more difficult. If the client has any language barriers, disabilities, misunderstandings, or a poor level of numeracy or literacy then it makes our job extremely difficult … legal aid is so tricky these days.

T: Yes, and then, on top of all that, you have to keep on top of everything to make sure clients are getting up-to-date advice both within the realms of the firm, as well as within the wider legal aid backdrop.
[*Rachel sighs*]

R: It's just so much to take on board … And even then, you often get clients asking you 'why am I answering all of these stupid questions if you can't offer me any help anyway?'

James (criminal solicitor) placed particular emphasis on reduced job satisfaction and the extreme stress and consequences of dealing with the demands of the Legal Aid Agency. 'A guy committed suicide due to increasing working hours … he worked every day until 10 pm and it all just got too much for him in the end'. The concepts of emotional labour and vicarious trauma will be discussed in Chapter 7. As Rachel (housing solicitor and partner) notes: 'we now have to fight for literally every bit of work we do' Likewise, Becky (civil liberties and human rights) states: 'the Legal Aid Agency has put so much pressure on us. They're just trying to inhibit and restrict in any way they can, which goes against all the principles of what they're trying to do initially with legal aid'. John (housing solicitor) concurs: 'the current legal aid bureaucracy has simply restricted our ability to offer holistic service like we did in the past because of the restrictions in funding … there have been significant changes in terms of what work you can do nowadays'. In this sense, balancing the scales of both altruism and reward proves difficult when faced with these external pressures. Ash (immigration solicitor) states that, because of the funding cuts, clients can only receive as good a service as the system will allow as they simply cannot afford it otherwise: 'It's no longer necessarily about helping humanity through a quality service, but more about churning out cases as quickly as possible to ensure efficiency is maintained … and that's bureaucracy for you!' This mirrors the findings of Newman (2013), likening the profession to a 'sausage factory', fashioning as many cases as possible in similarity to a production line. 'If I never had to speak to the Legal Aid Agency again, I'd be a very happy man … it is so hideously bureaucratic, and they drive me absolute insane! They have ruined the profession' (Nicholas, Housing Solicitor). Tom (housing solicitor) stated: 'multi-tasking is crucial. We've always got that added dimension of constantly having to battle with the Legal Aid Agency, which adds to all the other things we have going on with the client'.

Legal aid lawyers serve both the client and the government, but now appended to this dynamic, in discussing the decline in legal aid, is the complexity of the Legal Aid Agency. In England and Wales, there have been several administrative and legal failings by the Legal Aid Agency, meaning an urgent need for review is required. Due to cuts and insufficient resources, Rachel (housing solicitor and partner) argued that those working in the housing sector now experience far more face-to-face contact with their own clients, due to their current responsibility for the abundance of bureaucratic tasks previously performed by paralegals.[3] Rachel still retains a couple of paralegals and legal assistants in her firm, but her administrative duties have now increased significantly. This often distracts from other primary responsibilities such as providing legal expertise. As Rachel vented: 'I spend so much time doing stupid little tasks like photocopying, sending letters, and arranging appointments that it restricts my time doing the legal duties that I should be doing'. Zaloznaya and Nielsen (2011) term this 'task marginality', whereby those within the field spend more time doing menial tasks than using their advanced levels of professional and legal skills to help those most in need. Resultantly, Eleanor (family solicitor and partner) holds a deep sense of animosity towards the Legal Aid Agency, leaving her feeling demoralized:

> We must handle an awful lot which we are just not paid for. Just to set the scene … I have a few clients at the moment who have mental health issues whose first language isn't English, whose husband is being abusive, and you know my time has been slashed because objectively the legal aid agency take the view that I've taken too long but what they really fail to understand is that the nature of the client is that you have to do a proper, all-rounded job. The reality is we're not paid at all to do this, you're simply paid to do the quickest job possible and legal aid clients … because they struggle, they get themselves into extremely sticky situations, which makes it much more complicated in a legal sense. It's not like we just ignore that … it's like they just have *absolutely no idea* of what's happening on the ground. How can we help anyone when we are so restricted in what we can and can't do within our practice? I feel more and more restricted and insignificant by the day. [her emphasis]

Several respondents in this research echoed Eleanor's frustration with the way that legal aid work is funded. Eleanor also indicated how, if a case

3 A paralegal is an assistant often working alongside lawyers. They are trained to perform legal tasks and can assist in legal matters, apart from 'reserved matters' (NALP, 2024).

required an expert, such as a translator or a psychiatrist, it had become almost impossible to access due to the changes in this process: 'the fixed fees[4] around experts have massively inhibited our ability to instruct experts in legal aid claims'. Even when a professional is employed in a case, more often than not they hold no experience in the field as the funding will not stretch to cover the more proficient. Yet, despite being aware of her precarious position, Eleanor still makes considerable effort to address her clients' needs: 'I do legal aid because I've always done voluntary work and I've always had a social conscience and will always continue to do so, but quite frankly the Legal Aid Agency is absolutely battering us'. She further states, however: 'what's going to happen, ultimately, is that all the decent solicitors are going to have to walk away and you're going to have a whacking great big firm that specializes with paralegals who don't have any on-the-ground experience, and make mistakes left, right and centre'. Here, Eleanor outlines a dangerous predicament; having less qualified staff is not only a disingenuous way to treat the public (who are unlikely to be aware of the difference in knowledge and expertise between paralegals and lawyers) but may result in further oversights and 'catastrophic blunders' if more junior staff are provided with work beyond their capabilities.

Discussing the exploitative nature of the 'fixed fee' regulation, Louisa (civil liberties and human rights) highlighted how the changes implemented by the Legal Aid Agency come at a cost to clients:

> Now many of us spend most of our time trying to justify the need for funding and, because we normally just work as much as the client needs, it means a lot of our cases go over the fixed fee level. It is an extremely tiring process. Especially in some of the cases I do, you often need to have expert evidence, you need interpreters, you need so many different bits of extra funding that you need to apply for and that's extremely wearing, you know? It also takes up the time I used to be able to spend with my clients. It makes me extremely frustrated.

Respondents' abilities to keep clients out of trouble is becoming harder and more restricted because of such changes, but they nonetheless often persist in their endeavours. John (housing solicitor) asserted: 'The current legal aid bureaucracy and lack of ability have really restricted us … in the past, you've

[4] A fixed fee arrangement works in opposition to a standard hourly rate. It is therefore previously set, and not dictated by time spent on a given case. This allows more certainty regarding legal costs and therefore allows clients to budget better. They tend to be used for more procedural cases where little face-to-face time is needed (Francis Wilks & Jones, 2019).

always been able to be holistic and now you struggle'. He further argued that there is now an increased need for efficiency in his work so as to not waste time. Louisa (civil liberties and human rights) agreed:

> What used to be the ideal for legal clients is providing a more holistic service for them so that you can address multiple issues at once rather than parcelling people off or just saying 'I can't deal with that', because we can't deal with everything but we try and discuss clients and any problems to see if there's something else that somebody else in the organization can help with and that's really *really* useful. But things have changed a lot now. I was resistant to it initially, but it was always very time consuming and it's becoming much more difficult to do that now. [her emphasis]

Marcus (housing solicitor) also applied this perspective to the housing sector. He stated that he had far more funding when he first started, but now the cuts mean that 'either the client has to go out and look for free advice to sort out their benefits issues or do it themselves, which is far from straightforward'. A greater reliance on pro bono work – legal services provided on a free basis to individuals, charities, and collective groups – has become so high that the system is overwhelmed because of the cuts, and ever more people are being turned away for legal advice. Traditionally it was held that the free advice and representation provided by lawyers was only used as a means of obtaining access to justice for those unable to access legal aid funding. Pro bono is by no means a substitute for a properly funded system. Despite little incentive other than social gratification, legal aid lawyers now have more pressure trying to do it themselves pro bono to defend possession proceedings. Jane (housing solicitor) stated, however, that 'pro bono work is really just a sort of sticking plaster on a massive wound because all you really get is a one-off appointment and to give advice on a massive issue and that's it … it's just not good enough'. While pro bono is often used in cases where funding is otherwise unobtainable, this is work performed voluntarily and therefore is not something that can be done persistently by those practising in the field, as Marcus (housing solicitor) indicated:

> Our system is at the breaking point, you know. Firstly, the fact that, as housing solicitor, we know the underlying causes and what's led our clients to this point, and where traditionally we were able to deal with that holistically, and stop them [the clients] relapsing and leading to more costs … we just can't do that anymore and, if we do it pro bono, that inevitably leads to a loss to the law centre which makes our organization less viable, which could potentially lead to the law

> centre closing, and, you know, not everyone being helped in the future. Unfortunately, it's a Catch-22 because either you just don't help them, in which case you've failed your mission, or you do help them and you close down and fail your mission because there won't be anyone to help and it just doesn't look like this is going to improve in the future in any way, unfortunately.

As Marcus demonstrates, constant reminders and anxieties surrounding the impact of cuts to legal aid permeate the current system. This creates an environment in which the occurrence and effect of the funding cuts appear in some form every day, persistently haunting those inside. Within this dynamic, it is likewise worth acknowledging that the legal aid lawyers in this sample frequently discuss the impact of the cuts with each other, and this exposure provides an ability to deal with it. This notion of relying on each other and sharing disdain towards the Legal Aid Agency with colleagues speaks to the 'shared orientation' model set out earlier on. As James (criminal solicitor) explained:

> For me, being entirely open with each other about the cuts to legal aid makes it a lot easier. You know, we all joke around our futures in this career and you have to take it all quite light-heartedly if you are going to stick around. No one really knows what's going to happen so there's no point worrying too much. The media blow everything out of proportion.

While the media serves as an echo chamber for many concerns surrounding the future of legal aid, those already anxious about further cuts see these worries amplified or expanded through news articles, often fuelling speculation further. As Maddie (criminal solicitor) alluded: 'it is of utmost importance that we try and maintain our compassion for the clients and try and continue to do so without letting the wider influence of the media get in our way'. Or, as Andy (criminal barrister) put it: 'we're the ones in the field. We are facing the consequences every single day. The worst thing we can do is speculate about what's ahead'.

Reconceptualizing the 'professional' legal aid lawyer

> We cannot survive without the legal aid profession. It's simple, society relies on our profession, it is a pillar of the welfare state, and always will be. (Rachel, housing solicitor and partner)

Considering the continuous disparaging portrayal and increased bureaucratic hurdles, the traditional understandings of professionalism are disintegrating as the legal aid 'profession' is undermined by the 'global neoliberal turn in the late 20th and early 21st centuries', altering how the lawyers now have to practise (Francis et al, 2017). As Harvey (2006: 50) argues: 'Neoliberalism facilities a form of wealth redistribution called capital accumulation by dispossession, in which wealth and power is funnelled upward, away from the poor'. Reducing public spending comprises one of the latest manifestations of neoliberalism, undermining the professional nature of legally aided work by weakening working values and morale. Yet, the legal aid profession remains a vital pillar of the welfare state, attempting to uphold equal access to justice. Using the concept of 'New Professionalism' (Egetenmeyer et al, 2018), which calls for a threefold analysis of how the legal aid sphere spans the societal level, the organizational level, and alongside the individual level, this section attempts to reconceptualize the 'professional' legal aid lawyer, considering the backdrop illustrated above.

Tensions have grown as legal aid work has bifurcated because of the dehumanized nature of the profession, to the extent that now the job is seen less as 'serving the community', and more effectively as information workers in lucrative positions. Negotiating the radical impact of LASPO and the associated erosion of legal aid funding has not only produced structural reform but, moreover, rising state intervention has fundamentally altered the very meaning of legal aid work. Currently, the profession is becoming increasingly detached from its original concept as it denies the rights of workers within it to serve justice and help people (Newman and Welsh, 2019). As Marcus (housing solicitor) reasons: 'The profession is now dominated by more standardized practices'. This goes against the grain, as legal aid is typically perceived as a highly individualized profession.

As Whittington and Boore (1988) comment, invariably, professions are viewed as vocations as opposed to jobs, and therefore uphold principles and values in line with their outlined professional standards. Karen (director of a legal aid practitioners' group) confirms this: 'To be a lawyer requires you to enter the world as your vocation, as opposed to your occupation. Your heart must be in it, it should be what you are inclined to do, as opposed to what you are forced to do'. Increasingly, as the profession restricts the ability of those to do this it is further undermined, and the potential for access to justice is ever more reduced. As Newman (2013) argues, however, 'it can be seen that the fabled public service ideal forms a central part of professional ideology – whatever the practical reality'. Sommerlad (1996) identified a distinction between 'ideology' and 'actuality', and the gap between the two is becoming increasingly distant as legal aid lawyers now have less ability to enact the public service ideal, which has typically been an integral feature of their professional ideology. Typically, the legal aid profession upholds specific professional values that correlate with the privilege and status of being a legal aid lawyer. If these values are not upheld, then this can have an adverse effect on clients. A devotion to serving in the public interest, and forefronting client-centred practice, are two key attributes that have traditionally defined the work. The more these are restricted, the less professionalism is maintained. As Maister argues however, 'professionalism is predominantly an attitude, not a set of competencies. A real profession is a technician who cares' (in McCallym, 2009: 1). As identified within this research, a large majority of the participants remain committed to upholding an 'idealized' profession to be resilient to wider macro-changes, though the extent to which this can be sustained in the long term is uncertain.

However, professional ideals and practices may vary because of different workplaces, with varying processes of professionalization. Larson (1977) 'conceives professionalization as a process of collective advancement towards market control and status gain'. Pivotal to this is the presentation to the state of a 'façade of homogeneity' in the form of a standardized knowledge base and control of competition across the wider profession (Francis, 2005). The profession itself was best placed to do so when 'supported by an effective professional association', well-organized and far-reaching on the national scale'. Francis (2005: 175) further argues that 'the increasing variety of workplace arenas within which discreet ethical choices confront lawyers means that fragmentation within the legal profession is exacerbated'. In this sense, while professional control may still be exercised this occurs on a contingent and individualized basis, fluctuating between the varying workplace arenas. In this sense, negotiating the professional nature of legal aid work becomes highly individualized and idiosyncratic.

However, in this context, a by-product of neoliberalist professionalization practices is a progression towards professional decline. While the lawyers in question have always been viewed in a typically subordinate light, a growing antipathy towards the adversarial role of lawyers increases as lawyers fail to be champions of justice given their reduced scope to do so (Cape, 2004). Kronman (1993) and Simon (1998) identify this crisis in professional work contributing to the key failings of legal professionalism. Simon attributes this to the lack of 'ethical discretion in professional decision-making' resulting in an 'ambivalent role morality'. Moreover, as outlined in the previous chapter, the rhetoric of legal aid professionalism creates unrealistic expectations as gaps between motivations, education, training, and realities of practice are vast (see also Boon, 2005).

A profession in decline?

Negotiating the radical impact of the erosion of legal aid provision has not only produced structural reform but, moreover, rising state intervention has fundamentally altered the very meaning of legal aid work. Understanding the impact of declining support and difficult working conditions remains vital.

The work is becoming increasingly detached from its original concept, as it increasingly denies the rights of workers within it to serve justice and help people – the very driving force holding the occupation together (Newman and Welsh, 2019). Carr-Saunders and Wilson outlined the professional as being an individual who 'brings asymmetrical knowledge to the service of his client, and thereby exercises power over the client. Therein lie the duties and obligations of a professional to his client' (1986 [1933]: 499). Through the sociological lens, professions typically upheld the view that the responsibilities of these professional groups were integral to the conservation of the 'conscience collective', in the sense that they are vital for aiding the functioning of society through their unionization of ideals and values (Durkheim, 1950: 10). Critiques of professionalism, by the likes of Merton (1957), argue that the increasing reliance of professions on bureaucracy and managerialism has weakened the functioning of professions (see also Wright Mills, 1956). This is because of the shift away from reliance on knowledge and skill. In the context of the legal aid lawyer, it is argued that, because of reliance on bureaucracy and managerialism implemented by the Legal Aid Agency and other regulatory boards, its professional status has been weakened by the stringent nature of the work confining legal aid practice. Many areas of legal practice that were once the domain of the traditional lawyer have been reduced to standardized procedures.

In the context of legal aid, the increased managerialism resulting from New Public Management raises 'difficult tensions about the relationship between professional autonomy and the individual moral responsibility' (Francis, 2015: 185; Sommerlad, 2001). While an exclusive feature of a profession is its erection of barriers to entry, that is educational requirements, qualifications, or training, these function as necessary components required for practice, underpinning the 'social cohesion of professions' within society (Boon et al, 2005: 474). Yet, the construction of additional barriers, such as the impact of LASPO, ultimately place pressures on the professional practice of legal aid lawyers, creating rising tensions between practice and moral obligations. Considering the precarious nature of the work resulting from cuts to legal aid, one could argue that the professional nature of the work is becoming subject to the type of degradation traditionally associated with blue-collar work (Standing, 2011). This is evident in the combination of low salaries, low social status, disregard for their professional skillsets, and poor working conditions – including long and unpaid working hours, as highlighted by solicitors James (crime) and Ash (immigration).

The relationship between precarity and social class here is important, as 28 out of the 30 interview participants in this research identified as middle class. Typically, 'precariousness' has been seen as having much more of an impact on the working classes. However, the legal aid profession, which situates itself within the 'solidly middle-class' wider lawyering backdrop, has become increasingly contingent and reliant on short-term working patterns and free labour. Likewise, the automation of knowledge work has meant that highly skilled workers are less sought after, resulting in a category of workers known as the 'middle precariat' (Standing, 2011). This category refers to the 'downwardly mobile middle class', who now face very different working conditions because of precarious terrains. Changes to the legal aid regime encourage – or in some cases, force – the enactment of acquisitive as opposed to altruistic modes of work, with the privatization of public services and the removal of state welfare systems potentially contributing to this precariousness. This has implications for the demoralization and professional diminishment of practice in addition to the lawyer's individual professional identity, which in turn may drive people out of the field entirely. Lawyers are having to 'sell their individual skillset to the market', as identified by Robert (criminal solicitor), resulting in a loss of professional independence and an inability to perform the work in the way that mirrors the motivations for wanting to work within the field.

Academic literature has identified the legal aid field as becoming more 'factory-like' (Newman, 2013). Sommerlad (2008) notes how the marketization of legal aid provision has altered the status of legal practitioners. This results in a significant gap between the aspirations and realities of practice as expressed continuously by participants, as will be explored in Chapter 7. Progressing or 'moving up' within the field likewise proves very difficult. This is unusual for 'professions', which typically encourage personal and professional development, as well the opportunity to 'climb the ladder' through the likes of promotions coupled with increased responsibility and success.

Capped progression: is it impossible to climb the ladder?

Evidence of lawyers' lack of progression emerged from the research because of the decline of support for legal aid. Legal aid lawyers undoubtedly face marginalization within society, but also within their education and training. Highlighting issues of (in)adequate training and preparation for working with clients demonstrated that the participants were alert to potential failings beyond their control early on in their careers. This indicates how legal aid lawyers' personal investment may not be matched by professional or institutional provision. The legal aid lawyer's limited professional capacity has been further exacerbated because of the restricted opportunity to progress within the field, with participants continuing to face capped progression. This is the case unless you are willing to undertake significant risks, such as secondment, self-employment, or switching your practice area away from legal aid-centered work. Assuming that specialisms are transferable can be problematic in the first place, as the work of the legal aid lawyer becomes increasingly generic and deskilled. Alistair (criminal barrister) states that, generally, legal aid and progression do not go hand in hand. For instance, James (criminal solicitor) moved from working within a criminal firm to practising as a self-employed solicitor advocate; however, he noted that it took many years to be in a position to be able to branch out on his own. 'Taking the leap was extremely stressful, you have to believe in yourself and trust yourself. It's a bit of a balancing act really'. James had only just branched out as a self-employed solicitor when he became involved in my research, but he said straight away that he already felt more confident and excited about his practice. Delivering a service on his terms and being able to control his own work–life balance were both significant positives for him. Additionally, he felt like he had 'moved up in the legal world', gaining more autonomy and control over his own actions despite still dealing with legally aided cases. Similarly, Peter (criminal barrister) took secondment to another field not funded by legal aid, after feeling an inability to survive on the rates of pay for the work he was doing:

> Like a lot of other barristers, I felt like I was getting in a lot of debt because of the career I'd chosen … then a six-month secondment came along, and I felt like that got me out of the black hole I was in … I can't stress how important secondment can be for junior barristers, honestly, it's the biggest bit of advice I'd give!

Practising in legal aid often leaves little time for focusing on career progression on managerial/partner routes unless you work at the same firm for a significant period, as indicated by Jay (housing solicitor). For instance, Rachel (housing solicitor and partner) and Mary (family solicitor) both hold positions as partners within their respective housing and civil liberties departments. Both are in their late 30s and have been in their firms for more than ten years. Understanding what it means to 'progress' within their world is important to keep the profession alive. As Peter (criminal barrister) recognizes:

> There isn't a progression in terms of formal hierarchy; I can't get promoted but there is progressing in terms of the types of cases, i.e. gone from being mostly in magistrates to mostly doing warrants to fully trials in a county court … now full trials in front of judges … then in a year or so I'll be a lot more in the high court … but taking it easy as I don't want to get swamped. I suppose you could distinguish progress as the moment you get tenancy.

Here we can recognize that, while Peter desires to progress and is aware of the stages of career progression within his specialism, he is also cautious to take his role slowly to ensure that he does not become too overwhelmed.

This tactic is not unique; Mary (civil liberties and human rights solicitor) spoke of taking her role each day as it comes: 'going into legal aid work now is career suicide ... but I just don't want to compromise and move over to the corporate side. I'm just taking things slowly and seeing how things go on a day-to-day basis ... as opposed to looking at long-term progression'. Recognizing that, likewise, Mary did not want to move to the corporate side proves highly interesting here. Even with the lack of room for career progression within legal aid work, several participants openly cited that they would not want to move 'over to the other side' (Alice, welfare solicitor; Louisa, civil liberties and human rights; Peter, criminal barrister; and Tom, housing solicitor). This was due to several reasons, such as a lack of professional respect, disillusionment, and scrutiny of the 'other side', building on the public/private divide within the wider remit of lawyering discussed earlier. One of the more significant reasons for this, recalling an earlier discussion in this book, is the notion of questioning the actual meaning of success in the context of doing the work. Here, success is not necessarily measured in monetary terms, but rather by helping those most need of assistance, as confirmed by Maria and Jane, both housing solicitors: 'At the end of the day, if you choose to work in legal aid, then your career progression is just about helping as many clients as you can in the best way possible'. As conceptualized through the 'shared orientation' model, it is the very *craft* of the work that is the glue needed to keep the legal aid field afloat.

Career trajectories

Consistent with other research, several participants in this study were disillusioned with their careers in legal aid. This sense of disenchantment crosses over various specialisms and manifested in unusual ways. 'It is important to encourage legal aid work as a journey rather than a destination' (James, criminal solicitor). Lack of career progression can and may influence those thinking of entering the legal profession to reconsider. Combined with the high levels of stress, lack of support, and the juggling of mountains of legal aid cases, this affects retention levels within the profession, as cited in research conducted by Young Legal Aid Lawyers (2018). Krieger and Sheldon's (2015) study also noted that the lack of autonomy and professional respect make lawyers unhappy. However, keeping the profession alive proves to be a challenge. As Thornton (2020) notes, the 'evaporation of goodwill' indicates that the future of the service cannot be guaranteed'. 'It's all very, very emotionally draining ... the clients, the media, the Legal Aid Agency. I would only encourage a young person to do this if, like, nothing else would do and that is what they wanted to devote their life to' (Sophie, criminal solicitor).

In this research, those practising within legal aid did not deny that undertaking the work was an extremely demanding experience, both physically and emotionally. As James (criminal solicitor) notes: 'I wouldn't encourage anyone to enter the profession now … there is no personal support, no money, and loads of stress. It's all become too overwhelmingly hard to manage'. Eleanor, a partner in a family law firm, openly stated that she would not encourage anyone to enter the profession, as 'you don't get any thanks' from anyone, including those you seek to serve, the public or the media. Ben (housing solicitor) would not encourage anyone to enter the field of legal aid due to the sheer cost of obtaining the necessary qualifications and the inability to recoup the debt due to low salaries. However, as James (criminal solicitor) argues:

> Do work in legal aid, but just modify your expectations … ultimately you can get a lot of job satisfaction so it can be a somewhat nice way of earning a living. You can go into court and have a bit of banter and all that … it can be quite social.

James went on to state that the passion was to 'share not curb the experience' and to use the 'united drive to recruit future generations without clouding the real experience'. Despite this, it is evident that the numbers still entering the profession remain high – almost too high – creating other ramifications, as referenced by John (housing solicitor): 'Unfortunately, the numbers of lawyers have altered drastically since the 1970s that I wouldn't be surprised if there's ten times as many now … but the status of being a lawyer has reduced dramatically'. The likes of Anna (immigration solicitor), Ben (housing solicitor), Grace (criminal solicitor), Marcus, and Jay (housing solicitors), to name just a few, fundamentally confirmed their career trajectories to be very much tied to working within the legal aid remit. As Jane (housing solicitor) notes:

> I hope so, I *really* do hope I stay working in legal aid … the only thing that would stop me would be funding cuts coming in and making it absolutely impossible … but we're trying to get some different sources of funding, so we are not entirely reliant on legal aid. Nothing else would make me want to leave this job; the emotional satisfaction is too great. [her emphasis]

She further emphasized the need for 'active legal aid ambassadors', returning to places where they studied and talking to prospective students and explaining the realities as, ultimately, it was down to the new recruits to 'keep the profession alive' as it is such a hidden occupation. This notion of passing down and sharing insight within the legal profession forms the basis of knowledge (Cooke, 2021). Jane went on to state that the passion was to 'share not curb the experience'. While there were mixed reactions from the research participants as to whether they might encourage legal aid work, 28 out of the 30 participants fundamentally confirmed their career trajectories to be very much tied to working within legal aid due to their social commitment to the role. The distinctive vocational aspect of the work is the glue that holds an otherwise broken profession together, as evidenced throughout this book. A devotion to serving in the public interest, and forefronting client-centred practice are two key attributes that continue to define the work. This chapter deduces that their work fits more into the category of being a vocation as opposed to a profession in its traditional form.

Legal aid work as a 'calling'

Considering all this, I suggest here that legal aid work should be seen as more of a 'vocational pathway' than a 'profession' in its current form. For example, it has been noted in the US context that poverty lawyers are ranked the lowest in prestige in comparison to their private counterparts, due to their 'allegedly distasteful work with the poor' (Heinz and Laumann, 1982: 1049; Wexler, 1970). Thornton (2019) also notes that, in the context of criminal defence work, only 'successful' lawyers can do private defence, and those that are not are forced to do legal aid work. Precarity has infiltrated the public side of the lawyering profession. Vosko (2010: 2) defines precarious employment as 'work for remuneration characterised by uncertainty, low income, and limited social benefits and statutory entitlements'. Typically, it was thought that elite professions, such as lawyers, doctors, and accountants would be protected; however, this is not the case for those working in legal aid. While legal aid lawyers cling on to a few professional values that correlate with the privilege and status of being a lawyer, such as continuing to serve the public interest, education, and training, the profession has undoubtedly been hollowed out. As this research has shown, provisions are depleting, working practices have become more constrained, caseloads are building, pay-slips are inconsistent, and a work–life balance is non-existent. The 'profession' is gradually becoming increasingly unsustainable and, combined with the backlog from the courts post COVID-19, access to justice is being denied daily. One year on from the first COVID-19 lockdown, the backlog in magistrates courts stood at 476,932 outstanding cases, and in crown courts at 56,875 (HMCTS, 2021). The number of cases where neither party had a legal representative went from 13 per cent in 2013 to 36 per cent in 2020, making the field more unstable that ever (Law Society, 2021).

Legal aid lawyers face a limited professional role, carrying out work that is personally confining and of both limited significance and routine. Katz (1982) recognizes that tight working restrictions, discontinuities between cases and 'unique' clientele, results in work that is often seen as insignificant. Lack of significance is one of the biggest quandaries of human service work. In the words of Katz, 'poverty' typically implies that little needs to be done. Those practising in the field have extreme pressure to deal with legal problems, without making much of a difference on the wider scale: 'so long as he or she is poor, a person's civil contact will rarely affect the interests of more than a small circle of others'. The lawyers' limited professional capacity has been further restricted because of the lack of opportunity to progress within the field, with its participants continuing to face capped progression. This is the case unless professionals are willing to switch their practice area away from legal aid work. Assuming that specialisms are transferable can be problematic in the first place, as the work of becomes increasingly generic and deskilled.

Yet, many lawyers working within the field continue to view their work as a 'professional honour' and embrace the working environment despite the hurdles they face. Boukalas (2013) argues, in the US context, that cause lawyers have been made a distinct professional category. In this category, cause lawyers are a distinct object of study characterized by ethicopoltical commitments through their work, in other words 'do-gooding' or working for the social good. A strong regard for the micro working environment therefore drives legal aid lawyers' self-esteem and working ethic. Katz (1982) describes this process as 'adopting reasonableness'. The organizational character of the work is therefore pivotal to the practice as it allows for the transformation of negative elements of the work to be turned into positives – for example, transforming cold calculations of their work into emotional commitment and loyalty to the working philosophy of poverty lawyering. Lawyers in this sense often speak of their work as a 'home', or a 'family with a heart'. As Mittal (2012) conveys, the glue holding the public side of the work together is the drive for social change, which mirrors the findings of this research. Taking part in community resistance and avoiding the 'magnetization of capital neoliberalism' can encourage transformative change. Legal aid lawyering in some areas is grassroots activism inspired, and two key motivating driving forces within that are altruism and activism (Shah, 2021). As Forbess (2022: 52) notes: 'workers can be absolutely instrumental in operations to turn the tables on austerity'. Those within the field have to uphold and create change from the ground up, in light of being constantly trodden on by austerity, misconceptions and toxic narratives from the macro level. The significance of upholding a strong working culture and ethic has likewise been identified in this research.

This chapter has drawn on notions of professions to outline why they no longer apply in their traditional form to legal aid work. Wilson and Hollis-Brusky (2014) explore the idea of 'law as a calling' in the Christian context. Arguing that law in this context has been actualized in distinct ways, they argue that practicing law as a 'calling' allows for lawyers to 'turn inward' and unite, but also to 'turn outward' to maintain social justice, which is a key motivator as remuneration for their work. Those within it do not just have the drive to work within the field despite its current challenges, but rather they feel they *ought* to do it (Koltonski, 2018). As Newman (2013) found, a lot of lawyers are still proud of what they do and their contributions to the civic service, and remain driven at the coalface of legal aid work.

Summary: A conceptual round-up

> We're trying *so* hard to stay afloat, but it really feels like the ship is sinking. I keep trying to keep the water out but sooner or later it will be too late. You just don't know what the future is going to hold. (James, criminal solicitor)

First, this chapter critically called for the lawyering profession, which is often viewed as unabridged, to be reframed into two distinct occupation categories: legal aid practice and private practice. Findings indicate that the cumulative impact of austerity and misjudgement makes legal aid work much harder to navigate than its private counterpart, and the 'fat-cat' narrative continues to conceal the 'church-mice' reality. Legal aid lawyers are subject to a limited professional role, in the sense that their capabilities, significance, and overall career progression is significantly restricted. As the work becomes increasingly hollowed out, the lawyers face a more demarcated, restricted, and difficult working environment, and larger chunks of society are facing injustice as resource becomes increasingly compressed. The consequences that reductions in funding and services have on the 'lived professional experiences' results in the lawyer being placed in the position of a precarious professional. Political and structural underpinnings likewise make it difficult to navigate from a professional perspective, combined with the increased erosion of professional privilege as budgets become more constrained. Legal aid lawyers undoubtedly face altered professional identities. The gap between aspirations and realities of practice has increased as educational, structural, and societal support becomes minimalized. Yet, the practical craft of legal aid work continues to resist barriers in legislation and policy because of altruistic motivations and strong internal working cultures (Cooke, 2021). The work in its current form should no longer be viewed through the lens of being a traditional 'profession', but rather more a vocational pathway. This offers a truer reflection of reality, given that the key form of remuneration is largely altruistic as opposed to financial. Viewing legal aid work through a vocational as opposed to a professional lens undoubtedly offers a more accurate conceptualization. This resonates with Heyes's (2005: 561) conceptualization of a 'vocation' that: '(a) that person is particularly devoted, going "beyond the call of duty" in doing their job, and (b) they do the job because they like doing it or feel they need to do it (they "care")'.

7

One-Stop Shop: 'It's Not Just About Being Someone's Lawyer'

For many, legal aid work can be seen as a marginalized practice due to insufficient resources, restricted practice, and low rates of pay in comparison to their private counterparts. Post-pandemic, some practitioners are barely surviving. Not only do lawyers working in the field feel marginalized with regards to their status, ideologically, but they also struggle due to the gap between their aspirations and the realities of their practice. This results in unstable lawyer–client relationships and occupational burnout. By contrast, in line with the work of Zaloznaya and Nielsen (2011), the reason why the lawyers remain committed to working in an effective and idealized manner, demonstrating altruism, resilience, and determination, is because their deep engagement with their clients and broader social justice orientations allows them to 'make do' in an occupation whereby they are otherwise marginalized professionally. Evidently, legal aid practitioners are also, as a result, increasingly exposed to the risk of 'vicarious trauma', as they face harm from prolonged exposure to the trauma of their clients, which again is often very much overlooked (Fleck and Francis, 2023; Scott and Freckleton, 2024). Given this backdrop, considering why people continue to work within legal aid also remains vital for its very existence. Importantly, this chapter lays out and determines the particulars amid the journeys of individuals choosing to (and continuing to) practise within this remit. This proves crucial in respect of recent changes to legal aid work, outlined in the earlier chapters. These current fluctuations have forced those within the field to retreat from zealous advocacy, leaving the resultant role somewhat 'neutered'. Therefore, it is vital for future debates to question why those within the field nevertheless choose to become and to practise as legal aid lawyers, by reason of the fundamental role performed by these actors in upholding access to justice. This also sits well with the call for a vocational conceptualization made in Chapter 6. Whether or not lawyers actions vs their responses in interviews match up will also be explored here.

Why do people continue to work in legal aid?

People desire to work within legal aid for several (related reasons). For most, preserving access to justice is a passion, and fulfilling this drives individuals to work in the field. In similar vein, protecting human rights and the rule of law is crucial to maintaining democracy and, for many, this drives their work. As a result of the growing impact of economic austerity, building a career in legal aid work is becoming increasingly difficult. Chapter 5's exploration of demographics suggests some persistent bias – particularly within the barrister remit – of lawyers tending to be predominantly male, middle class, and white, especially in positions of seniority. The increased demoralization of the legal aid lawyering profession through cuts to funding and restrictions to legal practice results in a domain demonstrably deserted by an advantaged middle class. Making a living from an occupation offering little financial reward thus requires other incentives for attracting people to the field. This research suggests that it is the moral alignment that just does that.

This section explores the reasoning of individuals to become legal aid lawyers and/or to remain working within the legal aid field, before delving into how this situates into their day-to-day working lives. McDonald's survey, the first chronological study in an English context looking at 'lawyer motivations', situated 'satisfaction in helping people' below 'income' and 'prospects' in its resultant list of desires (1982). Sherr and Webb (1989) found that those entering the legal field tended to place their own individual objectives over altruism, likewise, mirrored in Boon's (2005) findings suggesting the resultant financial prospect of a law degree overrode any other public service aspiration. The reasons explored here are: (1) working in legal aid by default because their area of expertise/specialism is largely funded by legal aid; (2) individual aspirations, that is financial/educational; and (3) altruistic or 'do-gooding' motivations. Since the late 1970s, studies have demonstrated that defence lawyers have not always functioned as zealous advocates, instead displaying greater apathy towards their clients (Baldwin and McConville, 1977; Sommerlad, 2001). In contrast to popular perception, this research located altruistic motivations emerging from over half its participants (17/30). In short, many of the lawyers in this research are driven by the desire to make a difference to somebody's life.

Default: working in a legal aid specialism

Some individuals enter the profession by default, as opposed to making a conscious choice to work specifically within the legal aid field. Certain areas of lawyering are predominantly funded by legal aid, and those who end up working as lawyers do so because of the way in which their practised specialism is funded. For example, invariably, working within the legal aid remit is par for the course for those within the criminal and housing sectors, as a large bulk of the work within these specialisms arrives via such means. This was outlined by several interviewees: 'I went into housing law because I was interested in housing law … the legal aid, if anything, is a massive barrier of my work' (Jane, housing solicitor). Ben (housing solicitor) described his eventual employment as 'purely opportunistic', taking the first presented secure training contract that happened to be in legal aid. Rachel outlined a desire to get into a subject area (housing) that happened to be funded by legal aid. Grace (criminal solicitor) confirmed her existence in the field resulted from the way the work was funded. Thirteen of the participants indicated no specific desire to be a legal aid lawyer, arriving there through the financing model of their specialism. The motivations of the remaining 17 are explored below.

Individual aspirations: financial/educational gain

Among the remaining participants, none cited individual aspirations in the form of financial or educational rewards as primary motivators for working within the legal aid remit. Typically, in the context of choosing to enter a profession, financial incentives serve as a primary rationale, with certain professions invariably commanding higher salaries, for example, accountants, private lawyers, and medical professionals. However, as Paul (criminal barrister) in his mid-30s recognizes, monetary gain was only ever a motivating factor for those who had been in the legal aid profession for some time: 'maybe there's an older generation who would get massive briefs in back in the hay day', before adding, 'you know, one old guy said to me, "when I came to the bar, I didn't know anyone who didn't have a house in France", but that is *completely* different to my generation as the pay just doesn't allow that anymore'. Building on the basis, Rhiannon (welfare solicitor) addressed media misconceptions related to monetary gain:

> I think there's a misunderstanding that legal aid is like spending actual public money, and we're all just pocketing it. People don't realise how little funding we get. We're so careful with every penny, yet clients still assume that I'm a big fat cat living in a mansion with futons and the lot … solicitors from the other side in private practice can also be quite disdainful about it as well, so there's judgement from both ways really.

Working six days a week, the average junior criminal barrister will earn £17,000. Criminal solicitors have gone 25 years without a pay increase (Law Society, 2022). In spite of these headline outliers, the average starting salary for a legal aid lawyer very much conflicts with the common perception of the 'fat-cat lawyer'. As ascertained in earlier sections, while privilege offers a cushion that might otherwise push people out of the industry, once inside the monetary gain is limited. Ben (housing solicitor) highlights that, consequently, some of his friends pity him:

> I have had some horrible, patronizing conversations with maybe kind of more right-wing friends, who are just kind of making tons of money working for big businesses, and you know, they just make comments about 'oh yeah, why don't you just go and make some real money' … and like 'oh don't worry I'll go and get the bill, Ben'.

Nicholas (criminal solicitor) emphasized that, when he started, the rates of pay for legal aid work were 'more or less the same as they are now'. Having been in the profession since 1996, Nicholas described how in 'those days', £15 an hour overtime for going to the police station appeared quite a lot of money. Yet in 2017, billing an average £80 for an entire case that took six to eight hours on average seemed rather incomprehensible. As he further reasons, 'private criminal lawyers tend to charge for an hour, what I'm capped at charging for a *bloody* day!' (his emphasis). As Taylor-Gooby (2016) recognizes, governments are increasingly committed to a neoliberal and consolidation agenda and, by doing so, they exacerbate social divisions within society. Consequently, the welfare state is under unprecedented attack from spending cuts on those services for 'women, children, low-paid people and claimers of working age', resulting in the fragmentation of services and an increase in private provision. The reforms to LASPO were founded on giving taxpayers 'better value for money' by discouraging unnecessary and adversarial litigation, essentially because the legal aid budget was perceived as 'being wasted', with too much spent on sub-groups in society (Bowcott, 2018).

This sense of economic fragmentation ensuing from financial struggles is extended to barristers and solicitors alike, most notably within the criminal sector. The resultant financial impact directed two of the criminal barristers in this research, Alistair, and Paul, to begin supplementing their income by significantly increasing their private case numbers. As Alistair put it: 'the significance is, you can't really survive on just legal aid rates'. This proves difficult for the likes of those practising within the remits of specialisms generally reliant on legal aid cases, such as crime, family, and housing. Despite Alastair's specialism in crime, branching out into other areas, such as property law, was considered an 'uninteresting safety net' if the lack of income became too overbearing.

Concern over lack of income was commonplace within other legal specialisms. Ash spoke of the struggles of being an immigration solicitor within a law centre:

> The situation in 2007 was that we had to report to the Legal Aid Agency monthly with the work we had done so that we got paid regularly. Now it's changed so that we must wait until we have completed the case, which can take months … even years. It's like building a project, and then all the builders working on the site are saying it will last for a whole year. You are present, and at work daily, so they have to wait for the whole building to be resurrected before receiving any payslips. How do they expect us to eat and live while doing the given task? It just doesn't make any sense.

As a result, lawyers have established ways of coping with this prospective financial burden. Some, such as Maria and Jane (both housing solicitors), have 'tried not to think too far ahead', taking each day sequentially to proceed with their day-to-day workings rather than dwell on the wider impact of economic cuts. In the past, reminders from the government, the media, the public, and even non-legal aid lawyers about the looming impact of legal aid cuts were regularly reported in the legal press: 'Dark days for legal aid' (Ford, 2017); 'The future of legal aid is depressing' (Fouzder, 2018); and 'Cuts to legal aid and courts make a mockery to equal access to justice' (Bach and Walters, 2018). Focusing on the more immediate, therefore, has seemed a preferred option. As Maria put it: 'If you thought too far ahead, then the financial burden will just become too overwhelming. You just get your head down and take each day as it comes'. In spite of this, lawyers quite often complain that the system is going to 'collapse' and yet it is still standing, even after the significant warnings in 2013 following the implementation of LASPO. While it clearly has collapsed in places, to some extent this prediction has not yet come to fruition in its entirety.

Lack of access to early legal advice is preventing clients from accessing justice. Across family, criminal, and housing there remains a significant imbalance between need and supply, and the realities of this has meant that the public legal system is in crisis. 'If nothing is done, then we won't be able to speak of a criminal justice system in five years' time' (Phil, criminal barrister). Nina (immigration) further emphasized her worries of victims, defendants, and witnesses waiting years for justice. James and Robert (criminal solicitors) also raised their concerns about the unjust nature of the legal system, which disproportionately affects both the clients and lawyers working within it. Clients are often put off by such onerous and heavily restricted legal processes. Accessing justice in this sense is surrounded by barriers that clients must overcome, and in lots of cases this kind of rhetoric means many problems go unresolved. As many of the participants in this research noted, funding is the single biggest challenge facing our legal system. Eleanor (family solicitor and partner) spoke about the need to treat legal aid work in the same way as healthcare: 'If we want a robust system that does the job it should do, then just as the NHS is funded to help everyone regardless of postcode, status or earnings, we need money injected into the legal aid system'. The 'fat-cat' myth that has tarnished the profession; as Alistair (barrister) notes: 'we need to start shouting about it, as for far too long we have resigned ourselves to these false beliefs that society upholds … it's time to truly educate the public about the work we do day in day out'. In similar vein to the NHS and the pressures the healthcare system is facing, legal aid warrants the same attention from the media and the public alike. This sentiment was evident throughout my ethnographic fieldwork, particularly on the days I was based in court observing the duty housing solicitors, Marcus and Jay. They both explained that it was almost impossible to think ahead when on duty owing to their inability to predict how many clients, if any, they might see on any particular day or how successful these cases may be. This sense of unpredictability permeated their daily duties. This reaffirms Standing's (2011) work arguing that those experiencing modern labour insecurity, including the lack of long-term contracts or employment protections, are placed in the position of the precariat. The unpredictability of legal aid work echoes Standing's definition, the result of a powerlessness to plan or predict their work, both on a day-to-day basis and within a long-term career. This was demonstrated by this description extracted from field notes:

> FIELDNOTE
>
> I turn up at court on a sunny Tuesday morning. Marcus has bought me a coffee and a croissant, and I find him sitting in the meeting room in the corner waiting for me. Upon entering the waiting area, which the small meeting rooms surround, I realize there is no one sitting waiting to be seen. Marcus very quickly pops his head out of the office and alerts me that as there is no case list, no judges have come in and so no cases are going ahead that day. He is very apologetic and quickly tells me that he gets no warning in advance if this is the case, so quite often just has to physically come in to see whether his services are required. While he said this doesn't happen very often, as normally he is overloaded with cases, when it does it is extremely frustrating as it is a waste of valuable working hours. Despite this, he states that, when you accept the role as a duty solicitor, you must be prepared to sit around and wait with the prospect of not seeing a single client, and therefore not getting paid. Instead, we proceed to have a quick chat with the solicitor next door about fluctuating nature of the work, and we leave the court to head back to his office.

Others like Rachel (housing solicitor and partner) indicated that most of her time is spent waiting for clients to turn up to the solicitor's office, also meaning that some days she faces the prospect of reduced pay resulting from no shows. To be granted pay within the legal aid remit, solicitors practising in this field must apply to the Legal Aid Agency. To be able to do so, the client needs to turn up so as to present the necessary paperwork for filing a case on legal aid grounds. The Legal Aid Agency only pays for the time they believe a particular piece of work requires, and so, consequently, every single second is valuable. As Rachel (housing solicitor and partner) notes:

> If your time is wasted because you have spent the last 20 minutes waiting for a client, it all counts. While you can spend this time doing paperwork for other cases, sometimes this is counterproductive as you never get to finish anything. Most of the rates of pay are set in stone for a complete task, regardless of how much time is taken to complete it. Therefore, you just cannot afford to wait around; otherwise, you'll essentially be working even more unpaid hours.

During my time spent in this solicitors' office, I regularly encountered solicitors running up and down the stairs frustrated at a client's lack of appearance. Quite often, these clients were struggling to juggle problems such as unavailability of childcare, immediate housing issues, long-term unemployment, and debilitating health issues. Their chaotic schedules impacted their chances of getting to client meetings on time, if at all. Solicitors often warned me that although that day they had five or six client meetings scheduled for me to observe, in probability at least half would prove no-shows. Despite being a hindrance, clients either not arriving or arriving very late was considered inherent to the job:

FIELDNOTE

> Rachel had emailed me to say that I was welcome to observe a meeting with a client she had arranged for today. I replied, saying I was very grateful and asked her what time we should meet downstairs. She replies by saying 'erm ... 11ish? They will be late, it's a given'.
>
> I meet Rachel at 11 am downstairs in meeting room one for the new client meeting. The client doesn't arrive until 12.10 pm, by which Rachel has already got another client waiting. She had anticipated, however, that this would be the case and catered accordingly and had passed over one of the clients to her paralegal.

Just as Rachel managed to work around the complexities of meeting and organizing unreliable clients, overcoming this lack of security nevertheless meant that the client always needed to come first. Johnson (1980–81) coined the term 'hypothetical alter-ego lawyer' – in the interests of their clients, the lawyer exclusively works to please the public service ideal. Employing a public service ethos, Sophie (criminal solicitor) suggested that 'if you go into the types of law that don't make money, but for other reasons, such as the clients, then you just need to be prepared that you're never going to earn anything', adding that 'it's not about you, it's about the clients'. This sense of adopting an 'alter ego' in line with Johnson's (1980–81) model became further evident when expressed by Ben (housing solicitor): 'At the end of the day, we're just there to help the clients, and therefore, despite the lack of our own personal monetary benefit, we still do whatever we can to make sure we get a good legal outcome for them'. The 'do-gooding element' motivated over half the respondents in this research to work within the field of legal aid, as will be further elaborated below. This coincides well with the call for a vocational conceptualization that emerged in Chapter 6. It remains clear here that financial gain and personal advancement, as key benefits of working in a sought after 'profession', are non-existent in the legal aid context.

Altruistic motivations: representing the underdog

> It's the opportunity to use professional skills to make a definite difference to someone's life and to help them to bring a case where there's so much inequality, you know, between my clients and the British government, the Home Office on the other side; so there's quite lot of job satisfaction in helping somebody to address and overcome that inequality. The legal aid cuts are just something we must fight together. (Ben, housing solicitor)

Boon examined the implied meaning of public service in legal work, arguing that altruistic tendencies should be better understood as forms of intrinsic satisfaction, as opposed to a more outward facing conception of public service (2005: 253). Yet, fighting structural level injustice while attempting to gain justice for their clients was identified as a regular occurrence by these individuals. This reflects the partisanship identified by Scheingold and Bloom (1998), requiring the lawyer to serve both the client and the government, a process coined 'the ideology of advocacy' by Simon (1978). Referring to the legal aid cuts as a fight for their clients against the government, Home Office, or Legal Aid Agency was frequent throughout the discourse. Rachel (housing solicitor and partner) admitted that 'you literally have to fight for every little thing you do' within the housing sector. Despite her willingness to help those most at need, she said that 'it is definitely not an easy ride'. Marcus (housing solicitor) likened the legal aid workplace to a school playground:

> It's almost like you are at school … you are constantly going against people who have power and they have the power over you and push you around, and it's completely unfair because no one can do anything about it … they've got the *entire* state, you know, up against them, whether it's the Home Office trying to evict them, multimillion-pound

> local authority with a minuscule legal aid department trying to evict them, or a benefit system, you know, agency who are making decision they don't understand and they have absolutely no idea how to challenge.

Marcus recognizes the client as an underdog against those in positions of power, with the lawyer bridging the two sides. Despite their principal function as legal professionals primarily seeking to regulate legal matters, the very presence of the lawyer is often professionally compromised through assuming the wider battles of social justice. In reality, clients may be facing issues such as homelessness, discrimination, battles with local authorities, immigration control, mental health, to name just a few. Yet, as Newman and Welsh (2019) argue, lawyers – particularly within the criminal defence remit – are becoming progressively powerless, swamped by the increased bureaucratic and managerialist processes consuming their valuable time. The ability of those within the field to retaliate is increasingly difficult, as those within it feel continuously inadequate. Overly politically driven practice is difficult. For instance, besides referring to herself as a 'fire-fighter', Jay (housing solicitor) describes being the '*only* one standing between the person and actual disaster' (her emphasis). In line with this sentiment, as Sarat and Scheingold recognize, '"cause lawyers" are often positioned at the furthest margins of the lawyer occupation, persistently situated on the periphery of the personal and the political, in addition to the personal and the public' (1998: 331). Nevertheless, having been practising as legal aid lawyers for several years, many respondents still found pleasure in attempting to cleave to their role's altruistic tendencies. Alongside the previously outlined concerns surrounding the lack of financial incentive, this enjoyment came to represent one of the biggest appeals of working in the field, notwithstanding the more restricted nature of practice. This subsection outlines how and why those working within legal aid still find gratification in 'serving the community', given the current macro conditions.

This notion of 'representing the underdog' is entertained by many legal aid lawyers. Robinson and Bell's (1978) findings reflect an important cultural distinction between the UK and the US in approaching equality and social justice. In the UK, there exists a strong belief in a 'just society', while in the US greater emphasis is placed upon monetary success. Likewise, Lipset found that the Eglish value system emphasizes 'ascription', compared to a US value system underlining 'achievement' (Lipset, 1963: 517). Turner (1960) observed that in the American system everyone is taught that, no matter your origins, if you work hard then you will attain success. By contrast, the English system teaches everyone to 'reconcile themselves to their lot in life'. As Marcus (housing solicitor) outlines, ascription is part and parcel of being a legal aid lawyer. While some lawyers perform their role merely in accordance with the nature of winning or losing cases, other lawyers introduce, wherever possible, a notion of pursuing justice through the lens of decency. This links to Rutherford's (1993) work on 'humanizing' legal practice, a method often preventing the process of justice becoming both apathetic and repressed. This is particularly evident within the context of criminal justice. According to Phil (criminal barrister), 'it is very old fashioned to say you should be dispassionate in this role'. While never expected in earlier times, he added that delivering personality beyond the typical barrister role, by drawing on both emotion and a human connection, proves vital not only for the client's sake but also assists in winning a case.

However, Phil argues that criminal barristers are becoming increasingly demoralized by the impact of austerity and the ensuing intensified pressure. Nevertheless, he asserts that 'goodwill must be maintained as there is an even stronger notion of need now than ever before', with the work becoming ever more forced to depart from humanized justice. However, this is often demanding in practice. Below, in an extract taken from my field notes, I observed an interaction between Marcus (housing solicitor) and his client regarding an eviction, during his duty solicitor shift at a county court:

[*Based in a small meeting room at the side of a large waiting room*]

Marcus (M) to Client (C): Right, you have two ways to stop this.

[*Marcus is particularly frantic because of time restraints and, additionally, is faced with a very nervous client*]

M: [*Going through the figures*] Costs are prohibitive and it won't be worth court doing this as you've got three children … but the good news is they are not going to evict you … [*Grins*]

C: [*With a smile*] Who said that?

M: Your housing association solicitor – but you will be liable for costs … while I accept your situation but I'm not sure the judge will.

[*M frantically looks through the written law while chatting away*]

C: This is just a waste of court's time.

M: Well, I don't disagree with you on that … landlords are a bit trigger happy … the main thing is that your home is safe, but you do need to make sure you keep on track financially …

C: I think I've learnt my lesson.

M: Can I take a look? [*Grabbing evidence papers from the client*] I find it much easier to read things – thank you very much.

M: [*Continuing*] The thing is we need a legal argument, not a moral judgement here … that doesn't really wash with the judge I'm afraid.
[*Explaining to her what is going to happen in court, mid-sentence M says, 'just trust me' and grins. He then uses his phone to check something in the client meeting*]

C: I really need some water.

M: Just out there is a fountain … look, stop worrying, all you need to do is just sit next to me and listen, that's it.

C: I really hope you don't let me lose my home.

M: Don't worry, we've got this, I promise.
[*Client grins nervously and leaves to wait to be called in the waiting room. Marcus then turns to me and explains that he was slightly worried that he wouldn't win the case, but he had to show that he was confident to the client*]

There are several things revealed by this extract. First and foremost, Marcus states that 'we need a *legal argument*, not a *moral judgement*'. Likewise, his compassionate approach shows his desire for pursuing the humanistic motivations outlined in his interview. However, his lack of confidence ending the exchange proves the difficulty of its practical implementation. This notion of 'looking confident' and attempting to adhere to an ideal featured regularly within this research. This mirrors the contrasting positions of the lawyer presented by Katz (1982) who, on the one hand, speaks of their work as a 'project of professional honour', but, on the other, questions the 'limited professional role'. It seems here that the disparities between the two are becoming greater as the role of the legal aid lawyer undoubtedly suffers greater restrictions.

To this end, the needs of the clients remain consistent regardless of the macro backdrop. In line with this principle, respondents summarized their work as 'all-encompassing' (Jay, housing solicitor). Nicholas (criminal solicitor) likened some of his cases to a soap opera: 'Some cases I really bloody enjoy, it's just like watching an episode of *EastEnders* or something. You don't know what problem or ailment they are going to talk about next. They come at me like buses and sometimes I can help and sometimes I can't!' This excerpt suggests that, to some extent, Nicholas relishes the tourism into other people's lives, likening it to watching a television programme. Despite being restricted as to his ability to resolve all the issues outlined; it makes for a more entertaining role. This highlights further that, in some cases, relishing such cases could be for the benefit or entertainment of the lawyer, as opposed to the desire to want to assist with the clients' complex and wide-ranging needs. This undermines the ability of the lawyer in this case to want to always work in an altruistic manner, as sometimes, while it may be assumed that the work is being carried out to 'do good', in another sense, as illustrated in this case, concern into a client's wider 'ailments' may be more driven by self-interest. Maria (housing solicitor) reasons, however, 'we often understand the very awful situations that people are in, and we do of course have empathy … but the law is what it is … and, therefore, there's only so much we can do. We only have *so much* agency'.

For those comparatively new to the field, such as Grace (crime), Ben (housing), and James (crime), sometimes it is easier to merely focus on the fundamental legal matter at hand, despite their desire to be altruistic or to 'do good'. Increased amounts of regulation from the Legal Aid Agency mean that, bureaucratically, the assessment of need is much harsher, the resultant outcome of funding cuts attempting to marshal against weak cases. The purported aim is to avoid overburdening the legal system; however, these changes encourage more acquisitive than altruistic modes of work, which in turn contribute to increased precarity levels. In other words, rather than offering a client-centred practice, the work becomes case-centred and focused on finding cases eligible for legal aid funding, regardless of how deserving or desperate the client is. Given the cuts, some argue that it has almost become impossible to be altruistic in any way or form. As Nicholas (criminal solicitor) states: 'Attempting to put a bandage on a system that has crumbled … is frustrating to the extreme … these are humans we are dealing with, not inanimate objects! The Legal Aid Agency *forces* us to treat these beings as robots almost; it's just unacceptable and not appropriate' (his emphasis). Standing (2011) maintains that this 'unfamiliar zone of security' means that some professionals feel further insecurity in their roles, with those entering the legal aid profession to 'do good' now facing insecurities surrounding the ways in which they should practise. For example, Nicholas (criminal solicitor) draws a link between the fractured nature of the legal aid system and the increased amount of regulation from the state, resulting in a loss of access to rights for some of those most in need.

Even those clients who can access services often experience substandard practice from lawyers facing increasingly stringent time constraints. Regardless of the moral nature of a case, bureaucracy impedes the social need: 'The legal aid lawyer really has very little control and agency when it comes to it. In some sense, we are the *little guys* who are often taken for granted, placed into very precarious positions, and forced to confront some extremely morally difficult situations on an everyday basis' (Nicholas, criminal solicitor; his emphasis). Alistair (criminal barrister) notes: 'while the public good is being played down because of the cuts, we are all helpful people, so we just give in'. Likewise, Karen, the director of a membership body representing practitioners, refers to the role as a 'giving occupation'. She goes on to state that, 'in her world, success isn't determined through monetary gain, or corporate schmoozing, rather it is through the social good that we come to have a *real* existence. Nothing in the corporate world could ever rival that' (her emphasis). James (criminal solicitor) further argues that, since 'they don't really have to answer to anyone', it makes for a much more enjoyable role. However, James commands a better position than others as a self-employed solicitor and, therefore, he has more autonomy in the cases he chooses to accept. He spoke as to the flexible nature of the role, allowing him to conduct his work without having to please anyone in higher positions. 'Making the world a better place', he states, 'only takes one person at a time you know … being self-employed you can really see the difference that *you* make on a personal level' (his emphasis). In this sense, James maintains his sense of wanting to 'do good' because he has slightly more room to do so without anyone looming over him. Further research into the disparities between self-employed and non-self-employed legal aid practitioners would prove useful here.

Despite increasing hurdles, those practising within legal aid remain in the field. As Obama (2007: 135) notes: 'often [the lawyers'] poverty is proof of their integrity'. In rhetoric and practice, some of these lawyers are capable of acquiring much better-paid, higher status work, but instead opt to work within a more altruistic profession. For example, Alice (housing) recognized that, while she had the skillsets to work in a 'higher paid job', she had chosen to remain at an advice centre because she felt she was contributing to society. Furthermore, Eleanor (family solicitor and partner) outlined that, despite being offered a position at a private family law practice, her work within legal aid ultimately provided a much more 'honest' perspective on life, dealing day in day out with those battling the realities of real life. Rhiannon (solicitor at a law centre) concurred, claiming her nature entailed an affinity with the role: 'I'd always known I wanted to go into legal aid, I just suit it, I suppose I'm one of those bleeding-heart people'. Insight may be gained from questioning the structural (in)security of the legal aid lawyer actively opting to work in a more altruistic, as opposed to acquisitive, sphere. This being the case, traditional understandings of 'professions' may not fully capture the field to its full extent, further building the case for a more vocational understanding.

In line with this, a key finding here is that the potential benefits of working in legal aid can supposedly 'prevail' over a sense of macro structural insecurity, with several interviewees stating an enduring motivation to stay in the role, and a professed comfort with doing so, such as in the case of Eleanor (family solicitor and partner), Rhiannon (welfare), Maria (housing), and Sophie (crime). Legal aid lawyering was valued because respondents found it personally rewarding – in other words, they enjoyed personal benefits from working for the common good. As Ben (housing) remarked: 'life's not all about money you know, we can really make a difference here'. For some, clinging to this ideal seems inseparable from working in the legal aid field, despite the inability of some to continue to work in such a humanistic manner.

Tata (2007) attributes this model of working as the 'client-centred approach', whereby the duties and perspectives of the lawyer adapt according to the individual needs of each client. Despite some scholars suggesting certain lawyers maintain very low opinions of their clients and therefore treat them as 'undeserving of good treatment' (McConville et al, 1994; Newman, 2013), in my sample this appeared only occasionally. Tom (housing solicitor) said: 'at the end of the day, your work is all about the client. It is very much client-centred, and this is something that cannot be overlooked. Your client is relying on you to help them'. Unlike Newman's (2013) argument that, to portray a good image, many lawyers merely claim to uphold positive relationships with their clients, throughout my observations, many cases showed an identifiable rapport between the lawyer and their client, as strongly evidenced in the extract below:

	[*At the solicitor's office*]
Rachel (R) (partner and housing solicitor):	[*On the phone to a client*] How was your birthday meal, [*client's name*]? Did you get that dress you wanted?
	[*Client responds*]
R:	Well, I can't wait to see it. How's your mother doing?
	[*Client responds*]
R:	That's good to hear. Right, take care and I will see you next Thursday – make sure you eat properly this week!
	[*Client responds*]
R:	No worries, I'm only looking out for you … remember those documents next week too! Bye for now!

Quite often, during periods of my observation, the lawyers went above and beyond their role as a legal advisor by upholding pastoral care within their client relationships. It was perceptible during my research that solicitors frequently began their client meetings with general chit chat, prior to delving into legal matters. This contradicts the increasing restrictions on legal aid practice as, despite an intensified administration creating further time constraints on those practising in the field, the lawyers still took time to interact with their client in a personable manner. This was illustrated in one of the field notes taken during a day at the solicitor's office:

FIELD NOTE

I enter the meeting room with both James (criminal solicitor) and the client. Before we have even sat down, James is joking around with the client about

> the recent football scores. The night before the team that James supports had beaten the team that the client supports, so James took this opportunity to build up a rapport before addressing the matters of that meeting.

As Rutherford (1993) recognized in his work on the criminal justice system based around 28 interviews with practitioners, in the institutional practice there is an attempt to 'humanise the system from within'. Otherwise termed 'professional survival', Rutherford speaks of the way in which individuals within the criminal justice system come to maintain positions of influence, while maintaining some level of integrity. We can draw comparisons within this research, as evidenced by Phil (criminal barrister):

> The role of being a barrister is a very personal one. The rapports you build, the standards you maintain, the ethics and values you uphold, and the integrity you preserve remains vital. Yes, we are in a profession, whereby a lot of rules and regulations are enforced; but, at the end of the day, if we don't actively try to personalize the role, then you aren't really doing your job properly. Also, it wouldn't be nearly as enjoyable.

Despite this, this internal 'personalized' nature of the role is often contradicted by a depersonalized external perception – a significant theme identified in this book, causing further implications for the 'professional' identity of the legal aid lawyer. 'We're seen as representing people who don't deserve to be represented … we're seen as taking cases entirely for the money … but this is just not the case. We emotionally invest ourselves day in day out' (Maddie, criminal solicitor). Working with the 'undeserving' brings unwarranted attention from certain quarters. Both Alistair (criminal barrister) and Marcus (housing solicitor) were openly concerned about the increased level of stigmatization of both lawyers themselves and their eligible target groups, the clients. As Ben (housing solicitor) reasons, often he finds that he gets judged for working with 'poor people', particularly from his friends working in the corporate world, or those who identify as more right-wing. Some would perceive legal aid clients to be 'undeserving' as previously discussed. Ben argues that they deserve to be represented as often they are dealt a bad hand.

As Cape (2004) recognizes, discourse surrounding 'typical' legal aid clientele tends to portray victims and defendants as somewhat 'irreconcilable'. Yet, in some cases, this research uncovered the opposite, as observed during the fieldwork. Many of the lawyers interviewed tried to offer a good service even if they were not always able to do so. Marcus (housing solicitor) encompasses this well:

> It really doesn't matter who the client is, what their background is, what their legal issue is, or where their funding is coming from. At

> the end of the day, as a lawyer, I will treat everyone the same regardless of any of that, and I know that, across the board, this is the case too. I always enjoy meeting the clients that I have because you … I learn so much from them, I feel very privileged to represent them and *I am always challenged by them*, and you know, yes, they've been through terrible experiences, but I enjoy seeing them grow, and gaining courage in themselves to speak out. And, you know, that is always a massive privilege. [his emphasis]

Sophie (criminal solicitor) suggested: 'It's that sense of helping the neediest and vulnerable in society that makes me feel incredibly grateful'. This sense of power inversion, almost placing the client in the more powerful position in the relationship, proves highly significant. It is argued that the short-term nature of the work renders it difficult to maintain the lawyer–client relationship (Sarat and Felstiner, 1988). James (criminal solicitor) recognizes that, making his client meetings predominantly client-led, facilitating the conversation but allowing them to digress into what they feel is necessary, makes the overall process a lot easier. While this increases the level of rapport between the lawyer and client, this ultimately has implications regarding the time-consuming nature of this approach.

Renumeration rates ultimately affect the service that defendants receive, as the lawyer becomes torn between acting efficiently and providing a good level of service (Welsh, 2017). Legal aid practitioners are increasingly split between business needs and client needs, which has challenged their occupational identities. Morale is low among both workers and clients, and the stress of finances, combined with frustrating work methods, has meant that legal practice has changed (Thornton, 2020). Funding cuts have made the work ever more unpleasant, undermining the very ability of the lawyer to advocate for their clients (Peter, criminal barrister). Resilience is at an all-time low (Deghani and Newman, 2022). This was a consistent story spoken and observed among respondents. Jane (housing solicitor) refers to herself as a 'fire-fighter' as she feels like she is often the only one 'standing between the person and actual disaster'. Eleanor (family solicitor and partner) refers to her role in a 'giving occupation' and that 'in her world, success isn't determined through monetary gain, or corporate schmoozing; rather it is through the social good that we come to have real existence'. Grace (crime) stresses that 'it's the human connect that keeps legal aid work alive'. Insight may be gained from questioning the structural (in)security of the legal aid lawyer actively opting to work in a more altruistic as opposed to acquisitive sphere. The potential benefits of practising legal aid can supposedly prevail over this sense of structural insecurity, with many participants stating an enduring motivation to stay in the role and a professed comfort with doing so.

Clinging on to a client-centered approach

The next part of this chapter interrogates the everyday 'lived experiences' of the legal lawyers through a forensic examination of their day-to-day working lives, invoking the ethnographic and interview data to address the extent to which the wider social, economic, and political conditions shape their everyday experiences. I felt this was necessary given that the legal aid world is so hidden. Similarities and differences between the findings from the interview and ethnographic data are also examined to see if lawyers 'talk the talk but not walk the walk' (Newman, 2013). In other words, claims made in the interviews will now be drawn comparatively with the working practices observed. Participants can often present an idealized picture; however, this may not transfer to their practice. Does (and can) the moral alignment outlined above feasibly exist in practice given the (constrained) scope of legal aid?

The argument presented is that legal aid lawyering is more demarcated in the context of the post-2012 cuts, as established in previous chapters. LASPO has significantly restricted access to justice by reducing the budget by almost one-third. Lawyers have had to adapt to a new way of working in an increasingly resource-stretched environment or make difficult decisions about cases, and are having to turn people away despite them being in great need. This is at odds with the 'ideology of advocacy' (Simon, 1978), which maintains that the lawyer must serve clients and the government in a just and equal manner. The ideologically driven marketization of justice, coupled with legal reforms, undermines the modern lawyer's ability to execute their responsibilities effectively. Despite the ongoing threats to their occupation, many of these workers *do* grind tirelessly to always cling on to a 'client-centred' approach, as will be demonstrated.

The 'new' lawyer straddles the chasm between legal and political domains more so now than ever before, which results in their expectations not always being turned into reality. As Dehaghani and Newman (2019: 13) note: 'the ideal of the healthy lawyer-client relationship ... has been tarnished and faces serious practical impediments'. In the context of criminal work, this is a result of barriers to procedure, increased formal regulation, the disincentivization of lower fees, as well as the marketization of legal services. Ideal lawyering principles become compromised for 'practical business concerns'. As task characteristics become harder, workloads increase, resulting in emotional exhaustion and burnout; combined with unmet career expectations, those within the field become increasingly dissatisfied. Increasing emotional burden and burnout, in turn, leads to disaffection, which can make it difficult to derive any form of intrinsic satisfaction from their work.

In many instances, the lawyers' concerns with making their work entirely 'client-centred', and their subsequent enthusiasm for 'doing good' is very evident in the examples emergent from this research, as well as their ongoing dedication to their roles. Several of these individuals embody and maintain the quest to want to 'uplift society' in some way or form, whether it is stopping people committing suicide or acting as a resource for the unemployed or homeless, despite the inherent complexities of legal aid funding and the work.

As a society, we often overlook these humanistic obligations as being valid vocational components. The unflattering portrayal of legal aid lawyers in the media often fails to recognize the benevolence of those working in the field, and may even cause them to doubt their worth. Energized by real encounters with scenarios in which professionalism, empathy, and compassion for clients are regularly displayed, undoubtedly legal aid lawyers remain a pillar for society despite the challenges they currently face.

The holistic nature of legal aid work

> You've got to be able to deal with difficult clients. We do get some *extremely* vulnerable people who usually have severe mental health problems, for instance. You can get some very difficult and very highly vulnerable clients I think, and that can be a huge shock to people [legal aid lawyers] that aren't expecting it. You need to have more of a people skillset than a lawyer skillset. It's not about just being someone's lawyer. Sometimes you are their only hope. (Rhiannon, welfare; her emphasis)

Rhiannon's emphasis on the need to have more of a 'people skillset' than a 'lawyer skillset' illustrates how some aspects of legal aid work require extended interpersonal efforts. Similar comments were made by some other research participants, such as Grace (criminal solicitor), Jane (housing solicitor) and Marcus (housing solicitor), who likewise described their work as being 'holistic' in nature. Binder et al (2004) encourage lawyers to focus on the 'holistic entity' of the case as opposed to just the legal problem. Focusing on the notion of legal aid lawyering as a 'one-stop shop', the chapter explores how lawyers act as a source of multiple services whereby clients can have their legal (and selected other) needs met in just 'one stop', especially in cases situated within the wider theme of access to justice.

Those within the field are required to utilize their skillsets to focus not just on the immediate legal needs of the client, but also on the bigger picture. James (criminal solicitor) alluded to this, indicating that, as the criminal justice system tends to be the last stop for the client, often their need for assistance is at its greatest and most complex. Advice may be sought around housing eviction, deportation, or loss of parental authority, among other things. While these problems may be considered by some to override the 'traditional lawyering role', legal aid lawyers tend to assist with these other difficulties as a matter of course. Respondents in the research referred to this tendency as 'do-gooding', although Robin Steinberg, in the US context in 2006, originally coined the more formal term 'holistic lawyering'. Steinberg highlights how the importance of 'working compassionately with indigent clients means seeing first-hand that the problem and challenges they face stretch farther than the confines of the criminal cases before them' (2006: 626). Physical elements of this holistic imperative were rendered evident in Silverman and Co's office space, as the excerpt below illustrates:

FIELD NOTES

This particular firm is distinguishable from the others. While it looks like a typical solicitor's firm from the outside, with a small plaque stating the firm's name and slogan, you almost miss it because it blends in with the other buildings in that street. As I squeeze past a group of people congregated at the bus stop situated directly outside, I manage to locate the public entrance. Inside the door features a large waiting room, with colourful pictures, a toy box, and a bookshelf. The interior is painted in bright orange, and there are comfortable chairs scattered around, where clients are waiting to be seen. Kids are playing on the mat on the floor, and clients are chatting among themselves congregated at one side of the waiting area. On the other side of the room is a board, which hosts a variety of different posters ranging from counselling services, homeless shelters, NHS posters, as well as other helplines, including talk to FRANK and crisis hotline.

Several observations can be drawn from this extract regarding the situational design of the law firm. For example, in line with notions of 'holistic lawyering' (a trend since the 1960s), particular care had been taken with the décor of the waiting room and how it was read by potential clients and/or members of the public. For example, the physical space was far from being a clinical, corporate space with its brash bright-coloured walls, scattered toys, comfortable chairs, and lively images on the wall almost reminiscent of somebody's living room. The importance of structuring the waiting area in such a way has two core functions: to increase client satisfaction and, more importantly, to accommodate the holistic imperative. The solicitor's firm in this example was situated next to a bus stop, making it easily accessible for those who rely on the use of public transport. Furthermore, the expectation that clients may turn up with their children was evident by the number of available toys and the dedicated play mat in the centre of the room. If clients are bringing their children with them, it also highlights the possibility that they are unable to pay for childcare or may also be unemployed. Acknowledging this, the firm itself has specifically designed their waiting room in a way that reduces the stigma and shame of those facing these broader social issues. Something else notable is the absence of a television in the room encouraging those waiting to interact and engage with each other, in turn creating a much more relaxed and social environment. This is somewhat unique in comparison to other waiting areas observed in this research, such as the courts, which typically feed into the image of being very neutral, bare, and austere. This could be attributed to the fact that the firm, in this case, is on the side of the client, advocating on their behalf, whereas the court is not. Within Silverman and Co, it also seemed apparent that the posters on the notice board were placed intentionally and carefully constructed with the idea that the types of individuals visiting the firm may need further support with other welfare-related issues. Physical elements of the holistic imperative here were constructed with the direct purpose of prioritizing the clients' needs over everything else. This was likewise evident in the law centre, as their raison d'être typically focuses on the idea of tackling wider socio structural as well as individual legal issues. Thus, similar elements were observed, such as posters and helplines for other welfare-related matters. The law centre likewise had a cupboard that contained donated items for clients in great need. These items included nappies, trainers, tinned foods, as well as toiletries.

The ethos of these spaces is reminiscent of, and informs, the ethos of the type of lawyer who works there. Marcus (housing solicitor) explained that while, traditionally, the lawyer has arguably focused very much on the 'case at hand' as opposed to 'defending a case, the proper legal aid lawyer is very much about defending the client'. Holistic advocacy is a principal mechanism through which those in the field can make a difference in the long term; while those practising in the field face marginality within the wider legal profession, offering holistic legal assistance can add a further layer of significance to their work (Katz, 1982). This may prove invaluable to offset issues related to the perceived lower status afforded to vocations, as recognized Chapter 6. Ben (housing solicitor) draws an interesting analogy between lawyering and football teams: ' while commercial law firms are likened to, say, Chelsea as a football team, in general legal aid lawyers are equivalent to, say, Scunthorpe United'. In line with this notion, Rachel (housing solicitor and partner), argues that, while commercial lawyers may be described as 'extremely wealthy', 'fat cat', and 'privileged', legal aid lawyers should be described as 'committed', 'modest', and 'charitable'. The different discourses inevitably highlight the distinct ends of the lawyering profession, each of which offer very different measurements of satisfactory outcome. Jane (housing) similarly placed public and private lawyers into 'two different camps', situated at different ends of the spectrum within the wider remit of practising law. The benevolent nature of the reward that comes with legal aid funded work, however, may act as a priceless form of remuneration, as recognized in Jay's (housing) response: 'working for the social good is the one thing that we have over those working within the private sectors. It might not be a lot in the grand scheme of things, but it's the one thing we can get respect for'. Sophie (crime) also recognized how unpicking clients' complicated lives could often bring much more job satisfaction, which becomes an essential facet as workloads increase. As demonstrated earlier, a concern for the public good was identified as one of the biggest motivators for working in the sector: 'We all eat and breathe the same ethos … we're all here to help people, and because of that, it translates not only into our work but into our wider relationships'.

This holistic imperative, therefore, upholds two purposes. On the one hand, it meets the needs of the socially progressive orientation of the legal aid lawyers. And, on the other hand, it ultimately acts as a form of reward, allowing those in the field to feel significant in an otherwise marginalized environment. Several of the research participants continued to adapt their working practice to reconcile their original motivations of wanting to 'do good', despite external pressures. In line with Katz's (1982) work on 'self-tranquilising attitudes', individuals, such as Marcus, Rachel, as well as Tom (all housing solicitors), now focus on the 'smaller picture', such as being just a voice for their clients, as opposed to aiming to bring about wider socio-economic justice. This mirrors the findings of Zaloznaya and Nielsen (2011). Jane (housing) said: ' it's now just about being *that voice* for those who are entitled to justice. We may not be able to make any drastic changes to the wider justice imbalances in society, but *we can try* to achieve victories for those individuals that need us the most' (her emphasis). Ash (immigration) also stated: ' it's not about changing the world; it's just about making a difference step by step'. While Marcus (housing) suggested: ' it's just about knowing you singularly made that life-changing difference to that person's life'.

Adapting to the post-2012 cuts environment has meant adopting new or different strategies to ensure lawyers' continued investment in a manner that echoes sentiments of 'ideological marginality' (Zaloznaya and Nielsen, 2011). This concept of ideological marginality argues that legal aid lawyers face two conflicting ideological bases within their practice. On the one hand, their commitment to social justice requires a level of emotionality and compassion and, on the other hand, the professional constraints of practice inhibit their ability to maintain this. A comment from Marcus (housing solicitor) reflected this notion: 'It is so hard to maintain an acceptable level of commitment with your clients. This presents us with difficulties'. While Katz (1982) acknowledges that this is a well-established issue, he states that those practising in the legal aid field (in the US context) may struggle to maintain this dual commitment. Sophie (criminal solicitor) indicated this, stating that 'it is sometimes very easy to get caught up with clients that sometimes you forget what you are actually primarily there to do, which can ultimately have an impact on your job performance'. As she explains, while inevitably working for the social good is an integral part of the role, it is about finding the appropriate balance between being 'a lawyer' and being 'a holistic provider', which, as evidenced, is becoming much more difficult in this resource-stretched environment. Likewise, while typically a law centre often has projects that enable a more holistic approach, or internal referrals to address other welfare-related problems, private firms can rarely do that.

Krieger (2004–05) argues that it is impossible to separate personal and professional satisfaction. Changes to the legal profession, however, have meant that personal satisfaction levels have been adversely affected as practice is far more restricted due to monetary and time constraints. It has previously been argued that a 'combination of skill enhancement and service in the advancement of the public good has allowed some lawyers the opportunity to do well by doing good' (Granfield, 2007: 115; Wilkins, 2004). Granfield (2007: 120) further argues that, at the same time, lawyers are very restricted in their ability to challenge the root causes of most legal problems of the poor, such as inequality. There remain organizational differences that place 'unique pressures on lawyers in different practice areas, leading to distinct types of lawyering ideologies that shape legal practice'. It is therefore clear that both personal and professional satisfaction levels are internalized to each given field. While this may vary between solicitors and barristers, likewise this may differ between solicitors' firms, barristers' chambers, and law centres. Personal satisfaction that comes with this form of holistically natured work can be seen as enticing for some, especially to those who may be happy to be one of the lower earners in contrast to their corporate counterparts. It also gives those practising within it the chance to make impactful 'bottom-up changes', as stated by Alice (welfare). For instance, as Grace (criminal solicitor) put is: 'we like to go above and beyond for our clients because we act in their best interest. It is just about achieving the best outcome for the client'. Some of the lawyers involved in this research had a great ability to take on multiple roles all at once, such as Andy (criminal barrister): 'You do everything from a counsellor, doctor, psychiatrist, social worker, and a lawyer. You're everything, and you obviously don't get nearly enough thanks for all that, but it's just kinda what you sign up for'. As Andy notes, choosing to work in legal aid means facing clients with additional social issues, which in turn means developing knowledge, skills, and understanding beyond the legal field. He attributes this further to the decline of the welfare state in their ability to serve the clients as well as they should be served.

Despite this, exposure to and engagement in such a diversity of arenas brings with it a wealth of benefits for both lawyers and their clients. Exploring the social work side specifically, Sophie (criminal solicitor) described how it is essential to be open to the range of issues that might be relevant to a client:

> You're kind of a social worker at the same time …, that is an important aspect of the job, and *I do like that*. You've got a lot of homelessness issues or, you know, human rights issues and it kind of cuts across the board, and you are looking at all of those aspects of clients, and you are kind of dealing with some of the wider issues in our society today. [her emphasis]

Legal aid lawyers' unique relationships with their clients can have reciprocal positive outcomes, as Nicholas (criminal solicitor) showed: 'if you believe in them and help motivate them to make changes to their wider lives … this is even more effective than just winning a case, and the job satisfaction goes through the roof'. Similarly, Marcus (housing solicitor) alluded to this before a client meeting one day in my fieldwork: 'the fact we can help people and change people's lives … to make sure they have a roof over their head or have at least like the correct income to … kind of like get the necessities like food and stuff. That's just so rewarding in itself'. The following extract, taken from ethnographic field notes, demonstrates how Marcus works holistically in action:

	[*Sat in the meeting room with Marcus and his client as he carries out his housing duty work*]
Marcus (M):	So, why are you in arrears? You seem to have enough money [*looking through the client's bank statements*]
	[*Client shrugs his shoulders*]
M:	Oh, I see … loans! Loans are very scary aren't they, not very nice at all
	[*The client looks down into his lap in embarrassment*]
M:	Right, well, we can try and sort that … Do you have any other problems, anxiety, or anything?
	[*Client nods*]
M:	Do you think that you maybe just didn't open the letters when you should have done then?
	[*Client nods*]
M:	Ok, well if you are suffering from anxiety or depression do go and see a doctor, alright? Your health is very important, so make that a priority. Do you want me to find out the number of your local doctors' surgery?
	[*M proceeds to find the details for him before letting him answer*]
M:	Don't worry, we're in this together, you'll get through this. Shall we ring them now? You can go outside in the waiting area and speak to them?
Client:	Yes, please, that would be a great help.
	[*Marcus proceeds to ring up the doctor's surgery and hands the phone to the client*]

A discussion with Marcus after the exchange, however, highlighted how this 'do-gooding' notion is deemed to be an incredibly 'romanticized view' of the work of the legal aid lawyer:

> The fact that we'll win your case, we'll clear your rent arrears, we'll stop your eviction, we'll solve your mental health issues, and they're just going to go off like [in] some sort of romcom and live happy lives and drink in Starbucks, but truthfully they just won't survive if you leave them to their own devices.

His reference to a romcom evokes the idea that legal aid lawyering (in the eyes of others) solely has happy and positive outcomes. While Marcus's exchange from the field notes demonstrates that holistic work does sometimes happen, his doubts raised in the conversation immediately afterwards makes one question how often this is done in principle vs practice. Likewise, the excerpt could be read in a patronizing manner, as the language used by Marcus here is almost childlike, with phrases used such as 'loans are very scary' and 'do you think that you maybe just didn't open letters when you should have done then?'. In addition, Marcus's offer to ring the doctor's surgery could likewise be viewed as a way of finding a solution, but also deferring the problem on to someone else.

In some cases, working 'holistically', or putting on a holistic front, may often just be a quick and easy solution to offer a quick fix. Evidence of this is given in an exchange between Marcus and another duty solicitor:

M: Thank god she's out of my hands now!
[*He explains that the previous client had just broken down in front of him*]
[*Other duty solicitor laughs and puts his hand on his head*]

Duty solicitor: Tell me about it! It's not our job [to] be dealing with stuff like that, is it? Makes our lives so much bloody harder. I think she needs significant help to be honest.
[*M nods*]

M: I know, right. I'm not a bloody doctor am I? I don't know what they expect sometimes. [*laughs*]

DS: I know, right. God bless them.

Pleasence et al (2004) identified that people often experience multiple legal problems at once because of certain characteristics, thereby making them more vulnerable. These may include having a disability, a low income, or being unemployed. As such, it has been argued that providing 'timely assistance' with such matters may reduce the likelihood of more problems arising. This often proves difficult, particularly within the legal aid remit, as it becomes very difficult to deal with the 'problem clusters', as identified by Pleasence et al (2004), when lawyers are already on a budget from one specific legal problem, let alone multiple. Additionally, dealing with wider moral issues likewise raises questions over the professional ethics – and boundaries – of the lawyers in this field. Boon (2004: 250) argues that lawyers face 'twin pillars' of legal ethics; on the one hand, the 'principle of neutrality' means that 'they take clients, irrespective of the moral worth of their cause'; on the other hand, the 'principle of partisanship' necessitates them to act 'to the best of their ability or, in some formulations, zealously'. Boon (2004) therefore argues that 'cause lawyers'[1] are placed in a morally ambiguous position in which they deviate somewhat from traditional notions of justice, but likewise sometimes seek personal commitment with clients. As Boon (2001) reasons, 'transgressiveness' distinguishes 'cause lawyering', or legal aid lawyering, from the wider lawyering remit, as it relates to the degree to which the lawyer is willing to 'take sides' with clients representative of unpopular causes (Scheingold and Bloom, 1998: 212). The work of the lawyers in this research similarly 'demands adaptation to the circumstances of representation, including degrees of commitment to the purposes of clients … some of which may involve challenging conventional professional expectations' (Scheingold and Bloom, 1998: 267). However, Dehaghani and Newman (2021: 11) argue that: 'The ideal lawyer will forge good relations, providing a figure that can be trusted to listen to and support those suspected and accused of crimes'. In this sense, Marcus (housing) argues that it was always necessary to put the client first and he always seeks to maintain this ideal, as that is what the job requires him to do. This requirement, however, often blurs the lines between neutrality and partisanship, and this becomes a central feature of their role. As Bond (2004: 266) further notes: 'The ideal type cause lawyer selects clients but is guided by the moral imperative of the cause rather than their interests'.

Concerns have been raised, given LASPO, over the ability to continue offering holistic services, and helping the clients out with such matters may not be entirely in the lawyers' hands anymore. Reflecting on rapid changes within the legal aid field, Marcus (housing) explained that it is now more sensible to go ahead with a case on the basis 'that you might not be able to get quite as attached emotionally and physically as you did before to the client if they are in a position of great need; you have to be even more detached nowadays'. Marcus's comment, however, is somewhat paradoxical. When a solicitor is on duty in court, each appointment is no

1 'Cause lawyering denotes the practice of law by those committed to furthering through the upholding of a particular cause by legal means, the aims of the good society' (Sarat and Scheingold, 2001:1).

longer than, roughly, 10–15 minutes. This leaves little time for the lawyer to get attached; however, the length of the meeting matters less than the hurdles to be cleared because of changes to legal aid. The amount of paperwork required for any application has increased due to bureaucratic processes, as outlined in Chapter 6. As a result, lawyers now spend most of their time carrying out administrative tasks as opposed to interacting with the client. The Legal Aid Agency has made accessing legal aid through their online portal far more onerous, as they are now much stricter in the way that they assess applications. According to Karen (director), the Legal Aid Agency has made everything far more complex; the amount of information required to open a matter is 'ridiculous', and the system itself often 'keeps cases pending for weeks and weeks'. This proved to be problematic for several respondents in this research, including Marcus, John, and Jay (housing), as well as Paul (criminal barrister), who argued that efficiency now completely overrides quality in their services, which fundamentally challenges the idea of being able to provide a holistic service. Most dangerous perhaps is, as Paul further outlined, the broader sense of 'social demotivation' across the board. Those within the field are beginning to question their fundamental purpose; a theme that has been very evident from the start.

Vicarious trauma

Increasing pressures can also exacerbate the emotional toll of the work on the lawyers. This can be problematic, as legal aid work is typically both sensitive and emotional. Working in the sector requires an emotional component that goes beyond typical feelings caused by working practices, due to the nature of the cases and the clients. Therefore, this necessitates a form of emotional labour. Hochschild (1983: 7) defines emotional labour as 'the management of feeling to create a publicly observable facial and bodily display'. The legal aid lawyer is not only required to have face-to-face contact with their client, but is also required to have a form of emotional state that he/she has some control over. Emotional labour is further defined as the ability to 'induce or suppress feeling to sustain the outward countenance that produces the proper state of mind in others' (Hochschild, 1983: 7).

The cases that legal aid lawyers deal with span, and invoke, a range of emotional issues that cannot be displayed in front of clients. Drawing on this, Sophie (criminal solicitor) spoke about the private struggles she faces when dealing with challenging cases: 'At first, I used to just go home and absolutely sob my heart out about cases I had dealt with that day, but you can't live like that. After a while, you begin to learn how to manage these a bit better – but it's still so *so* hard!' (her emphasis). Hochschild (1983) identifies two approaches: 'surface acting' and 'deep acting'. The former is the ability to deceive others about what one is feeling so as to be able to respond in the right manner. The latter is the ability to encourage or self-induce feelings to produce the desired emotion for the sake of the audience (Hochschild, 1983; Stanislavski, 1965). Individuals such as Maddie (crime) often found it difficult to balance their emotions because 'we often have to work with our heads, and not our hearts because sadly we cannot always give the answer that our clients are looking for'. She went on to state that this has been made far worse by the cuts to legal aid, as 'even though sometimes we know that there will be very little chance of getting legal aid funding, we still must maintain a positive manner for the sake of the clients'. This is made even more difficult within the context of legal aid work, as the clients tend to be in positions of absolute desperation, as further confirmed by Maddie. Goffman's dramaturgical framework (1959) employs the image of a theatrical performance to offer an insight into face-to-face interactions. Goffman uses the terms 'frontstage' and 'backstage' to capture all elements of interaction in a social situation. For example, 'frontstage' refers to the use of impression management to present to the audience in the best possible manner, while 'backstage' refers to a place that is only inhabited by the performer. Maddie admits that she particularly struggles to hide her emotions from her clients sometimes, and therefore must work hard to maintain an 'appropriate and professional front' when facing sensitive cases within the remit of criminal law – such as cases of abuse, sexual assaults, and those involving young children, to name just a few.

Goffman further argues that one can 'take off' and 'put on' character, and this seems very fitting for someone in Maddie's position. While in front of her clients she acts in a manner that is guided and constrained by her position as a professional, she quickly 'takes off' this character once she is out of that given situation: 'sometimes I have to just take a minute and have a little cry in the toilet'. Grace (criminal solicitor) likewise argued that she sometimes used to 'lay awake at night thinking about these kinds of cases if she had come across them on that given day'. To this end, as evidenced in the research carried out by Scott and Freckelton (2024: 12), it is 'reasonably foreseeable' that lawyers could potentially face psychiatric harm from the vicarious trauma that they experience. As opposed to their private counterparts, as Phil (criminal barrister) maintains, 'quite often we are required to go above and beyond legal obligations which can mean that we are exposed to a lot of difficult situations to deal with both emotionally and physically'. Maddie, a criminal solicitor, further builds on this to say that, while in the private world you would 'have strong occupational health and support networks inbuilt within the workplace', in the context of legal aid this is not the case, due to significant funding issues and official support systems. It is therefore vital that those working in the field have a form of emotional outlet, justifying the need for the 'shared orientation'. Offering more of a holistic service can likewise be very emotionally debilitating for legal aid practitioners. Respondents expressed concern over not being able to help their clients holistically because sometimes it is impossible to draw that line professionally. In this context, the emotional burden becomes too much to manage. As Rhiannon (welfare) put it:

> Sometimes there is nothing you can do for the client; they've used up every chance, and you know the next step for the client is probably going to be a life on the street – and that's the worst situation because we get people who, you know, ... there's just nothing we can do to physically help them, and they're going round and round in the system, and there's nothing more, and that is absolutely heart-breaking because they are just trapped in a cycle. The emotional toll is so hard to manage.

Rhiannon stressed that there is very little formal emotional support within her firm, so managing the emotionality of her work can be even more difficult and isolating. As highlighted earlier, however, a form of working culture can be a particularly useful as a tool to 'vent' or to further 'release' any emotions to others in the field that 'you trust and can confide in', especially in situations when you are faced with difficult colleagues. As the findings show, resilience is critical in this field. Having some form of 'camaraderie' with colleagues can be the emotional outlet that is needed when dealing with ongoing traumas. Robert (criminal solicitor) placed particular emphasis on this within the criminal sector: 'otherwise defence lawyers get absolutely no emotional release whatsoever and, frankly, that is just not ok'. The impact of not having any emotional support or outlet can take its toll in the form of occupational burnout. Burnout refers to 'a persistent, negative, work-related state of mind in "normal" individuals which is primarily characterised by exhaustion, which is accompanied by distress, a sense of reduced effectiveness, decreased motivation, and the development of dysfunctional attitudes and behaviours at work' (Schaufeli and Enzmann, 1998: 19). Brotheridge and Grandey (2002) explored the impact of two types of emotional labour as predictors of burnout. They looked at 'job-focused emotional labour' as well as 'employee-focused emotional labour'. The former relates to work demands and the latter to the regulation of feelings. In line with the work of Hochschild (1983), one of the most significant contributors to burnout for legal aid lawyers is the role of 'surface acting' as it ultimately leads to emotional exhaustion. Rachel (housing solicitor and partner) stated that, for her, having that constant feeling of guilt of always having to try and put on a brave face was a constant strain. Likewise, as Grace (criminal solicitor) reasoned, having to respond in an emotionally suppressed manner to her clients, particularly in the case of very sensitive cases, can lead to very high levels of occupational stress. She further stated that this emotional toll places an 'immense weight of pressure' on the lawyer themselves as they are having to always act in a manner that deviates from their natural human emotional response. Maslach and Jackson (1981) identify three features of burnout, including emotional exhaustion, depersonalization, and diminished personal accomplishment.

Ultimately burnout is a crucial concept to consider, as this can ultimately affect how employees carry out their work. Exhaustion combined with low workplace support can collectively lead to occupational burnout, to the point that this can have long-term ramifications on the individuals working within that given environment. This is evidenced in a response from Ash (immigration solicitor): 'Some days, I want to absolutely give up. I get so exhausted that I just can't cope, you know, then I don't perform in the way that I should, and it is just a vicious circle'. This coincides with Maslach and Jackson's (1981) three stages of burnout. Evidence of burnout can be seen in this research, not only because of the emotional demands due to the work's holistic underpinnings, but also due to increasing workloads and restrictions on time. For example, James (criminal solicitor), argued that, because of the increased bureaucracy and the increased level of admin required, often 'you really struggle to feel that you have accomplished anything. There's just no time'. As further evidenced in the extract taken from my field notes below, due to the frantic nature of legal aid work, it is not surprising that this can take its toll on those working in the field. Time is so restricted that this can impede the work of the lawyer, particularly within the duty solicitor scheme, which has an 80 per cent success rate, as further stressed by Marcus (housing solicitor). More than this, behind every client seen through the duty solicitor scheme is a different human tale. Marcus further alludes to this as being 'an element of thrill' as you do not know who is going to turn up next, which he found quite exciting. At the same time, Marcus argued that time is one of the biggest negatives of being a legal aid lawyer.

While the disorganization of time and spontaneity are both pivotal to the work, this can lead to a lack of secure work-based identity and professional diminishment due to the lack of instrumentality within the day-to-day running of the role. However, Grace (criminal solicitor) enjoyed having no shadow of the future hanging over her in this sense. She enjoyed the temporal, short-term nature of her work, saying it 'keeps her on her toes'. Arguably, legal aid lawyers have never had a linear time structure as their work has always been very much short term in its nature, and this is true of lawyers more generally.

Summary: Is 'do-gooding' still feasible?

Given that legal aid lawyering has previously provided impetus and means to address broader social issues, there are limits as to what is achievable considering the funding cuts. The consequences that the reductions in funding have had on the lived experience of those working within the field have been highly detrimental as they begin to take their toll both emotionally and physically. While those in this sample pool are facing significant hurdles to being able to practise holistically, surprisingly, within their aspirations, they still attempt to cling very tightly to the holistic imperative. While the fiscal cuts continue to batter the system, vitally the humanistic motivations remain just as compelling as they were before, despite the more detached lawyer–client relationship. A wider gap has been created between the lawyers' aspirations and practice, though they still typically uphold a desire to 'do good', as evidenced throughout. At the same time, the legal aid profession is being squeezed by external pressures restricting their day-to-day practice and their further capacity to address the wider social need, despite the status and need of the clients remaining the same. Nonetheless, Marcus (housing solicitor), given this, stresses the absolute need for a holistic approach to be maintained:

> Saving that home is key because if you don't do it, that family and that person is potentially street homeless, or they're sofa surfing, or at best in the private sector and the amount of money they will spend on, you know, moving and accommodation will really affect their life chances and you can just see how their lives will go completely downhill. You'll then struggle at work, your kids' education will be affected, and it's like sliding doors, you know, where you have this moment, this moment where your life can change and that often is the possession proceedings, you know, and you lose absolutely everything … that's why it's so important to fight hard for it, and why the lack of legal aid provision in the area can be so *so* devastating. [his emphasis]

Jay (housing), a colleague of Marcus, reasoned that it can even be down to a simple thing like knowing beforehand when to put in certain applications and, unless you have the chance to be advised by a duty solicitor, you will not know what to do. For example, he states: 'if you don't make an application for support or your housing cost by the time you reach your first hearing, even if the court has the discretion to save you, it will just be an outright possession order … and that's just the attitude the judges tend to take'. Without legal advice, those most in need are often completely unaware of the legal consequences that could occur if legal proceedings are not carried out correctly. Marcus's response sums this up nicely: 'You're the only person standing between these people and disaster. You could ignore it and just go to the pub, but it's *always* on your conscience. You at least want the satisfaction that you did everything you could and had the chance to save that client'.

This notion encapsulates the profound character that some legal aid lawyers possess. While sharing these narratives highlights the complexities of working within such a precarious world, importantly, by doing so, it also gives voice to those who seek to maintain a strong sense of altruism within an otherwise economizing profession. Yet, while it is of the utmost importance to show the encouraging and heartening side to legal aid lawyering, as has been done in the previous sections, addressing the undesirable or adverse features of the day-to-day working lives of these individuals is just as important.

In line with the work of Newman (2013), what is suggested here is that, to some extent, there were competing narratives between the interview and ethnographic data. This demonstrates further the ever-widening gap between the aspirations and reality of practice among legal aid lawyers. For example, Marcus stresses the absolute need for a holistic approach, but this was not implemented in every client meeting I observed. In some cases, I witnessed him very swiftly rushing through the legal matters to move onto the next client, without taking any time to make sure the client was ok. This tended to be on the busier days during court duty service, where he had eight or more clients. This evidences that where time is restricted because of limited legal aid allocation this can have an adverse effect on how practice occurs in reality. On one occasion, I observed James making a phone call to a client who was in prison. Due to technical difficulties, the line kept cutting out and, rather than persisting to keep ringing back, James gave up after the second attempt because he did not have the time. Rachel also cancelled a couple of client meetings while I was at Silverman and Co because she had other clients who she thought would be more likely to be granted legal aid funding. Tom (housing solicitor) likewise maintained a very blunt manner in his meetings with clients and said outright if he thought the client had no chance. In most cases, he was not even willing to attempt to get funding for these individuals as he knew how onerous the task would be. Clients were turned down at least once a day. Perhaps the ability to refuse cases is only feasible within the housing sector, however, as 80 per cent of housing matters are legal aid funded and therefore the demand for it is excessively high.

This section has likewise highlighted that many have had to sacrifice the broader holistic elements of their roles, which has unsurprisingly attracted a lot of pessimism not only among those practising, but also the clients, as their access to justice becomes increasingly restricted, as stressed by Marcus (housing solicitor). Undoubtedly, due to limitations on services, the professional marginality of the legal aid lawyer has been accentuated to the extent that the lawyers are becoming increasingly detached from their clients. 'Just getting by' in the profession, as stressed by Nicholas (criminal solicitor), is now the fundamental focus day-to-day, as otherwise 'it can be too much to take on as we are only human after all'.

Despite this, legal aid lawyering's existence is still noticeably underpinned by the legal aid lawyers' enduring actions in supporting their clients in a lot of cases. In many instances, the lawyers' concerns with making their work 'client-centred', and their subsequent enthusiasm for 'do-gooding', is very evident in the examples that have been given, as is their dedication to their roles in spite of being on a sinking ship. In their compelling narratives, from stopping people committing suicide to acting as a resource for the unemployed or homeless, several of these individuals embody and maintain the quest to 'uplift society' in some way or form, despite the inherent complexities of the work and associated vicarious traumas. While some participants did more 'talking' than 'walking', in the sense that the lawyers were not always able to live up to the way they wanted to work, they were still committed to it. To this end, the moral alignment of the work is what keeps people going, and that is very much shared across the board. But, to keep that moral imperative going, a strong collaborative 'working culture' is needed in order to cope with the emotionally heavy work and vicarious trauma that can accompany working with legally aided clients. This justifies the 'shared orientation' conceptualization well.

8

Concluding Remarks: Revisiting the 'Shared Orientation' Model

It is not unusual to see criminal barristers being mentioned in the news. They have been at the forefront of public media vilification for the past two decades, and Tony Blair's branding of lawyers as 'fat cats' in 2001 has been lurking around ever since. For most people, the thought of barristers striking may seem absurd. Yet, people continue to confuse work publicly funded by the state (legal aid) with privately funded work, and this book has fundamentally called for a clear separation and conceptualization to be made. Following the industrial action by rail workers and junior doctors, barristers practising in criminal legal aid followed suit over a long-running dispute over their lack of pay. Members of the Criminal Bar Association (CBA) – a body that represents all practising barristers in England and Wales – have rejected a proposed 15 per cent pay increase from the government following an independent criminal legal aid review, arguing that it is just not enough. As a reminder, barristers involved in legal aid work at the start of their careers receive an average salary of just £12,200 after expenses, chambers' rent, clerks' fees, tax, insurance, and travel. This could not be further from the 'fat-cat' image presented, in contrast to the 'church-mice' reality of those working in the legal aid field. The public side of the profession has undoubtedly been surviving on barristers' commitment to justice and goodwill, and it is now creaking more than ever, as the lawyers continue to hold onto their altruistic imperative. To the public, the profession has always been seen as elite and well-paid. But the stark reality is far from this when it comes to legal aid work. The iconic gown, wig, and briefcase do not always represent a privileged position; rather, this uniform continues to conceal the austere reality. While not all superheroes wear capes, in this case they do. In a system that is designed to deliver 'justice for all', defence remains pivotal. If the government will not take sufficient responsibility and educate the public on the stark differences between publicly and privately funded legal work, then the legal aid practitioners themselves must take matters into their own hands in an attempt to uphold the very heart of justice. Defunding of public services is so ubiquitous in today's society that it has lost its bite. But it is so incredibly important not to overlook this less recognized area for, if the system fails, access to justice is denied for many and the rule of law is simply not upheld.

This exploration has been driven by these considerations, as well as the often hidden nature of the legal aid world. This book therefore critically analyzes and catalogues the interviewee narratives to shed light on the complex nature of the field in question. It is hoped that, by unlocking the door to the legal aid world, a deeper understanding of their work will inform academic, political, and public remits alike. This study was the first of its kind – to bring criminal justice and social welfare work – as well as solicitors and barristers together in one up-to-date exploration of working practice. Typically, research on legal aid lawyering has tended to separate different legal aid specialisms and/or areas of practice. The choice not to do this has enhanced the overall analysis and allowed for commonalities to be drawn across a diverse field. Consequently, a much fuller discussion has been developed. Legal aid lawyers have traditionally been both understudied and overlooked; however, they remain an essential part of the very mechanics of justice. By revealing the hidden world of the legal aid lawyer, this research has contributed to the broader socio-legal field, and wider literatures on the study of work, culture, justice, and altruism.

The preceding chapters have assessed the field in a threefold manner. The research presented throughout this book locates the complex and nuanced interactions between the socio-economic backdrop, the legal aid occupation, and the legal aid lawyer across the macro, micro and meso levels. In addition, it has explored the social milieu of the legal aid world in terms of personnel, modes of operation, and positionality within the wider legal profession. The macro, meso, and micro levels together have helped to produce an overview of the legal aid terrain, which would not have been encapsulated if each level was explored in isolation. In order to successfully capture the world of the legal aid lawyer, and seek to bring the field to light, all three levels must be addressed more.

This threefold framework likewise facilitated the discovery of the new conceptual lens, entitled the 'shared orientation' model, which offers a new way of understanding the ways in which work and culture interact in a rocky occupational field. This acted as a key conceptual model for the basis of this book and anchored the entire exploration. It is hoped that, going forward, this model might speak to other fragmented professions. Bearing that in mind, this final chapter highlights and offers final reflections on the key findings that emerge from this book, as well as their implications. Reflecting further on this book's contributions to broader academic literature, this chapter will then conclude with suggestions for future research. It is hoped that this research can ultimately benefit other 'professions' that are in similarly precarious and overlooked states.

Research summary

Capturing a snapshot of a depleted and diminishing occupational group provides a precious resource to aid in understanding and contributing to what it means to be a liberal professional in the 21st century in the legal context. Increasingly, those working with the field face precariousness as they attempt to cling onto legal aid contracts, resulting in uncertainty, instability, vulnerability, and insecurity. In the context of increasingly diminishing legal aid workplaces, however, observing labour under precarious working conditions is a matter that does not attract the attention it deserves. While the individualized legal aid lawyer is presented here as a precarious worker facing marginalization and fragmentation, it is through their 'shared orientation' that they can maintain and attempt to cling on to their ideal occupation to challenge and overcome wider tactics of austerity. Fundamentally, the 'shared orientation' acts as a meso-level catalyst to manage macro-level threats, which in turn affects how legal aid lawyers go about their everyday micro practice

The opening of this book presented a composite character who highlighted the plight of the legal aid lawyer. The purpose of this was to capture the nuances of the role in terms of expectations, sacrifices, and outcomes, while indicating how personal and professional identities and values overlap. An additional intention was to outline clearly some of the complex aspects of the findings in a dynamic and applied manner, thus communicating the core elements of the data in a more accessible format. This makes an original methodological contribution, and therefore set up the remainder of the book nicely.

After a discussion, in Chapters 2 and 3, of the research context and the biographies of the participants in this research, Chapters 4, 5, and 6 addressed the consequences of the reductions in funding and services on the lived experience of the legal aid lawyer, as well as their working identities. Advancing understanding has paved way for the construction and development of a fresh, yet original, perspective on the changing legal aid world, by capturing changing working practices on the ground level – something that has been very much overlooked in the past. This has resulted in the ability to offer a new conceptual lens to aid understanding going forward.

Research findings

Establishing that the legal aid lawyer is situated in the position of a precarious worker, this research investigated the changing nature of what it means to be a lawyer in light of the cuts to legal aid funding, following the implementation of LASPO 2012 (and additional consultations across the board). Close attention has been paid to the effects that reductions in funding and services have had on the 'lived' professional experiences of legal aid lawyers, as well as the relationship between precarity and the lawyers' professional identities. The experiences of the 30 professionals interviewed for this research, as well as those encountered within the ethnographic fieldwork, while each unique, can nonetheless be categorized into broader themes. The findings suggest that the legal world operates like, and should be viewed through, a vocational lens, given its multifaceted, socially-driven, and professionally marginalized status, which contrasts with its private counterparts. The identity work of the legal aid lawyer is multifunctional. Within their role, they are expected to adapt as a precarious worker as they are forced to take on multiple roles that would have traditionally been occupied by paralegals or administrative assistants. The meaning they attribute to their profession, however, as stressed by the participants in this sample, consists of a fragmented identity, adopting the roles of 'a counsellor, doctor, psychiatrist, social worker, and legal aid lawyer', which gives them meaning considering the constrained macro picture, which is slowly causing ever more destruction.

Beyond this, shedding light on the nature of contemporary legal aid work, the capacity for state institutions, professional groups, and individuals to 'do good', this research did just that. More so, it examined how the cuts to funding and provision affect the structural (in)security of white-collar professionals (lawyers) who chose to work in a more altruistically minded as opposed to acquisitive sphere. Crucially, tensions have arisen between the desire to want to 'do good' in a profession that has typically been underpinned by altruistic tendencies, and the capacity for those in the profession to practise in such a way persistently and effectively. The gap between legal aid lawyers' aspirations and the realities of their practice has been widened. This exacerbated existing issues, such as a lack of reward (that is financial and/or social), lack of career progression, restrictions on time to be able to perform their roles, occupational burnout, and increased emotionality due to ongoing vicarious trauma.

This research has provided a cultural exploration of legal work, exploring the ways in which the dynamics of culture and work interact within the post-2012 cuts context. In response to this, a 'shared orientation' conceptual framework has emerged. The framework seeks to offer a new understanding, incorporating the macro, meso and micro levels. The findings outlined the development of a strategy aligned to coping mechanisms. This was explored as a process that allows those in the field to cope in light of broader structural changes, which may variously impede daily practice. Embodying a form of 'shared orientation' encourages cohesion in an otherwise fragmented occupation and allows those within it to affect the more desirable features

Figure 8.1: Threefold analysis evidencing findings on the macro, meso, and micro levels

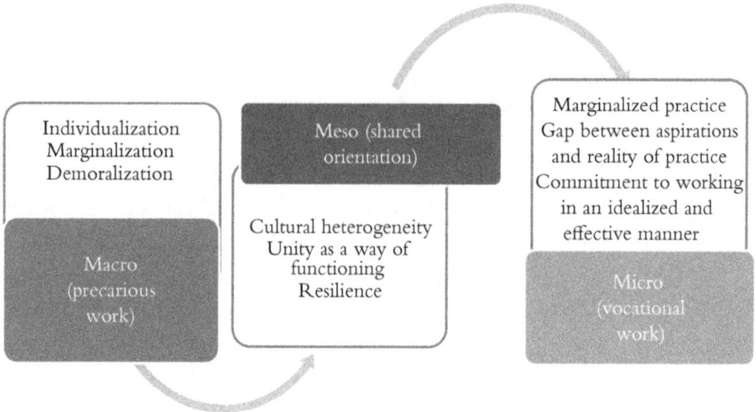

Source: Author's own elaboration.

of their 'ideal' occupation. The findings make an original contribution to knowledge through an assessment of how a framework of 'shared orientation' functions to consolidate individualized labour in adverse circumstances.

The three levels of exploration are summarized in Figure 8.1, which illustrates the research findings in a visual manner:

As shown in Figure 8.1, on the macro level, the legal aid lawyer can be identified as a precarious worker as they face variability and uncertainty, spanning different workplaces, specialisms, job titles, caseloads, and barriers to their work. The field faces further fragmentation and marginalization in the context of the post-2012 cuts. The findings demonstrated that some lawyers remain loyal to their engagement in an 'ideal occupation', as their ability to practise in a humanistic manner allows them to get by in an occupation in which they are otherwise marginalized (in line with the findings of Zaloznaya and Nielsen, 2011). As stated, their work is therefore better understood through a vocational lens, due to the social motivations that drive entry into the field. On the meso level, a working culture in the form of a 'shared orientation' was demonstrated to be of more use in understanding both the nature and response of legal aid lawyering in uncertain times. This cultural mechanism helps to navigate broader macro changes and allows for individuals within the domain to maintain a sense of unity and cohesion. On the micro level, despite their marginalized practice, the lawyers here were seen to hang on to some elements of the 'one-stop shop', extending their efforts in some cases beyond just the legal remit. The data demonstrated how the gap between lawyer aspirations and the reality of practice is widening, which calls for close attention going forward.

The marginalized legal aid lawyer

Findings suggest that the legal aid lawyering profession faces significant marginalization. This is twofold: because of increased pressures on legal aid provision and through occupational marginalization because of disparaging attention from private lawyers, the media, and broader society. Inadequate training and preparation for working within the field, demonstrating that participants are alert to potential failings beyond their control early on in their careers, exacerbate this marginalization. This places them on the peripheries of the profession, as their personal investment and motivations are not matched by professional or institutional provision. Also, while the field is becoming somewhat more diverse, some inequalities in social class, gender, and race remain, particularly within the remit of being a barrister.

As this research found, the most significant motivator for career entry and continuance in the field was the ability to 'do good' or to work for the wider social good. This contrasted with the high level of frustration as the lawyers were being forced to become increasingly detached from their clients, resulting in feelings of being undervalued, frustrated, and powerless to do their jobs. They did so with a degree of resignation and acceptance, as the restriction on their practice was just 'how things are going to be'. Participants in this research were not driven by monetary gain at all due to the low salaries associated with the work, and the remaining participants were working in legal aid by default because of how their specialism was funded. A couple of the participants stated that, if anything, the legally aided element of their work was a significant barrier to their everyday practice. Recognizing what motivates individuals to enter the profession is essential, as the current terrain has the potential to dissuade new recruits.

The research also showed that the participants with altruistic motivations were keen to follow their motivations by putting the client first. While the participants indicated that they enjoyed representing the 'underdog', working for the social good was often visible in more intrinsic ways as opposed to being public facing. For example, those within this sample often just accepted the macro situation and, due to pressure and time restraints, did minimal campaigning on the wider scale against the cuts to legal aid funding. They discussed the issues among their fellow workers to support each other, but remained professional in their approach with an inward-facing front, venting only within the walls of their workplace. This could be attributed to their marginalized position, lack of overall confidence, and the inability of legal aid lawyers to do anything about the situation brought about by broader austerity agendas. As changes to the regulation of the legal profession continue, likewise the future of the work is uncertain, and its formation may significantly alter from how it has traditionally been perceived for centuries (Boon, 2015).

A reconfigured professional identity?

These motivations can be linked to the context in which the legal lawyer works and the impact it has on their professional identities. Wider cuts to funding, combined with the marginalization created as a consequence of increased bureaucracy from the Legal Aid Agency, have resulted in a precarious backdrop. In this research, the 'new' lawyer straddles the chasm between legal and political domains more than ever before, as they are placed in a position where their agency is very much restricted. The cuts to funding came as part of the UK government austerity programme – a fiscal policy that consists of sustained reductions in public funding. As the Ministry of Justice tightens its grip on the Legal Aid Agency, those inside it become increasingly alienated, as the gap between their aspirations and practice gets ever wider, creating a strong sense of structural insecurity. The findings, while limited by the size of the sample group, do suggest some support for the hypotheses outlined by Newman and Welsh (2019: 64), who argue that 'English criminal defence lawyers currently present as alienated workers' as a result of 'structural change – most notably funding cuts and demands for efficiency'. Evidence of this can be seen across both civil and criminal remits in this study; however, further research is undoubtedly needed as macro changes continue to occur.

Not only has the relationship between the lawyer and client changed, but so too has the relationship between the lawyer and the state. The professional status of the legal aid lawyer has been undermined, and they face an even more 'limited professional role' (Katz, 1982). The role is limited in the sense that multi-tasking becomes crucial in an already resource-restricted environment. As argued by Zaloznaya and Nielsen (2011), lawyers are now subject to 'task marginality' whereby those in the field spend far more time doing menial tasks than using their advanced levels of professional and legal skills to help those most at need. This results in extreme frustration, as it inhibits and restricts the ability of the legal professionals to follow their aspirations of working for the social good. An emergent finding was how the professional identity of the legal aid lawyer has weakened in line with alterations to their way of practising. As a result of the unpleasant processes implemented by the Legal Aid Agency, the work is being increasingly dominated by standardized practice. Therefore, the professional advantages of the role are becoming increasingly less. This results in a crisis of professional identity due to a growing antipathy towards the adversarial nature of the work. In line with the work of Boon (2005), this widens the gap between expectations and reality, as the gap between motivations/training and the realities of practice become even vaster. These findings may increasingly make it difficult to attract and retain people in legal aid work.

Confined practice imposed by the Legal Aid Agency further determines and constrains knowledge and practice and has resulted in legal aid lawyers facing a shift in their own autonomy and professionalism. As they are required to carry out more administrative duties, they can be seen to be slipping into roles that are typically seen as being lower middle-class jobs. While lawyers would previously pay other people to write letters and carry out administrative duties on their behalf, restrictions have resulted in the lawyers having to do a lot of these jobs themselves. The combination of low salaries, low social status and disregard for professional skillsets all contribute to the precariousness of the work. The loss of professional independence, as well as the restricted ability of those in the field to carry out the work in the way that mirrors the motivations for many wanting to work in the field in the first place could help drive people out of the field of work. The more resources and time are being squeezed, the more difficult it is to 'do good', undermining the very purpose of legal aid work. Consequently, this contributes to the diminished professional status of the lawyers, which is problematic, as 'lawyers serve an important constitutional importance' (Boon, 2015: 36).

The 'ideal' legal aid lawyer

Besides the difficulty of 'doing good' under the constraints found, this research suggests that legal aid lawyers nevertheless attempted to sustain the 'ideal' legal aid lawyer identity. The participants remained positive, as the desire to continue to 'do good' remained important. The legal aid lawyer's deep engagement with their clients and wider social justice orientations simply allow the lawyers to 'make do' in an occupation in which they are otherwise marginalized, not only by their private counterparts but also by broader society. As the findings showed, legal aid lawyers were, therefore, willing to endure personal and professional sacrifices, resulting in practice restriction, occupational burnout, and capped progression. The commitment to working in an effective and idealized manner, demonstrating altruism, resilience, and determination, was evident across both civil and criminal remits alike, and again contributed to the suggestion of viewing the work as a vocation or a 'calling'.

The ability of the lawyers to continue to offer a 'one-stop shop', where the lawyers act as a source of multiple services through which clients can have their legal (and selected other) needs met in just 'one stop', has been somewhat sacrificed. This was indicative of earlier points, such as the widening gap between the aspirations and realities of practice, which, as a result, means the lawyers feel more dispirited. However, the quest to want to continue to fight for justice has been made easier through reliance on group networks. Networking played a significant role to enable the lawyers to connect and communicate virtually as well as in person. Likewise, a stable form of working culture enabled those within the field to cling on to their 'idealized profession', even if it was more fragmented in the realities of practice, speaking to the shared orientation model.

Coping mechanisms

Put simply, this research has demonstrated that the occupational terrain of the legal aid lawyer has changed, and will continue to change, because of the precarity of legal aid provision. Suitable coping strategies need to be identified to help soften the impact of this. Despite the many challenges encountered by participants on their legal aid paths, they were overwhelmingly positive in their pursuit for justice. Participants were resilient and accepted what was happening to the wider macro terrain because they were energized by and engaged with their fellow colleagues on the meso and micro levels – which was remarkable.

The existence of the 'shared orientation' was the solid foundation that allowed the participants to 'get by' on a day-to-day basis. It was as if their individual motivations were no longer significant in isolation but through group connection; the desire to belong and engage in a broader and more integrated network of lawyers was more important. This group element plays an even more significant role in which the professional typically acts as 'a company of one' due to the very individualized nature of the work. A 'shared orientation', or in other words, a legal aid lawyer's way of being, not only captures cultural dissonance among those working in legal aid; but also likewise acts as a coping mechanism and/or an emotional outlet from the wider fragmentation of the role as a result of funding cuts, which prioritizes efficiency over quality. This cultural framework, which is sustained by both teamwork and individualization, likewise attempts to keep the field alive, despite it being stretched at its seams.

The main functions of having a 'shared orientation' are offering unity as a way of functioning in a multifaceted and fragmented occupation; fortifying support systems and collegial relationships in the face of diversity and intense emotionality; transcending occupational boundaries as well as negotiating personal and professional overlap; and as a way of 'finding your feet' beyond the remit of formal education and training. The model fundamentally accommodates the cultural heterogeneity of the legal aid world that traditional models of occupational culture would otherwise overlook, offering a nuanced and more accurate picture. 'Shared orientation' was seen to be passed down from the more experienced lawyers to those newly entering the occupation. Legal aid lawyers chose to maintain this 'shared orientation' as opposed to being *obligated to* uphold a working culture. Legal aid lawyers uphold their working culture and holistic imperative because, on the one hand, they desire to but, on the other, it is imperative to their survival as their work becomes progressively more insecure. While the occupational terrain of the legal aid lawyer has fundamentally – and will continue to be – adversely affected by cuts to funding, the need for them to maintain a strong core and support each other is more necessary than ever. In a field where, typically, the core is hollow as each lawyer follows their own path, building and strengthening this 'shared orientation' is entirely in the hands of the lawyers themselves. It is one of the few mechanisms of control that remains authentic in their world, and valour must come from the ground up given that the terrain is so rocky.

Wider contributions to academic literature and theory

This research has made a definite contribution to the understandings of the 'modern' legal aid lawyer, wider socio-legal literatures on lawyering, and legal cultures, by offering a snapshot of their working world in the post-2012 context. It has also identified several themes found within the theoretical framework that reach out to the wider sociological academic audience. These include the study of professions, white-collar work, precariousness, occupational culture, and altruistic modes of work. Theories of precariousness have been used here to explore the changing nature of a traditionally white-collar, altruistic profession. An original contribution to the study of occupational cultures has been made, as a nuanced and more-fitting framework of how culture and work interact in the legal aid context has emerged. Overall, this book sheds light on a subject matter that is very much aligned with broader political dynamics. This, therefore, offers an insight into what it means to be a middle-class 'liberal' professional in the 21st century.

Broadening out from specific research goals, the findings have also encouraged the need to reflect on wider questions going forward. To what extent have we devalued work? And to what extent have we said that the only work that can be rewarded is financially orientated? The interviewees described a prevailing sense of the devalued nature of working for the common good as bureaucratic practice is prioritized over humanized practice. Moreover, while having the title of being a 'professional' used to give agency to be able to make or implement social change, here we see a significant shift in what it means to work in an altruistic profession. This is a result of the deprofessionalization of key actors within the world of work. The structural insecurity of working in a traditionally altruistic sphere brings to light challenges that are not often faced within the acquisitive sphere. Reward comes in the form of a discourse of 'giving', in the sense that an interaction between the lawyer and the client is not merely just a 'transaction', but rather an emotionally informed reliance on each other.

The portrait of the contemporary legal aid lawyer that has been presented in this research is one that is enveloped with the outward and inward desire to 'do good', yet the effect of austerity continues to question the very nature of this identity. As further evidenced here, working in legal aid requires those within it to have a form of moral obligation to move away from self-interest and to want to help others. As the work becomes increasingly precarious, those within it face meagre rates of pay, occupational burnout, and marginalized practice, which limits the level of client care one can offer. This research has demonstrated that what is needed in the role is the balance between finding a suitable level of altruistic practice and professionalism that fits with the complex nature of modern society and under the umbrella of wider austerity measures. Maintaining a sense of altruism – even if it is in the form of informal mechanisms such as a 'shared orientation'–may help professions to maintain some traditional characteristics, slowing down the trend of deprofessionalization.

Despite this, the way in which economies and governments are changing could mean that the whole question of what it means to be a legal aid lawyer could continue to change drastically and could thus almost become extinct in a generation's time if things continue the way they are. This calls for continued research and attention.

Recommendations for future research

Since this research began, the climate in which legal aid lawyering exists has continued to evolve. This research offered a snapshot between 2016 and 2017, when the fieldwork was carried out and the data was obtained. Due to the changing nature of legal aid provision, research needs to be able to 'keep up' with the ongoing changes to the macro context. There is, therefore, an ongoing need for further research and this needs to happen quickly and fluidly to be able to adapt to the ever-changing landscape. Future research should consider the impact of continued economic change; the effect of the LASPO review recommendations on legal aid; what a legal aid lawyer study with a wider geographical span would look like; what would make a useful piece of client-focused research; and how further study of the 'shared orientation' model should proceed. These would all benefit scholarship within the different areas of legal aid, the legal profession, as well as contributing to work carried out by scholars on occupations and public services generally, but especially under austerity.

In line with this, the Government published a post-implementation review of part 1 of LASPO (February 2019), alongside a separate review of legal aid for inquests, as well as a Legal Support Action Plan that laid out the government's 'vision' of the modern system of legal support as a consequence of LASPO (Justice Gap, 2024). The review sought to assess the extent to which LASPO has met its four original objectives:

1. making significant savings
2. discouraging unnecessary litigation

3. targeting legal aid at those who need it most
4. delivering better value for money.

The overall conclusion is that LASPO was only 'partially' successful in meeting these objectives. While significant savings have been made, evidently this has had serious knock-on effects on the occupation, which has somewhat rationed justice. As noted by the Law Society (2024a), the number of legal aid cases started has dropped by 805 per cent since 2000. In January 2023, the government announced a review of civil legal aid and the report is due any day, but projections from the Law Society (2024a) show that the number of legal aid providers could drop by a third by 2025. A recent review by the National Audit Office (2024) found that the Ministry of Justice had achieved its aim of reducing legal aid spending. Emergent from the report findings, it is vital that legal aid is available to all who are eligible and, until that happens, it is impossible to demonstrate that it is meeting its core objectives and securing value for money. The Law Society (2024a) have called on the government to raise fees by 20 per cent, which would cost £134 million. Change is accompanied with both positive and negative commentary and, while some change may help reform legal aid provision, it may also exacerbate existing problems as there is a 'risk of being seen as just kicking the can down the road' (Bob Neill MP, chair of House of Commons Justice Select Committee, 2020). To this end, legal aid provision is also very much tied up with the political agenda, so as the political landscape faces imminent changes over the coming years, legal aid may go in and out of focus even more so.

The sample for this research was both small and purposive, and simply granted by means of opportunity. While the findings are neither comprehensive nor definitive, they offer a vital snapshot of the occupational world of the legal aid lawyer. A wider geographic span, as well as more prolonged research with more barristers, solicitors, and other professionals within the legal aid backdrop in the form of multisite research, will assist with further understanding of the occupation and the ways in which it both functions and endures in its precarious context. This would benefit both civil and criminal remits. Clients are likewise obvious respondents for further research, as they would offer a different perspective overall. As Rhiannon (welfare solicitor) noted: 'Clients still assume that I'm a big fat cat living in a mansion'. A very different vision may emerge from the clients' perspectives, as they have a very different way of seeing the legal aid world. While lawyers can present themselves in a manner in which they seem fitting, painting an idealized picture, research with clients may reveal further that lawyers 'talk the talk' but do not always 'walk the walk' (Newman, 2013).

The research set out to address the complexity and multifaceted nature of the resource-constrained legal aid world. The ability to look at lawyers practising in both civil and criminal remits allowed for various layers of analysis, which fundamentally helped construct the institutional identities that emerged out of this research. In particular, the extensive sample benefited the construction of the 'shared orientation' model, as it would have been harder to justify if fragments of the profession were explored in isolation. While this meant that the breadth of the field could be explored, likewise depth was achieved due to the threefold analyses. As previously. mentioned, civil lawyers often seek a 'remedy', whereas criminal lawyers often seek to penalize. The findings emergent here were more positive than expected, as previous research has indicated adverse findings. For example, Newman's (2013) ethnographic work on criminal defence lawyers evoked more of a negative outlook on the work. This could be attributed to the fact that he focused on the lawyer–client interaction solely within the remit of criminal defence. Again, this likewise justifies the need to also research from the perspective of the clients as they could paint a different picture to the legal aid lawyers.

Further research is also required into how features of a 'shared orientation' model manifest across the field. While this new conceptual model has been addressed on the surface level here, and its existence is evident, a future study should build on this by further assessing the extent to which the 'shared orientation' is applicable across 'multiple sites' with varying actors. By applying this framework in differing geographic, economic, and demographic backdrops, the extent to which it is both a viable and suitable model to understand the legal aid lawyer's working practice can be assessed. As the macro context becomes precarious to an increasing extent, the ability of 'shared orientation' to withstand external pressures and continue to act as both a response to the lawyer's marginality, as well as a coping mechanism, needs further exploration. A greater understanding of the working culture of the legal aid lawyer is likewise needed to understand further how flexible and adaptive the framework of analysis is, as it is very much in its experimental stages. The model of 'shared orientation' that emerges from this research, as a flexible framework allowing for differing levels of engagement, may prove valuable in the study of other complex occupations that have multiple layers (for example, medicine, social work, or education) as a valuable framework of study where a blanket model of occupational culture may not suit.

Final thoughts

Overall, I believe that this research has met the aims it laid out initially and, as such, offers a valuable contribution to the knowledge on the subject of the legal aid lawyer, and the challenges that are faced in their everyday work. Existing academic work was not able to move us beyond looking at the more specific features of the legal aid world in isolation from each other, whether that be a particular aspect of their work or a specific specialism. The threefold analysis adopted here has encapsulated legal aid work in a detailed and nuanced manner. Legal aid lawyering cannot be explained solely through macro theories of sociology of work and precariousness alone, as this misses out the interactions on the organizational and individual levels. Likewise, without situating the work in the macro context, an accurate and valid representation of the legal aid world would not be given as the cuts permeate every layer of the occupation. Social reality in the context of the lawyer is multifaceted and complex, and therefore such an eclectic approach is needed to give real insight. It is through this threefold model that a richer picture of how precarity and austerity refract down the varying levels of the occupational terrain emerges. The humanity of lawyers is not something that is regularly spoken about. External characteristics are very one-dimensional, and they ignore the day-to-day professional roles. This research has sought to address that. While the individualized legal aid lawyer has been presented here as a precarious worker facing marginalization and fragmentation, it is through their collaboration that they can maintain and attempt to cling on to their ideal occupation in an attempt to challenge wider tactics of austerity. Fundamentally, their shared way of being acts as a meso-level catalyst to manage macro-level threats, which in turn affects how the lawyers go about their everyday micro practice.

To round up, encapsulating this occupational world in full was a hugely daunting task; however, it is a crucial time to have obtained a richer understanding of what it means to be a legal aid lawyer in times of precariousness. While 'fat-cat' narratives continue to conceal the 'church-mice' reality, there has been a slight shift in sentiment recently because of public legal challenges such as Grenfell, COVID-19 and barrister strike action. Yet a change in public perception is urgently needed given the remaining gap between the perception and reality of legal aid work, as well as its broader decomposition. This is also necessary for the future health of the *whole lawyering profession.*[1] Ultimately, as Mary (civil liberties and human rights) states: 'working on the legal aid frontline is still an absolute privilege'.

[1] See also Bleasdale and Francis (2020).

References

Abel RL and Lewis PSC (eds) (1988) *Lawyers in Society: Vol I The Common Law World*. Berkeley: University of California Press.

Abel RL and Lewis PSC (eds) (1989) *Lawyers in Society: Vol III Comparative Theories*. Berkeley: University of California Press.

Abel RL, Sommerlad H, Hammerslev O, and Schultz U (2020) *Lawyers in 21st-Century Societies: Vol 1: National Reports*. Oxford: Hart Publishing.

Abel RL, Sommerlad H, Hammerslev O, and Schultz U (2022) *Lawyers in 21st-Century Societies: Vol 2: Comparisons and Theories*. Oxford: Hart Publishing.

Abel-Smith B and Stevens R (1967) *Lawyers and the Courts: A Sociological Study of the English Legal System 1750–1965*. London: Heinemann.

Allamby L (2019) Sinking not swimming – personal litigants and access to justice. https://lag.org.uk/article/205977/sinking-not-swimming-personal-litigants-and-access-to-justice

Allen TD (2001) Family-supportive work environments: the role of organizational perceptions. *Journal of Vocational Behaviour* 58(3): 414–435.

Andreoni J (1989) Giving with impure altruism: applications to charity and Ricardian equivalence. *Journal of Political Economy* 97(6): 1447–1458.

Atkinson M and Hammersley M (2007) *Ethnography: Principles in Practice*. London: Routledge.

Atkinson P, Coffey A, Delamont S, Lofland J, and Lofland L (2001) *Handbook of Ethnography*. London: SAGE.

Atkinson P and Drew P (1979) *Order in Court: The Organisation of Verbal Interaction in Judicial Settings*. New Jersey: Humanities Press.

Aubert V (1976) The changing role of law and lawyers in nineteenth- and twentieth-century Norwegian society. In DN MacCormick (ed), *Lawyers in Their Social Setting*. Edinburgh: Green: 1–17.

Bach W and Walters C (2018) Cuts to legal aid and courts make a mockery of equal access to justice. https://www.theguardian.com/law/2018/aug/17/cuts-to-legal-aid-and-courts-make-a-mockery-of-equal-access-to-justice

Baldwin J and McConville M (1977) *Negotiated Justice*. London: Martin Robertson.

Bar Council (2023) Access to justice can't survive further budget cuts: new report from the Bar Council. https://www.barcouncil.org.uk/resource/access-to-justice-can-t-survive-further-budget-cuts-new-report-from-the-bar-council.html

Bar Standards Board (2024) Diversity at the Bar 2023. https://www.barstandardsboard.org.uk/static/3c0b96c6-2bef-4584-be7ded60a8747498/Diversity-at-the-Bar-2023Final-Version.pdf

Beck U (1992) *Risk Society: Towards a New Modernity*. London: SAGE.

Beck U (2000) *The Brave New World of Work*. Cambridge: Polity Press.

Becker H (1968) Whose side are we on? *Social Problems* 14(3): 239–247.

Becker H and Geer H (1957) Participant observation and interviewing: a comparison. *Human Organization* 16(3): 28–32.

Bellini A and Maestripieri L (2018) Professions within, between and beyond: varieties of professionalism in a globalising world. *Cambio* 8(16): 5–14.

Bennett W (2001) *The Lawyer's Myth: Reviving Ideals in the Legal Profession*. Chicago: University of Chicago Press.

Binder A, Bergman P, Price S, and Tremblay P (2004) *Lawyers as Counsellors: A Client-centred Approach*. Eagan: West.

Bleasdale L and Francis A (2020) Great expectations: millennial lawyers and the structure of contemporary legal practice. *Legal Studies* 40: 376–396.

Bond S (2004) Organisational culture and work-life conflict in the UK. *International Journal of Sociology and Social Policy* 24(1): 1–24.

Boon A (2001) Cause lawyers in a cold climate: the impact(s) of globalization on the United Kingdom. In A Sarat and S Scheingold (eds), *Cause Lawyering and the State in a Global Era*. Oxford: Oxford University Press: 143–184.

Boon A (2004) Cause lawyers and the alternative ethical paradigm: ideology and transgression. *Legal Ethics* 7(2): 250–268.

Boon A (2002) Ethics in legal education and training: four reports, three jurisdictions and a prospectus. *Legal Ethics* 5(1): 34–67.

Boon A (2005) From public service to service industry: the impact of socialisation and work on the motivation and values of lawyers. *International Journal of the Legal Profession* 12(2) 229–260.

Boon A (2015) *Lawyers Ethics and Professional Responsibility*. Oxford/Portland: Hart Publishing.

Boon A, Flood J, and Webb J (2005) Postmodern profession? The fragmentation of legal education and the legal profession. *Journal of Law and Society* 32(3): 473–492.

Boukalas C (2013) Politics as legal action/ lawyers as political actors: towards a reconceptualisation of cause lawyering. *Social and Legal Studies* 22(3) 395–420.

Bourdieu P and Wacquant L (1992) *An Invitation to Reflexive Sociology*. Cambridge: Polity Press.

Bowcott O (2018) Legal aid: how has it changed in 70 years? *The Guardian*. https://www.theguardian.com/law/2018/dec/26/legal-aid-how-has-it-changed-in-70-years

Bradley K (2019) *Lawyers for the Poor: Legal Advice, Voluntary Action and Citizenship in England 1890–1900*. Manchester: Manchester University Press.

Breger MJ (1982) *Legal Aid for the Poor: A Conceptual Analysis*. Washington DC: Scholarship at Catholic Law.

Brewer JD (2000) *Ethnography*. London: Open University Press.

Brooke H (2016) The history of Legal Aid – 1945–2010. https://sirhenrybrooke.me/2016/07/16/the-history-of-legal-aid-1945-to-2010/

Brotheridge CM and Grandey AA (2002) Emotional labor and burnout: comparing two perspectives of 'people work'. *Journal of Vocational Behavior* 60(1): 17–39.

Cape E (2004) The rise (and fall?) of a criminal defence profession. *Criminal Law Review* (1): 401.

Carlen P (1976) *Magistrates Justice*. London: Martin Robertson and Co.

Carr-Saunders AM and Wilson PA (1986 [1933]) *The Professions*. Oxford: Clarendon Press.

Chamberlayne P, Bornat J, and Wengraf T (eds) (2000) *The Turn to Biographical Methods in Social Science: Comparative Issues and Examples*. Hove: Psychology Press.

Chambliss E (2010) Measuring law firm culture. *Studies in Law, Politics, and Society* 52: 1–31.

Chan J (1996) Changing police culture. *British Journal of Criminology* 36(1): 109–134.

Chan J (2014) Conceptualising legal culture and lawyering stress. *International Journal of the Legal Profession* 21(2): 213–232.

Choonara E (2011) Is there a precariat? *Socialist Review*. http://www.socialistreview.org.uk/article.php?articlenumber=11781

Christensen W and Crank JP (2001) Police work and culture in a nonurban setting: an ethnographical analysis. *Police Quarterly* 4(1): 69–98.

Connelly T (2017) Female barristers granted access to top London court's male-only robing room. *Legal Cheek*. https://www.legalcheek.com/2017/08/female-barristers-granted-access-to-top-london-courts-male-only-robing-room/

Cooke E (2021) The working culture of legal aid lawyers: developing a 'shared orientation model'. *Social and Legal Studies* 3(5) 704–724.

Cooke E (2024) 'Fat cats' versus 'church mice': unveiling legal aid practice from behind the shadows of private legal practice in England and Wales. *Legal Studies*: 1–18. doi: 10.1017/1st.2024.19.

Coutu M (2020) Economic crises, crisis of labour Law? Lessons from Weimar. *Journal of Law and Society* 47(2): 221–239.

Cownie F (2004) *Legal Academics: Cultures and Identities*. Oxford: Hart Publishing.

Criminal Bar Association (2022) Criminal Bar Association – parliamentary briefing. https://www.criminalbar.com/wp-content/uploads/2022/09/CBA-Parliamentary-Briefing-31.8.22.pdf

Crossley M (2000) *Introducing Narrative Psychology*. Buckingham: Open University Press.

Daily Mail (2007) £500,000 lawyer tops legal aid fat cat league. *Daily Mail*. https://www.dailymail.co.uk/news/article-463504/500-000-lawyer-tops-legal-aid-fatcat-league.html

Daily Mail (2011) How crime DOES pay: 500 barristers earning more than the PM. *Daily Mail*. https://www.dailymail.co.uk/news/article-2004915/500-legal-aid-barristers-earning-David-Cameron.html

Daily Mail (2013) Legal aid payouts to fat cat lawyers will be slashed by a third, says Justice Secretary. *Daily Mail*. https://www.dailymail.co.uk/news/article-2306630/Legal-aid-payouts-fat-cat-lawyers-slashed-says-Justice-Secretary.html

Davey JP, Obst PL, and Sheehan MC (2001) It goes with the job: officers' insights into the impact of stress and culture on alcohol consumption within the policing occupation. *Drugs: Education, Prevention and Policy* 8(2): 141–149.

Deal TE and Kennedy AA (2000) *Corporate Cultures*. Reading: Addison-Wesley.

Deering J (2011) *Probation Practice and the New Penology*. London: Routledge.

Dehaghani R and Newman D (2019) Can – and should – lawyers be considered 'appropriate' appropriate adults? *Howard Journal of Crime and Justice* 58(1): 3–24.

Dehaghani R and Newman D (2021) The crisis in legally aided criminal defence in Wales: bringing Wales into discussions of England and Wales. *Legal Studies* 41: 365–384.

Dehaghani R and Newman D (2022) Criminal legal aid and access to justice: an empirical account of a reduction in resilience. *International Journal of the Legal Profession* 29(1): 33–52.

Denvir C, Kinghan J, Mant J, and Newman D (2023) *Legal Aid and the Future of Access to Justice*. London: Bloomsbury Publishing.

Denzin NK and Lincoln YS (2011) *The SAGE Handbook of Qualitative Research*. London: SAGE.

Dingwall D and P Lewis (eds) (1983) *The Sociology of the Professions*. Hampshire: Macmillan Press.

Duff E, Shiner M, Boon A, and Whyte A (2000) *Entry into the Legal Professions: Law Student Cohort Study*. Law Society Research Study No 29. London: The Law Society.

Dukes R and Streeck W (2020) Labour constitutions and occupational communities: social norms and legal norms at work. *Journal of Law and Society* 47(4): 612–638.

Durkheim É (1950) *Leçons de sociologie: physique des moeurs et du droit*. Paris: Presses Universitaires de France. Foreword by H. N. Kubali; Introduction by G. Davy.

Durkheim É (1957) *Professional Ethics and Civic Morals*. London: Routledge.

Egetenmeyer R, Breitschwerdt L, and Lechner R (2018) From 'traditional professions' to 'new professionalism': a multi-level perspective for analysing professionalisation in adult and continuing education. *Journal of Adult and Continuing Education* 25(1): 11.

Emerson RM, Fretz RI, and Shaw LL (1995) *Writing Ethnographic Fieldnotes*. Chicago: University of Chicago Press.

Erlanger HS and Klegon DA (1976) Socialisation affects of professional school: the law school experience and student orientations to public interest concerns. *Law and Society Review* (13): 11.

Evetts J (2003) The sociological analysis of professionalism. Occupational change in the modern world. *International Sociology* 18(2): 395–415.

Ferrell J (1997) Criminological verstehen: inside the immediacy of crime. *Justice Quarterly* 14(1): 3.

Ferrell J (2015) Cultural criminology as method and theory. In J Miller and WR Palacios (eds), *Qualitative Research in Criminology*. Routledge: New York.

Ferrell J and Hamm MS (1998) *Ethnography at the Edge. Crime, Deviance, and Field Research*. Boston: University Press of New England.

Fielding NG (2011) Judges and their work. *Social and Legal Studies* 20(1): 97–115.

Fleck J and Francis R (2021) *Vicarious Trauma in the Legal Profession: A Practical Guide to Trauma, Burnout and Collective Care*. London: Legal Action Group.

Flood J (1987) Anatomy of lawyering: an ethnography of a corporate law firm. PhD Dissertation. Evanston: Northwestern University.

Flood J (2013) *What Do Lawyers Do? An Ethnography of a Corporate Law Firm*. New Orleans: Quid Pro Books.

Forbess A (2022) Redistribution dilemmas and ethical commitments: advisers in austerity Britain's local welfare state. *Ethnos* 87(1): 52–74.

Ford J (2017) Legal aid, judicial review and the fight for justice. *New Law Journal*. https://www.newlawjournal.co.uk/content/legal-aid-judicial-review-fight-justice

Fouzder M (2018) Criminal defence solicitors facing extinction. *Law Society Gazette*, 17 April. https://www.lawgazette.co.uk/practice/criminal-defence-solicitors-facing-extinction/5065695.article

Francis A (2005) Legal ethics, the marketplace and the fragmentation of legal professionalism. *International Journal of the Legal Profession* 12(2): 173–200.

Francis A (2015) Legal education, social mobility, and employability: possible selves, curriculum intervention, and the role of legal work experience. *Journal of Law and Society* 42(2): 173–201.

Francis A and others (2017) *Lawyers in Society: England and Wales Country Report* (Law and Society Association International Meeting, Mexico City, June).

Francis AM (2004) Out of touch and out of time: lawyers, their leaders and collective mobility within the legal profession. *Legal Studies* 3(24): 322–348.

Francis Wilks & Jones (2019) Fixed fee retainer agreement. https://www.franciswilksandjones.co.uk/fixed-fee-retainer-agreements/#:~:text=Fixed%20fee%20solution%20provided%20by%20Francis%20Wilks%20%26%20Jones&text=For%20example%2C%20we%20could%20agree,agreement%20to%20a%20minimum%20term

Friedman LM (1989) Law, lawyers, and popular culture. *Yale Law Journal* 98(8): 1579–1606.

Friedson E (1973) *The Professions and Their Prospects*. Beverly Hills: Sage Publications.

Geldart W (1995) *Introduction to English Law*. Oxford: Oxford University Press.

Giddens A (1991) *Modernity and Self-Identity: Self and Society in the Late Modern Age*. Stanford: Stanford University Press.

Goffman E (1956) *The Presentation of Self in Everyday Life*. New York: Anchor Books.

Goffman E (1990 [1959]) *The Presentation of Self in Everyday Life*. St Ives: Penguin Books.

Goffman E (1967) *The Nature of Deference and Demeanour' in Interaction Ritual: Essays on Face-to-Face Behaviour*. New York: Pantheon Books.

Gosling GC (2017) Gender, money and professional identity: Medical social work and the coming of the British National Health Service. *Women's History Review* 27(2): 310–328.

Goulandris A (2020) *The Enterprising Barrister: Organisation, Culture and Changing Professionalism*. London: Bloomsbury Publishing.

Gouldner A (1968) The sociologist as partisan: sociology and the welfare state. *American Sociologist* 3(2): 103–116.

Granfield R (2007) The meaning of pro bono: institutional variations in professional obligations among lawyers. *Law and Society Review* 41(1): 113–146.

Green BA (2016) The lawyer as lover: are courts romanticizing the lawyer–client relationship. *Touro Law Review* 32: 139.

Griffiths J (1986) What is legal pluralism? *Journal of Legal Pluralism* 24: 1–55.

Guba EG and Lincoln YS (1994) Competing paradigms in qualitative research. In NK Lincoln (ed), *Handbook of Qualitative Research*. London: Sage: 105–117.

Hamilton M (2021) The fat cat lawyers will be banned from mounting last-ditch appeals to stop foreign criminals being booted out of Britain. *The Sun*. https://www.thesun.co.uk/news/14332061/ban-appeals-to-stop-foreign-criminals-deportations/

Harper D and Lawson D (eds) (2003) *The Cultural Study of Work*. New York: Rowman and Littlefield.

Harrington B and Seabrooke L (2020) Transnational professionals. *Annual Review of Sociology* 46: 317–337.

Harvey D (2006) *A Brief History of Neoliberalism*. Oxford: Oxford University Press.

Heidensohn F (1992) *Women in Control? The Role of Women in Law Enforcement*. Oxford: Oxford University Press.

Heinz J and Laumann E (1982) *Chicago Lawyers: The Social Structure of the Bar*. New York/Chicago: American Bar Foundation/Russell Sage Foundation.

Heinz J, Nelson R, Sandefur R, and Laumann E (2005) *Urban Lawyers: The New Social Structure of the Bar*. Chicago: University of Chicago Press.

Henry S (1983) *Private Justice*. London: Routledge.

Heyes A (2005) The economics of vocation or 'why is a badly paid nurse a good nurse? *Journal of Health Economics* 24(1): 561.

HMCTS (2021) HMCTS weekly management information during coronavirus: March 2020 to February 2021. https://www.gov.uk/government/statistical-data-sets/hmcts-weekly-management-information-during-coronavirus-march-2020-to-february-2021

Hochschild AR (1979) Emotion work, feeling rules, and social structure. *American Journal of Sociology* 85: 551–575.

Hochschild AR (1983) *The Managed Heart: Commercialisation of Human Feeling*. London: University of California Press.

Hodson R (2001) *Dignity at Work*. Cambridge: Cambridge University Press.

Holdaway S (1983) *Inside the British Police: A Force at Work*. Oxford: Basil Blackwell.

House of Commons Justice Select Committee (2020) Coronavirus (COVID-19): the impact on the legal professions in England and Wales: Seventh Report of Session 2019–21. https://committees.parliament.uk/publications/2227/documents/26119/default/

Hunter R, Roach A, and Mack K (2016) Judging in lower courts: conventional, procedural, therapeutic and feminist approaches. *International Journal of Law in Context* 12(3): 337–360.

Hynes S and Robins J (2009) *The Justice Gap. Whatever Happened to Legal Aid?* London: Legal Action Group.

Johnson E (1980–81) Lawyers' choice: a theoretical appraisal of litigation investment decisions. *Law and Society Review* (1): 15.

Johnson SD, Koh HC, and Killough LN (2009) Organizational and occupational culture and the perception of managerial accounting terms: an exploratory study using perceptual mapping techniques. *Contemporary Management Research* 5(4): 317–342.

Jorgensen MB (2015) Precariat – what it is and isn't – towards an understanding of what it does. *Critical Sociology* 42(7–8): 959–975.

Jupp V (1989) *Methods of Criminological Research*. London: Unwin Hyman.

Justice Gap, The (2024) Criminal legal aid firms warn of 'mass rejection' of new contracts due to serious concerns about fees. *The Justice Gap*. thejusticegap.com/criminal-legal-aid-firms-warn-of-mass-rejection-of-new-contracts-due-to-serious-concerns-about-fees/

Kadushin A (1962) A study of adoptive parents of hard-to-place children. *Social Casework* 43: 227–233.

Katz J (1982) *Poor People's Lawyers in Transition*. New Brunswick: Rutgers University Press.

Kemp V (2010) *Transforming Legal Aid: Access to Criminal Defence Services*. London: Ministry of Justice.

Kinghan J (2021) *Lawyers, Networks and Progressive Social Change: Lawyers Changing Lives*. Oxford: Hart Publishing.

Kivell NM, Evans SD, and Paterson SE (2017) Community power structure analysis and the ethical considerations of 'studying up'. *American Journal of Community Psychology* 60(34): 467–475.

Koltonski D (2018) Vocations, exploitation, and professions in a market economy. *Social Theory and Practice* 44(3): 323–347.

Korczynski M (2003) Communities of coping: collective emotional labour in service work. *Organization* 10(1): 55–79.

Krieger L (2004–05) The inseparability of professionalism and personal satisfaction: perspectives on values, integrity and happiness. *Clinical Law Review*: 425.

Krieger L and Sheldon K (2015) What makes lawyers happy: a data-driven prescription to redefine professional success. *George Washington Law Review*: 554.

Kronman A (1993) *The Lost Lawyer*. Cambridge: Belknap Press.

Kuna S and Nadiv R (2018) Divided we stand? Occupational boundary work among human resource managers and external organization development practitioners. *Employee Relations* 40(5): 848–867.

Kwan N, Farndale E, and Park JG (2016) Employee voice and work engagement: macro, meso, and micro-level drivers of convergence? *Human Resource Management Review* 26(4): 327–337.

Labour Party (2010) Manifesto. https://manifesto.deryn.co.uk/labour-manifesto-2010-a-future-fair-for-all/

Lamont M (2000) *The Dignity of Working Men: Morality and the Boundaries of Race, Class, and Immigration*. New York: Russell Sage Foundation/Harvard University Press.

Larson MS (1977) *The Rise of Professionalism: A Sociological Analysis*. Berkeley: University of California Press.

Law Society (2017) LASPO four years on. https://www.lawsociety.org.uk/topics/research/laspo-4-years-on

Law Society (2019) Annual statistics. https://www.lawsociety.org.uk/topics/research/annual-statistics-report-2019

Law Society (2021) Civil legal aid: a review of its sustainability and the challenges to its viability. https://www.lawsociety.org.uk/topics/research/civil-sustainability-review

Law Society (2022) U-turn makes bad situation worse: solicitors left behind by government deal. https://www.lawsociety.org.uk/topics/criminal-justice/u-turn-makes-a-bad-situation-worse-solicitors-left-behind-by-government-deal

Law Society (2024a) Criminal duty solicitors: a growing crisis. https://www.lawsociety.org.uk/campaigns/criminal-justice/criminal-duty-solicitors

Law Society (2024b) LASPO Act. https://www.lawsociety.org.uk/topics/legal-aid/laspo-act

Law Society (2024c) New National Audit Office report shows legal aid is 'on its knees'. https://www.lawsociety.org.uk/topics/legal-aid/national-audit-office-report-shows-legal-aid-on-its-knees#:~:text=in%20real%20terms%2C%20government%20spending,2012%2F13%20and%202022%2F23

LeBaron M and Zumeta ZD (2003) Windows on diversity: lawyers, culture, and mediation practice. *Conflict Resolution Quarterly* 4: 463–472.

LeCompte MD and Schensul J (1999) *Designing and Conducting Ethnographic Research*. Walnut Creek: AltaMira Press.

Legal Futures (2018) Barrister should not have been suspended for 'robing room gossip'. https://www.legalfutures.co.uk/latest-news/barrister-should-not-have-been-suspended-for-robing-room-gossip

Levenson H (1977) Legal aid for mitigation. *Modern Law Review* 40(5): 523–532.

Lipset SM (1963) The value patterns of democracy: a case study in comparative analysis. *American Sociological Review* 28: 515–531.

Lipset SM, Trow MA, and Coleman JS (1956) *Union Democracy: The Internal Politics of the International Typographical Union*. New York: Free Press.

Lively KJ (2001) Occupational claims to professionalism: the case of paralegals. *Symbolic Interaction* 24(3): 343–366.

Loftus B (2010) Police occupational culture: classic themes, altered times. *Policing & Society* 20(1): 1–20.

Loweth J (2022) Talk of 'fat cat barristers helping criminals' is designed to stir up public emotion over strikes, says Bradford lawyer. *Telegraph and Argus*. https://www.thetelegraphandargus.co.uk/news/20717576.talk-fat-cat-barristers-helping-criminals-designed-stir-public-emotion-strikes-says-bradford-lawyer/

Mack K and Roach Anleu S (2007) 'Getting through the list' judgecraft and legitimacy in the lower courts. *Social and Legal Studies* 16(3): 341–361.

Mant J (2020) Placing litigants in person at the centre of the post-LASPO family court process. *Child and Family Law Quarterly* 32(4): 421.

Mant J, Newman D, and O'Shea D (2023) Blended advice and access to justice. *Ministry of Justice Analytical Series*. https://assets.publishing.service.gov.uk/media/642569452fa848001 3ec0fac/blended-advice-access-justice.pdf

Mant J and Wallbank J (2017) The mysterious case of disappearing family law and the shrinking vulnerable subject. *Social and Legal Studies* 26(5): 629–648.

Maslach C and Jackson SE (1981) The measurement of experienced burnout. *Journal of Organizational Behaviour* 2(2): 99–113.

McConville M, Hodgson J, Bridges L, and Pavlovic A (1994) *Standing Accused. The Organisation and Practices of Criminal Defence Lawyers in Britain*. Oxford: Clarendon Press.

McCormack C (2004) Storying stories: a narrative approach to in-depth interview conversations. *International Journal of Social Research Methodology* 7(3): 129–136.

McDonald P (1982) 'The class of '81' – a glance at the social class composition of recruits in the legal profession. *Journal of Law and Society* 9(2): 267–276.

Mead GH (1934) *Mind, Self and Society: From the Standpoint of a Social Behaviorist*. Chicago: University of Chicago Press.

Merrill B and West L (2009) *Using Biographical Methods in Social Research*. London: SAGE.

Merton RK (1957) *Social Theory and Social Structure*. Glencoe: Free Press.

Mieg HA (2016) Profession: Begriff, Charakteristik, Zentralwerte. In MW Dick, R Marotzki, and H Mieg (eds), *Handbuch Professionsentwicklung*. Bad Heilbrunn: Klinkhardt: 27–40.

Miles S (2005) *Foreword to Simone Weil: An Anthology*. London: Penguin.

Miller CL (1994) What a waste – beautiful, sexy gal – hell of a lawyer: film and the female attorney. *Columbia Journal of Gender & Law* 4: 203.

Miller PC (2000) Strategies of representation in collective biography. In T Hägg and P Rousseau (eds), *Greek Biography and Panegyric in Late Antiquity*. Berkeley: University of California Press: 209–254.

Mittal R (2012) *Legal Aid: Catalyst for Social Change*. Delhi: Legal Aid Society.

Ministry of Justice and the Legal Aid Agency (2018) Legal Aid statistics in England and Wales. https://assets.publishing.service.gov.uk/media/5a82a6e1e5274a2e87dc2483/legal-aid-statistics-bulletin-jan-mar-2017.pdf

Moorhead R (2010) Lawyer specialization – managing the professional paradox. *Law and Policy* 32: 226–259.

Moreira JI (2022) Arbitration vis-a-vis other professions: a sociology of professions account of international commercial arbitrators. *Journal of Law and Society* 49(1): 48–67.

Morgan RI (1994) The introduction of civil legal aid in England and Wales. 1914–1949. *Twentieth Century British History* 5(1).

NALP (National Association of Licensed Paralegals) (2024) Qualifications. https://www.nationalparalegals.co.uk/qualifications/

Nash K (2018) Neo-liberalisation, universities and the values of bureaucracy. *Sociological Review* 355: 60.

National Audit Office (2024) Government's management of legal aid. https://www.nao.org.uk/wp-content/uploads/2024/02/governments-management-of-legal-aid.pdf

Natt Gantt LO (2004) Integration as integrity: postmodernism, psychology, and religion on the role of moral counseling in the attorney–client relationship. *Regent University Law Review* 16: 233.

Newman D (2013) *Legal Aid Lawyers and the Quest for Justice*. London: Hart Publishing.

Newman D (2016) Are lawyers alienated workers? *European Journal of Current Legal Issues* 22(3): 2–25.

Newman D, Mant J, and Gordon F (2021) Vulnerability, legal need and technology in England and Wales. *International Journal of Discrimination and the Law* 21(3): 230.

Newman D and Welsh L (2019) The practices of modern criminal defence lawyers: alienation and its implications for access to justice. *Common Law World Review* 48(1–2): 64–89.

NKLC (2019) About North Kensington law centres. https://nklc.org.uk/about/?

Noordegraaf M (2016) Reconfiguring professional work: changing forms of professionalism in public services. *Administration & Society* 48(7): 790–791.

Oakley E and Vaughan S (2019) In dependence: the paradox of professional independence and taking seriously the vulnerabilities or lawyers in large corporate law firms. *Journal of Law and Society* 46(1): 109.

Obama B (2007) *Dreams from My Father*. Edinburgh: Canongate.

O'Hara EA and Ribstein LE (2009) *The Law Market*. Oxford: Oxford University Press.

O'Neill M (2020) Biographical research on the move: theorising, experiencing, imagining (the Chicago School reloaded). *Polish Journal of Sociology/przegląd Socjologiczny* 68(4): 99–124.

O'Neill M, Penfold-Mounce R, Honeywell D, Coward-Gibbs M, Crowder H, and Hill I (2021) Creative methodologies for a mobile criminology: walking as critical pedagogy. *Sociological Research Online* 26(2): 247–268.

O'Nions H (2020) 'Fat cat' lawyers and 'illegal migrants': the impact of intersecting hostilities and toxic narratives on access to justice. *Journal of Social Welfare and Family Law* 42(3): 319–340.

Parsons T (1939) The professions and social structure. *Social Forces* 17(4): 457–467.

Parsons T (1954) The professions and social structure. In T Parsons, *Essays in Sociological Theory*. New York: The Free Press: 39–49.

Paterson A (1971) *Legal Aid as a Social Service*. London: Cobden Trust.

Philips J, Waters J, Westaby C, and Fowler A (eds) (2020) *Emotional Labour in Criminal Justice and Criminology*. London: Routledge.

Pleasence P, Buck A, Balmer NJ, O'Grady A, Genn H, and Smith M (2004) *Causes of Action: Civil Law and Social Justice*. London: Stationery Office.

Poelmans S, Chinchilla N, and Cardona P (2003) Family-friendly HRM policies and the employment relationship. *International Journal of Manpower* 24(3): 128–147.

Post RC (1987) On the popular image of the lawyer: reflections in a dark glass. *California Law Review* 75(1): 379–389.

Pue W (1998) Lawyering for a fragmented world; professionalism after God. *International Journal of the Legal Profession* 5(2/3): 125–140.

Punch M (1979) *Policing the Inner City: A Study of Amsterdam's Warmoessraat*. Hamden: Archon Books.

Punch M (1985) *Police Corruption: Deviance, Accountability and Reform in Policing*. London: Routledge.

Regan F, Paterson A, Goriely T, and Fleming D (1999) *The Transformation of Legal Aid*. Oxford: Oxford University Press.

Reiner R (1985) *The Politics of Police*. New York: St Martin's Press.

Reiner R (2000) *The Politics of the Police*. Oxford: Oxford University Press.

Robinson R and Bell W (1978) Equality, success, and social justice in England and the United States. *American Sociological Review* 43(2): 125–143.

Robson P (2017) The portrayal of the corporate lawyer on TV: the US and British models from LA Law to Trust and Suits. *Journal of the Oxford Centre for Socio-Legal Studies* (2): 46–58.

Rogers J (2012) Representing the Bar: how the barristers' profession sells itself to prospective members. *Legal Studies* 3(2): 202–222.

Rosener JB (1990) Ways women lead. *Harvard Business Review* 68: 119–125.

Rutherford A (1993) *Criminal Justice and the Pursuit of Decency*. Oxford/New York: Oxford University Press.

Samuel G (1983) Public and private law: a private lawyer's response. *Modern Law Review* 46(5): 558–583.

Sanchagrin KJ (2014) Career trajectories among lawyers: the evolving role of social capital. Thesis: Iowa: University of Iowa.

Sandberg S (2015) *Narrative Criminology: Understanding Stories of Crime*. New York: New York University Press.

Sarat A and Felstiner W (1988) Law and social relations: vocabularies of motive in lawyer/ client interaction. *Law and Society Review* 22(4): 737–770.

Sarat A and Scheingold S (1998) *Cause Lawyering: Political Commitments and Professional Responsibilities*. Oxford: Oxford Socio-Legal Studies.

Sarat S and Scheingold S (2001) *Cause Lawyering and the State in a Global Era*. Oxford: Oxford University Press.

Schaufeli W and Enzmann D (1998) *The Burnout Companion to Study and Practice: A Critical Analysis*. Abingdon: Taylor and Francis.

Schein EH (2010) *Organizational Culture and Leadership*. San Francisco: Jossey-Bass.

Scheingold S and Bloom A (1998) Transgressive cause lawyering: practice sites and the politicization of the professional. *International Journal of the Legal Profession* 5(2–3): 209–253.

Scott R and Freckelton I (2024) Vicarious trauma among legal practitioners and judicial officers. *Psychiatry, Psychology and Law* 31(3): 500–522. doi: 10.1080/13218719.2024.2339323.

Sennett R (1998) *The Corrosion of Character: The Personal Consequences of Work in the New Capitalism*. New York: Norton.

Shah J (2021) Community lawyering in resistance to neoliberalism. *Michigan Law Review* 120(6): 1061–1084.

Sherr A and Webb H (1989) Law students, the external market, and socialisation: do we make them turn to the City? *Journal of Law and Society* 16(3): 225.

Silverman D (2000) *Doing Qualitative Research*. Thousand Oaks: SAGE.

Simon WH (1978) The ideology of advocacy: procedural justice and professional ethics. *Wisconsin Law Review* 29: 34.

Simon WH (1998) *The Practice of Justice*. Cambridge: Harvard University Press.

Smith T and Cape E (2017) The rise and decline of criminal legal aid in England and Wales. In MRMZ Alexander (ed), *Access to Justice and Legal Aid: Comparative Perspectives on Unmet Legal Need*. Cham: Springer: 63.

Solicitors Regulation Authority (2024) Diversity in law firms' workforce. www.sra.org.uk/sra/equality-diversity/diversity-profession/diverse-legal-profession/

Sommerlad H (1996) Criminal legal aid reforms and the restructuring of legal profession-alism. In R Young and D Wall (eds), *Access to Justice*. London: Blackstone Press.

Sommerlad H (2001) 'I've lost the plot': an everyday story of legal aid lawyers. *Journal of Law and Society* 3(28): 335–360.

Sommerlad H (2004) Some reflections on the relationship between citizenship, access to justice, and the reform of legal aid. *Journal of Law and Society* 31(3): 345–368.

Sommerlad H (2008) 'What are you doing here? You should be working in a hair salon or something'. Outsider status and professional socialization in the solicitors' profession. *Web Journal of Current Legal Issues* 2(1).

Sommerlad H (2010) The implementation of quality initiatives and the new public management in the legal aid sector in England and Wales: Bureaucratisation, stratification and surveillance. *International Journal of the Legal Profession* 6(3): 311–343.

Sommerlad H (2013) Let history judge? Gender, race, class and performative identity: a study of women judges in England and Wales. In U Schultz and G Shaw (eds), *Gender and Judging*. Oxford: Hart Publishing: 347.

Sommerlad H and Sanderson P (1998) *Gender, Choice and Commitment: Women Solicitors in England and Wales and the Struggle for Equal Status*. London: Routledge.

Sommerlad H and Sanderson P (2013) Social justice on the margins: the future of the not for profit sector as providers of legal advice in England and Wales. *Journal of Social Welfare and Family Law* 35(3): 305–327. https://doi.org/10.1080/09649069.2013.802108

Souleles D (2018) How to study people who do not want to be studied: practical reflections on studying up. *Political and Legal Anthropology Review* 41: 51–68.

Standing G (2011) *The Precariat: The New Dangerous Class*. London: Bloomsbury.

Stanislavski C (1965) *An Actor Prepares*. New York: Theatre Art Books.

Steinberg R (2006) Beyond lawyering: how holistic representation makes for good policy, better lawyers and more satisfied clients. https://www.nycourts.gov/ip/partnersinjustice/Beyond-Lawyering.pdf

Stephen FH, Fazio G, and Tata C (2008) Incentives, criminal defence lawyers and plea bargaining. *International Review of Law and Economics* 28(3): 212–219.

Stephen F and Tata C (2006) 'Swings and roundabouts': do changes to the structure of legal aid remuneration make a real difference to criminal case managements and case outcomes? *Criminal Law Review* 8: 722–741.

Tata C (2007) In the interests of clients or commerce? Legal aid, supply, demand, and 'ethical indeterminacy' in criminal defence work. *Journal of Law and Society* 34(4): 489.

Tata C (2019) 'Ritual individualisation': creative genius at sentencing, mitigation and conviction. *Journal of Law and Society* 46(1): 112–140.

Taylor-Gooby P (2016) The divisive welfare state. *Social Policy and Administration* 50(6): 712–733.

Teubner G (1987) *Juridification of Social Spheres: A Comparative Analysis in the Areas of Labor, Corporate, Antitrust and Social Welfare Law*. Berlin: Walter de Gruyter.

Thornton J (2019) The way in which fee reductions influence legal aid criminal defence lawyer work: insights from a qualitative study. *Journal of Law and Society* 46(4): 559–585.

Thornton J (2020) Is publicly funded criminal defence sustainable? Legal aid cuts, morale, retention and recruitment in the English criminal law professions. *Legal Studies* 40(2): 230–251.

Travers M (1997) *The Reality of Law: Walk and Talk in a Firm of Criminal Lawyers*. Dartmouth: Dartmouth Publishing Company.

Turner RH (1960) Sponsored and contest mobility and the school system. *American Sociological Review* 25: 855–867.

UK Parliament (2025) *Poor Persons (Legal Aid)*. Volume 188. https://hansard.parliament.uk/commons/1925-11-18/debates/de1bda08-ad84-4382-9d62-19b3bd65e65c/PoorPersons(LegalAid)

Van Maanen J and Barley SR (1984) Occupational communities: culture and control in organisations. *Research in Organizational Behaviour* 6: 287–365.

Vosko L (2010) *Managing the Margins: Gender, Citizenship and the International Regulation of Precarious Employment*. New York: Oxford University Press.

Webb J (2003) Being a lawyer/being a human being. *Legal Ethics* 5(1): 130–151.

Weber M (1924 [1894]) Entwickelungstendenzen in der Lage der ostelbischen Landarbeiter. In M. Weber, *Gesammelte Aufsatze zur Sozial- und Wirtschaftsgeschichte*. Tübingen: JCB Mohr (Paul Siebeck).

Weber M (1978) *Economy and Society*. Berkeley: University of California Press.

Webley L (2020) Ethics and the family mediation process. In M Roberts and M Moscati (eds), *Family Mediation: Contemporary Issues*. London: Bloomsbury Professional Ltd.

Welsh L (2017) The effects of changes to legal aid on lawyers' professional identity and behaviour in summary criminal cases: a case study. *Journal of Law and Society* 44(4): 559–585.

Welsh L and Howard M (2019) Standardization and the production of justice in summary criminal courts: a post-human analysis. *Social and Legal Studies* 28(6): 774–793.

Westaby C, Philips J, Ainslie S, and Fowler A (2023) Pushed from above and pushed from below: emotional labour and dual identities amongst senior probation officers in England and Wales. *European Journal of Probation* 15(1): 40–59.

Wexler S (1970) Practicing law for poor people. *Yale Law Journal* 79(5): 1049–1067.

Wharton AS (1993) The affective consequences of service work: managing emotion on the job. *Work and Occupations* 20: 205–232. https://doi.org/10.1177/0730888493020002004

Whittington D and Boore J (1988) Competence in nursing. *Professional Competence and Quality Assurance in the Caring Professions* (1): 109–139.

Wilding J (2019) Droughts and deserts. a report on the immigration legal aid market. *Joseph Rowntree Trust*. http://www.jowilding.org/assets/files/Droughts%20and% 20Deserts%20final%20report.pdf

Wilding J (2023) *The Legal Aid Market: Challenges for Publicly Funded Immigration and Asylum Legal Representation*. Cambridge: Polity Press.

Wilkins D (2004) Doing well by doing good? The role of public service in the careers of black corporate lawyers. *Houston Law Review* 41: 1.

Wilson JC and Hollis-Brusky A (2014) Lawyers for god and neighbor: the emergence of law as calling as mobilizing frame for Christian lawyers. *Law & Social Inquiry* 39(2): 416–448.

Wright Mills C (1956) *The Power Elite*. Oxford: Oxford University Press.

Yakren S (2008) Lawyer as emotional laborer. *University of Michigan Journal of Law Reform* 42: 141.

Young J (1999) *The Exclusive Society: Social Exclusion, Crime and Difference in Late Modernity*. London: Sage.

Young R (2013) Exploring the boundaries of criminal courtroom workgroup. *Common Law World Review* 42(3): 203–239.

Young Legal Aid Lawyers (2018) Social mobility in a time of austerity. https://www.younglegalaidlawyers.org/sites/default/files/Soc%20Mob%20Report%20-%20edited.pdf

Zaloznaya M and Nielson LB (2011) Mechanisms and consequences of professional marginality: the case of poverty lawyers revisited. *Law and Social Inquiry* 36(4): 919–944.

Index

References to figures appear in *italic* type.